Remarkably Brighton

Still in Touch

a novel by Paul W. Weber

the Peppertree Press

www.peppertreepublishing.com

Copyright © Paul W. Weber, 2022

All rights reserved. Published by the Peppertree Press, LLC. the Peppertree Press
and associated logos are trademarks of the Peppertree Press, LLC. No part of
this publication may be reproduced, stored in a retrieval system, transmitted in
any form or by any means, electronic, mechanical, photocopying, recording, or
otherwise, without prior written permission of the publisher and author/illustrator.
Graphic design by Elizabeth Parry
For information regarding permission, call 941-922-2662 or contact us
at our website: www.peppertreepublishing.com or write to:
The Peppertree Press, LLC.
Attention: Publisher 715 N. Washington Blvd., Suite B
Sarasota, Florida 34236

ISBN: 978-1-61493-836-1
Library of Congress: 2022911756
Printed: Jujy 2022

Cover photos by J. Damon, J. Vichich and C. Kull

"Hail, oh Hail our Alma Mater,
Brighton we are proud."

DEDICATION

In Honor of the Greatest Generation, Friends and Family

Raising the Flag over Iwo Jima
(Photo Rosenthal)

TABLE OF CONTENTS

PROLOGUE

Roll of Honor   Sept 14, 1943

> *"Twice in my lifetime the long arm of destiny has reached*
> *across the oceans and involved the entire life and*
> *manhood of the United States in a deadly struggle."*
> —Prime Minister Winston Churchill,
> Harvard University Speech, Sept. 1943

WILLIS TOWNE SPED DOWN the sandy old drovers trail in his beat-up Ford pick-up faster than usual, reaching the main road in record time. It was a perfect late summer morning and the leaves of the maple trees lining Frank Rickett's farm had already begun to turn into varying shades of yellow, red and brown. Frances Griffin waved at him but the smoke from his cigarette and dust from the gravel he plowed to the side of the road made it impossible to see her. He had one thing on his mind anyway—getting to town in time to put the last names on the sign he had been working on for weeks.

Towne was a newcomer to Brighton. He had moved there only a few months before with his wife and her cats—eight at last count. They were living in the tenant house on the old Chamberlain farm that his son-in-law, Carlos Weber, owned. There was no rent to pay and it would serve the purpose for the time being. On Carlos's recommendation, he had been commissioned by the city of Brighton to paint a banner and the names of town men and women serving in the armed forces on the recently constructed roll of honor that had been erected on the southwest corner of Main and Grand River. The town fathers intentionally did not call it a war memorial, for there had been few casualties as yet in the area. Carlos's cousin Max Musch, the Proving Grounds talented young architect, designed it and the men and women of the volunteer fire department built it. The fourteenth was the appointed day for its dedication, just in time for the Conservation Club and Boy Scouts to finish their landscaping. Every diary entry in town and no less than four articles in the *Brighton Argus* that twenty-first month of America's Second World War noted that Brighton should indeed be proud of it.

Willis put his cigarette out and stopped at the parking spot that had been reserved for him adjacent to Mrs. Merchant's boarded up house. The job would not take long; there were only twenty-six

1

names to finish and his rheumatism was not as bad as it had been lately. Though he was adept at pulling every script he had mastered in his career out of his artistic cache—from Old English Dickensian, the flowery Edwardian in which he had been schooled to the modern Art Deco of the Jazz Age and Depression—he chose the ever popular Antiqua. He also chose to paint left-handed, for he was more precise as a southpaw, particularly with the myriad of flourishes he would be using. There were a great many onlookers already, forcing him to be more patient than usual. He hastily but meticulously added the last of the 275 names of the men and women that had somehow been omitted from the original list the Blue Star Mothers had collected. When he finished, he had but a few minutes to admire his work:

John Allen	Harry Hayes	Charles Sheffer	Doris Pitkin	*Roll*
Melbourne Morgan	Robert Singer	Helen Mullany	Frederick Hyne	
Harris Dannon	Robert Morlan	Troy Smail	Garnet Rollison	
Lyle Davenport	Edward Pittenger	Roy Thomas	Marguerite Dunning	*of*
Charles Dean	William Richmond	Azel Travers	Harry Herbst	
Homer Harrington	Edwin Roser	Frederick Waterbury	Earland Bert Bair	*Honor*
Earl Keyes	William Scroggins	Charles Smith	**sign by Willis Towne**	

Willis Towne, 1943

The Lansing native had never been at ease in crowds—perhaps because he had been intimidated by demonstrators once too often in the 1930s as a Deputy Ingham County Sheriff, perhaps because it was just his nature; in any case, he had not intended to stay for the dedication. But it was too late by the time he finished to leave without being noticed and Eric Singer, master of ceremonies, had told him he would be acknowledged, after which he would receive payment for his work. Yes, he would stay. Few would notice the rainbow of colors from other jobs that had penetrated from his painter's smock to the work suit he was wearing.

2

It had been an eventful day in town. Lloyd Pearsall did an outstanding job chairing the day's festivities. Coinciding with the unveiling of the honor roll, with its Liberty Bell motif, the bond drive opened and was hugely successful. Emma Westin, in her eighteenth year at the Brighton State Bank, later noted in her diary that the fourth Series E drive alone had recorded between eleven and twelve thousand dollars in sales. There was a parade down Main Street at mid-day in which two hundred military police from Grass Lake were featured as honored guests. And Hayes Bennett's Entertainers from WJR had been invited to the ceremony to lift the crowd's spirits after the singing of the National Anthem. They were scheduled to sing patriotic favorites and two of the most popular *Hit Parade* songs from 1942 and '43—*Til We Meet Again* and *I'll Get By*.

"A fine job," Singer said to Willis as he fingered the Brighton State Bank check in the pouch pocket of his printer's apron after the ceremony. "And thanks for including the names Lloyd didn't give me until yesterday." Eric's hair had become gray and there were deep furrows now in his usually calm and self-assured face. He had managed to disguise his feelings in front of the crowd but with his family and friends his voice cracked whenever he talked about his sons. Carlos Weber's father-in-law was an out-of-towner and with him Singer was free to reveal his true feelings. The paint was still drying on his oldest son, Robert's, name and Eric knew that his middle son's name would soon be added to the list that was already far too long. Robert had always been his brother's role model and not long before Frederick Singer had announced to him his intention after graduation to enlist in the army air corps.

"You're welcome, Mr. Singer," Willis answered, taking note of the tears that were forming in the town printer's eyes. "Hope everything..." He ended his sentence abruptly. Eric had already disappeared in the alley behind Rolison's Hardware leading to his small shop off Main and West Streets.

"Hope everything will be all right!" he shouted, though he knew in those days nothing ever would be all right.

Ruth, Carolyn and Louie Weber, 1942

CHAPTER ONE

The War **Winter, 1943**

Therefore, since the world has still
Much good, but much less good than ill,
And while the sun and moon endure
Luck's a chance, but trouble's sure,
I'd face it as a wise man would,
And train for ill and not for good.
"A Shropshire Lad" —A.E. Housman

THE SNOW WAS MELTING that February day when my uncle, Louie Weber, hoisted his six-year-old daughter and her young friend to the roof of the chicken coop on their farm just south of town. Tommy Comisky, who was eight, bragged that he had already climbed to the top with no help from any adult. It was an unusually mild day for winter, now on record as the coldest one in Michigan history. There had been a blizzard on the eleventh of the month and the mercury had plummeted to six degrees below zero only two days before. The three children were happy that they could play outside all day for a change. Their mothers had not made them put on heavy snow suits for the raucous snowball fight they planned and they were excited about watching the 10:30 Flint-Ann Arbor train zoom past.

Getting any closer to the tracks than the chicken coop was strictly forbidden since the time young Tommy had goaded his friends, my cousin Carolyn and Bobby Richmond, into hitching a ride on a slow moving caboose that had stopped in back of Comisky's. It crossed Rickett Road on the outskirts of town and made an abrupt halt at the depot on Main Street before Florence Richmond and Ruthie Weber managed to race to the west side of Brighton to rescue them. But train *watching* was a different matter. Carolyn had promised her Uncle Charles Smith that she and her pals would wave at him as he passed by in a fast moving coach taking him to boot camp in Indiana.

Charles "Chug" Smith was Aunt Ruthie Weber's brother. He was optimistic and good-natured, witty and straightforward. Chug played everything by heart on the guitar and piano and had a reputation as one of the funniest raconteurs Brighton had ever produced except for "Shag" Hacker. He was a guy you wanted to have on your side, not just because of his imposing stature but because he was a friend you could count on. Always a lover of fast automobiles and motorcycles with big engines, he saved enough money working at the Brown McLaren factory in Hamburg to buy a red Ford convertible. An adventurous type, he took everything in his stride. The Selective Service Law exempted him from the draft because he was the sole provider for his widowed mother. Chug enlisted anyway and Bea Smith was furious when she heard about her son's decision. Yet there was little she could do to dissuade him. Faye Knight, Jack Teeple and most of his other friends were volunteering—end of subject.

Chug didn't want to admit it, but he was homesick by the time he reached Fort Benjamin Harrison in Indiana. He hitched rides from everywhere he was stationed to come home on a pass, once from as far away as Miami Beach, where he qualified as a marksman. No visiting home, though, from Hobart, Tasmania, where he disembarked from a troop transport in mid-year. At the busy quay he smoked a Lucky Strike, staring at one of the southern hemisphere's most beautiful harbors, almost intoxicated by the color of the dazzling water in mid-winter. After the two-week trip from California evading the enemy, he was waiting for another transport to take him who knew where. Over the Japanese controlled "Hump"—the main land artery over the Himalayas to China—he flew, on his way to the southeastern part of China not far from Japanese-held territory. There he joined American forces in the China Offensive to help Generalissimo Chiang Kai-shek. When he got as far as Kweilin he was issued a gun, a shiny new motorcycle and assigned to the 1211th Military Police Company. How lucky could a guy get, he thought, when he met up there with a unit full of poker players who loved to listen to him play guitar and tell stories?

There were few advances for Allied Forces in the month after Japan's bombing of Pearl Harbor in December 1941 drew the United States into war. In the European Theater, Germany's relentless bombing of Britain never abated. Joseph Stalin, the Soviet Union's megalomaniacal dictator and former ally of Hitler, pleaded with President Roosevelt and Prime Minister Churchill to invade Western Europe as his Red Army came dangerously close to defeat during the German sieges of Stalingrad and Leningrad. Virtually the only Allied advance across the Atlantic was in North Africa, where American forces landed with far less resistance than anticipated. British Field Commander, Sir Bernard Montgomery, had already stubbornly fought German forces in the northeastern part of the continent. If the inevitable invasion of Europe across the Mediterranean from North Africa were to succeed, victories there against the Third Reich's most brilliant general, Erwin Rommel, were essential. Though Montgomery, his superiors, and American General Dwight D. Eisenhower were often at odds about strategy, some of the links in Hitler's chain of victories were at last wearing thin. The clever (and principled) Rommel, dubbed the "Desert Fox," and his *Afrika Korps* had at last met their match as the Allied armies advanced from the eastern and western parts of the continent to amass their armies in Algeria and Tunisia.

In the Pacific, the beleaguered American naval fleet struggled to recover from the surprise Japanese attack on Hawaii. Even though President Roosevelt had been steadily increasing defense funding and gotten Congress to institute a draft, dubbed by critics the "Old Man's Draft," it took months to transform factories into meeting the challenge of recovering from Japan's treachery, not to mention supplying troops fighting on two continents. There had been enormous Allied casualties in battles like the Coral Sea and Midway Islands, leading Japan to believe it could complete what it had set out to accomplish at Pearl Harbor—destroy American sea power. But its enemy's forces fought valiantly both on sea and in the air in what military historian John Keegan called "the most stunning and decisive blow in the history of naval warfare." Emperor Hirohito's warlords, who, like Hitler, had sustained no significant losses since the outbreak of hostilities in 1931, at last saw their hope for complete hegemony in the Pacific thwarted in just a few months.

Ultimately, President Roosevelt's war cabinet convinced the commander-in-chief that only one strategy would succeed in the Pacific: a multi-pronged path of westward island hopping, bloody conquest after bloody conquest, across occupied territory to the Japanese mainland. Sending troops to mainland China, where Chug found himself, was, however, a secondary strategy in the Pacific war, a gamble that met with only partial success. Civil War had torn the country apart for over ten years but it was believed that the antagonists, Nationalist leader General Chiang Kai-shek and Mao Tse Tung, commander of the communist Red Army, were necessary allies in diverting, if not defeating, the Japanese. Over-confidence in the Nationalist army and a determination to bomb Tokyo from far-off bases with planes not yet equipped for the mission were also causing major divisions in both civilian and military circles in Washington and China.

Unfortunately, the major Allied wartime strategy in China lacked cohesion and leadership. Not only was the Nationalist Generalissimo often off track and indecisive but American General Joseph Stillwell was also unpredictable. "Vinegar Joe" expected unrealistic major Chinese offenses on Japanese held cities and he was not always in good graces with Washington and Chiang Kai-shek. Nor did Stillwell see eye-to-eye with the popular leader of the 14th Air Force, Claire Chennault. A brilliant commander, Gen. Chennault had been a reliable cog in the wheel driving the American presence in China, ten years into what historians have called the Second Sino-Japanese War. Chennault's "Flying Tigers" had flown more successful missions over the "Hump" supplying troops in China than any other after the 1942 Japanese capture of the Burma Road, and he was immensely popular with men in combat, particularly the 1211th army. He was a soldier's soldier who played baseball with the troops and spent most of his free time commiserating with them about being away from their sweethearts or the chow served in the mess hall. But Chennault, like Stillwell, had his shortcomings. His judgment was often too colored by his successes. Would Chug witness a more unified command after his arrival on the Asian mainland or was there to be protracted military engagement with no clear victors?

"Last call for mail," a non-com announced as he entered the cavernous, canopied tent barracks at the base in Kweilin. Chug had just finished another letter home in time for mail call, encouraged that his last one had been published in the **Brighton Argus**. To console his mother, he had promised that he would always let her know where he was stationed. He was faithful in his correspondence and, though taboo, managed to slip an "I" for India, "B" for Burma or 'C" for China on the envelopes from Asia Bea Smith found in her mailbox.

"Hope we get to speak to the General, Smitty," Chug's buddy Dave Heck shouted as the corporal left with a leather bag that dwarfed him, filled to capacity with letters addressed to family members, sweethearts and friends in almost every state of the union. Heck was Chug's best MP friend but his nemesis at cards. It made him mad that the best damned blackjack player at the Western House in Brighton could not beat a guy from the South Side of Chicago. The next day the two MPs' motorcycles were as close as non-coms could get to the famed leader of the 14th Air Force. Chennault shook their hands and the envelope that Bea Smith got a few weeks later marked "C" contained three Kodak black and white snapshots of her son and the General. A fourth picture had been removed by a censor because it captured a P-40 fighter in the background with the Flying Tigers' trademark jagged shark's teeth on the fuselage. A fifth photo, precisely the same, remained in Chug's wallet for the rest of his life.

Private Charles Smith with General Claire Chennault, Kweilin China, 1944.

"Chennault was a real gentleman," Heck said to Chug that evening in the smoke-filled tent after he had won another fast hand of stud poker. "Now we need to convince General LeMay to fly in and pose for us."

Shorty Wong, who worked at the 1211th army camp doing everything from washing clothes to lining up dates for G.I.s with Chinese girls, had become one of Chug's best friends. He was reliable, had a genial personality and delighted in proudly showing Chug the most picturesque region in China. People gawked when the two friends walked into shops or cafes—Shorty was all of four foot eight and Chug measured six foot five.

In mid-1944, Chug seriously worried about his buddy. Kweilin, the ageless, beautiful city on the Li Chang River, Shorty's family, and the entire civilian population of the city were now in peril. Shorty had vowed not only to watch over his family but his American friend as well. Whenever the thought of a Japanese onslaught got the better of him, he looked to the mountains. "We see enemy close, we go mountains south with family," he assured Chug. "Not worry, take you with!"

Japan's Chinese Expeditionary Army had begun an all-out offensive, a gamble to defeat the Nationalist armies at Kweilin and other strategic areas in the country, including Kunming to the southwest. Kweilin would likely be left undefended. A Japanese victory in both cities was part of a plan to connect all occupied territory on the mainland of Asia then push southeast to Indochina. The enemy also intended to destroy American air bases supporting the Nationalist government headquartered at Chunking. Called "Ichigo," the Japanese committed 400,000 men to the operation, the Imperial Japanese Army now supplemented by retreating troops withdrawn from the Pacific.

Earlier in the year Chug and his buddies, as well as Capt. Bonjino, their commanding officer, had complete confidence in General Chennault to deal with the military threat. But by summer, men in the 1211th wondered if Operation Ichigo were about to succeed. American military advisors were pessimistic because Chiang Kai-shek's resolve to commit massive numbers of troops to the defense of Kweilin wavered. Adding to the problems plaguing the American command was General Stillwell's headstrong style. He was often in disagreement with General Chennault and Chiang Kai-shek, for whom he served as Chief of Staff, and he had never been a popular nor unifying leader in a region that sorely needed it. But luckily for the American initiative in China, Stillwell was at last replaced. He was succeeded by General Albert Wedemeyer—one of the war's most under-rated commanders and strategists—a personnel change that was not quick enough to change the immediate scope of the war but a break for the long term.

The misgivings Smitty and his friends had about the future of the city in the middle of summer were validated as fall approached. American troops were ordered to move out of Kweilin, leaving the airbases looking like concrete ghost fields. Juxtaposed with this was the evacuation of masses of people to the countryside by rail and foot and the withdrawal of large contingents of the Nationalist army. Kweilin had been deemed too hard to fight for and on Nov. 24 it fell—defended by only 20,000 troops and all but destroyed by the Japanese 11th army.

One hundred thousand Nationalist troops were killed or wounded and contemporary accounts reported as many civilian casualties in the whole province surrounding the city.

The 1211th and Chennault's 14th Air Force retreated successfully as far as Kunming, where the rear echelon of General Wedemeyer's forces were entrenched. Sadly, though, the fate of Kweilin and its neighboring city, Liuzhou, made the Mainland China retreat bittersweet. That story—so similar to the horrendous fate of China's capital, Nanking, in 1937—dare never be neglected, Chug often said. He remained safely ensconced under Wedemeyer and Chennault at the terminus of the Burma Road but the memory of a city surrounded by beautiful, fairytale-like mountains resembling inverted ice cream cones and the enduring friendship of Shorty Wong were lost for good now. *

Some information about developments in World War II following the bombing of Pearl Harbor in both the European and Asian theaters, particularly Japan's occupation of China, drawn from Wikipedia.

Shorty Wong and Chug Smith, 1944.

Private Charles H. Smith, 1943.

M.P. Chug Smith with Chinese children, Kweilin, 1944.

Eddie on the fender of Aunt Emma's Chevrolet Coupe, Second Street, 1944

CHAPTER TWO

The Homefront 1943

*"...There is one front and one battle where everyone
in the United States — every man, woman and child — is
in action and will be privileged to remain in action
throughout this war. The front is right here at home,
in our daily lives (and) in our daily tasks...."*
— Fireside Chat 21, April 28, 1942 Pres. Franklin D. Roosevelt

CHUG'S LETTERS TO HIS MOTHER AND SISTERS from the warfront expressed gratitude for being in Kunming yet were tinged with deep regret about the fall of Kweilin and intense sadness about the fate of his friend, Shorty Wong. Stateside, Smitty's family anxiously watched newsreels of events unfolding in China at the *Grand* Theater. On the surface, at least, Chug felt in reading letters from home that small town life had not changed much. Mail call one day in Kweilin brought him a letter from his sister, Doris Case. Baby Ann Sharon was adept at walking to the kitchen from the RCA Victor console radio in the front room. The twenty acres of field corn Doris's husband, Charlie, had experimented with on their Pleasant Valley farm was the proverbial "knee high." Doris only hoped that with a small child and producing his quota of crops on the farm Charlie would not get called into service. Chug was unaware that Livingston County's enlistments from the Old Man's Draft were tapering off and for the Case Family making any future plans was virtually impossible.

In Brighton there was renewed patriotic fervor and the single mindedness and drive necessary for a nation to secure victory on every front of the war. The Civil War cannon in Fairview Cemetery that children had played on for generations turned up missing early in the war. It fell prey to one of many wartime scrap metal collections, ignominiously removed from its scenic prospect on a hill overlooking Ore Creek next to the flagpole. Children in school wrote letters to G.I.s and collected supplies like decks of cards, toothbrushes and candy to send them. Women collected tin cans and stuffed paper bags with old nylon stockings full of runs. Because troops needed to be supplied first, consumer goods were in short supply. Children took their turns tearing stamps out of ration booklets for any number of commodities to expose ghoulish pictures of Japanese warlords and their minions. They felt proud and received praise from their parents if they were able to produce a coupon worth 70 points for a large beef roast for Sunday dinner and the leftovers it would yield. A beef rib roast cost $.33 per pound and required 18 points, a one pound ham $1.12 and 33 points.

Mom's sister, Emma Westin, an institution by the 1940s at the Brighton State Bank, wrote every day about these and other happenings in town in her 1943 and 1944 diaries. She kept herself well informed about prices and the availability of goods and services but also about who was engaged in patriotic endeavors. Customers at the two story brick bank building on the Mill Pond rarely just made routine deposits or withdrawals from tellers like Alice Newcomb, the bank cashier's daughter, or Evelyn Richmond. They made a point of stopping to visit, if just for a minute or two, with Emma. And rarely did Emma not write about conversations or observations she found of particular interest, from routine stories about children, church or soldiers' fates to village wartime occurrences, like the unveiling of the town's Roll of Honor or the repaving of Main Street in the middle of summer.

Like my mother's, my aunt's 1943-44 wartime diary is a treasure trove for later generations of people's aspirations and hopes, concerns and sadness, elation and reservations. She wrote about the progress of the war and letters she had sent and received from no less than five G.Is. Both of Emma's nephews were in the army, one cousin in the Women's Army Corps and her cousin's brother, Richard Larson, in the Army Air Corps. A native of Escanaba, he was home on furlough in New York, *"pale and thin, a quiver in his hands that would not go away"* from action in the Pacific. Emma had never failed to send letters of encouragement and presents to "Dickie," who had lost his mother to cancer at only 6 and been taken care of in Brighton by her for almost a year. One day alone in October 1943 she packaged and sent him two books—*Col. Effington's Raid and CO/Postmaster* along with a deck of cards, towels, a glass jar of almond chocolate candy and a toothbrush! Tragically, "Dickie" did not survive the war. Emma noted in her diary on May 15, 1944 that after three engagements in the Pacific, Tech Sgt. Richard Larson was killed with two other crewmen in a military test flight off the coast of Cherry Point, North Carolina.

Strick's Store displayed pictures of Brighton men and women serving in the armed forces during W.W. II, c. 1944.

She wrote about politics, happy occasions and sad things. On Aug 14 she noted that Chuck Sheffer *"died from Bright's disease, which he contracted in service in the Pacific."* In October she wrote that Wayne Plummer, a navigator on a B-24—the ex-boyfriend of Una Wagenknecht, a St. George member—was reported missing in action. She even wrote about bizarre things. Once the husband of a church friend, Peter Sater, sent her a memento of the Pacific war—a bracelet taken from the pilot of a downed plane in the Marshall Islands where he was serving! A few months later, on furlough, Peter proudly stopped by to visit Emma, a wad of pictures of dead enemy soldiers in hand to show her. There was a fire Oct 12, 1943 in the Lannar Building next to the post office, where the *Detroit Times* and *Detroit News* stored their newspapers, that caused considerable damage. Bud Pitkin buzzed over the town in his B-25 Dec. 4. One of Tillie Hill's twin sixteen-month-old sons died tragically from choking on an obstruction in his throat April 15. Common illnesses were recorded—there was a scarlet fever epidemic in Fowlerville in February; whooping cough sent students Donald Bandkau and Paul Shoup to bed in March. She noted that on June 28 Gov. Dewey of New York was nominated as the Republican candidate for President to run against Franklin Roosevelt, now seeking an unprecedented fourth term in office, and in October New York faced St. Louis in the World Series.

In July Emma wrote that Dr. Archie McGregor served as master of ceremonies for a tribute to the Brighton Advanced Stamping Company on Second Street. The "Advance," as most locals called the new factory in town, was honored for receiving an "E" award from the government for outstanding war production. The Brighton High School band played, many military officials were present, and a jeep and tank were on display. That same month, she noted, two hundred forty-seven donors showed up at the blood bank, some of whom were rejected, some of whom fainted. Despite objections from the local temperance society and at least two churches, the Red Cross Auxiliary wisely kept a bottle of whiskey on hand to deal with such an eventuality.

My aunt wrote praiseworthy things that might otherwise be lost in the annals of time about Brighton residents who worked ceaselessly in the war effort—men and women, children and adults—determined to do their part on the home front for victory. One such volunteer was Walt Carmack, owner of the *Grand* Theater on West Grand River. Walt worked with renewed energy in the early winter of 1943-44. Andy Robertson, Brighton's civil defense director, had made him chief air raid warden in 1942 after concern arose that Michigan's factories were making it vulnerable to the enemy. Tokyo and Berlin were a world away but that did not stop people from imagining the worst possible scenarios. In an editorial, *The Brighton Argus* had warned its readers not to be "complacent"—German bombers would only have to fly over Hudson Bay into Michigan to destroy key targets like factories down river in Detroit or Ypsilanti. Following his appointment, Walt set about organizing the town into three defense zones presided over by his friends Gus Karus, Joe Ulman and Frances Michaels. He ordered the fire department to cease the practice of sounding the noon fire alarm at the back of city hall so people could discern the difference between practice drills and—God forbid—an authentic bombing alert. And Brighton's chief air warden resolved to make the rounds himself in Brighton two to three times a week to set a good example for his volunteers.

There was good reason for Carmack's patriotic fervor. As one might expect, determination to mount an all-out effort to win the war was keenest in the ranks of the military and their families. Scores of men like Walt's two sons, Ray and Ted, were now serving. *The Detroit Free Press* reported in mid-1942 that 1,700,000 Michigan men between the ages of eighteen and sixty-five had registered for the draft and 100,000 between eighteen and forty-five were serving in the armed forces. Some of those inductees, like Chug Smith, the Singer brothers, Roy Thomas, Harry Herbst, Bill Richmond and his buddy Robert Morlan, climbed on the troop transport train in Brighton or Detroit with fanfare enough for an entire company. Others left for service unheralded, doing what was expected of them, few aware of what their lot would be in a world turned upside down.

Early in 1944, Willis Towne's list on the *Roll of Honor* approached four hundred. By then people interested in analyzing recruitment noted some interesting statistics. Many parents worried not just about one or two of their children in service but as many as four. Many long-time residents and recent transplants to Brighton had three or more family members serving on every front in Asia, Africa and Europe. Among them were the Cains, Tuthills, Wenzels, Leffers, Hidtlebaughs and Pelkeys. Moreover, a large number of women were volunteering for service. Marguerite Dunning, Helen Mullany, Doris Pitkin and Garnet Rolison were just a few daughters of Brighton, like sisters in arms throughout the country, to distinguish themselves in their respective branches of service.

Many local men were torn between duty to country and their responsibilities as providers for their families. Patriotism and loyalty to country was one thing; the cold reality of war and its effects on families, however, was another matter. Livingston County's draft board routinely received requests for exemptions from service for personal reasons that could not easily be dismissed. Young fathers often pled their case for exemption from the draft or even honorable discharges. Township boards upon which decisions often rested—one of which my father served on—struggled with cases requiring dismissal or review. They dutifully recommended more than once in interviews with the county's chief civilian draft director, Earl Grub, that neighbors with small children whose wives had no means of livelihood be recalled honorably from service.

Many men answered the call to service, but reluctantly. They dealt with handling guns, resolved to kill or be killed, strove to abide by military rules of conduct and faced basic training hardships with courage. But some could not accustom themselves to military discipline. Homesickness or simply making foolish decisions about accountability on bases was too much to deal with. Dan Leslie was one of them. Just eighteen when he enlisted in late spring 1943, he grew morose and was lonesome for his family despite the precious few hours he had to himself during basic training to think about them. He thought ten days of furlough would be enough time to make a difference but his leave only made things worse. His calculations seemed logical—hitchhike to Brighton, see his parents and buddies and work through the realization that he might never see them again. Everything went as planned. Dan visited every member of his family to show off his coast guard uniform. He played pool and cards with friends in his graduation class. Good furlough, he thought. He had mustered all the strength he needed to return to base then serve on some cutter patrolling waters off Greenland or escorting a troop ship across the Atlantic.

Word reached Brighton July 8 that Dan had been picked up by MPs in town after being reported AWOL. He had every intention to return to his base but the home cooking, camaraderie with his friends and seeing his old girlfriend made him think differently—like a civilian again. The MPs must have weighed over two hundred pounds and were six feet five inches, at the very least. Dan was scared. Long days in the brig, a court martial, and a dishonorable discharge were high prices to pay for miscalculating the day he was due back. The two men who picked him up were not as threatening as one might think. "Don't worry, kid," one of them who had been close-mouthed until then whispered to him as they reached the corner of Grand River and U.S. 23. "We've picked up more soldiers like you than I can count lately. It's like skipping school when the weather is nice—playing hooky to go to a ballgame. But Uncle Sam is your boss now and you recruits who are wet behind the ear have to learn the hard way. No trial. You'll get an Article 15 when you get back—kp and clean up some nasty latrines for a while. But I wouldn't advise you to forget what day it is on leave again just because you like hanging around your girlfriend."

Micky Faherty's case was different—tragically different, in fact. Mick was younger than Dan, the youngest of five siblings. The only boy in the family, the outgoing lad had everything going for him—good looks and intelligence—and he never refused to help someone in need.. He was not even eighteen when he joined the navy. Like Dan, he had a girlfriend—a serious girlfriend. The day he left for basic training in the navy, Faherty learned that he was going to be a father. There was no alternative in his mind. The first week of July 1944 he was married, a child due shortly. He went AWOL intentionally. The MPs who arrested him at home on East Main were nothing like the two men who took Dan back to his coast guard base. He was handcuffed, read the charges and court martialed soon after. Sentenced to five years in prison at Ft. Leavenworth and subject to further punishment by the navy afterward, Mick was allowed to return to Brighton before his incarceration to see his baby boy, born in August. That same day he burned his navy uniform.

Standing beside the French doors in our living room, next to the front vestibule facing Rickett Road, was a pine desk Dad had given Mom. It was a Christmas present from sometime before the war and he had purchased it, like the rest of the furniture in our house, from Beurmann's in Howell. Mom had made plans for a home office in that bright front room, away from other parts of the house where people tended to congregate. Once a show piece, complete with a portable Royal typewriter she had purchased with her first pay check from Landis Machine Company in the late '20s, her haven had seen better days by the time my brother Eddie, as a toddler, discovered that wing of our 12 room farmhouse. There were ink spots on top of the desk, in every drawer—even on the hardwood floor below. Numerous scratches covered its surface, the typewriter's keys were bent and the ladder-back chair with a red velvet seat that came with the desk was no longer sturdy enough to sit on.

Buried underneath stacks of insurance papers, bank statements, federal income tax returns and land titles in one of the double desk drawers were two small battered notebooks. At the top of one, red and more "used" looking because it was filled with entries, were the faded gilded words *"National Diary 1943."* The other was from the year 1948, a Christmas present to Mom in 1947 from my Uncle Joe. Already as a preschooler those books were intriguing to me—long after the *war* when I could not yet read and my only interest was scribbling drawings of farm animals or dogs and cats in it with a fountain pen my mother could never keep concealed from me.

I continued to be drawn to those daybooks, ever fascinated by my mom's writing. Depending on how much of a hurry she was in, some entries were in her neat hand while many looked more like shorthand than anything else. As I grew older, I became curious about some of the things Mom had written. Were they about me? Were they about cows? About Dad? I soon discovered that diary entries could be about anything—the weather (always a good topic when there were fewer things to write about), games we played, church, people getting married—even animals dying. When I finally mastered the art of reading cursive, I remember feeling sad about an entry from Valentine's Day in the 1948 daybook: *Jip, our faithful old dog who was 14 ½ years, died today. Lew's horse Bob also died today. We went uptown this afternoon, having at last started our car again. We went around to Mother's and had supper with them. The boys got valentines today from Emma.* I thought a long time about Jip—that "faithful" dog—about the litters of puppies she always hid in the barn that I always begged Dad to see. About Dad telling how she simply had to be told to "fetch the cows" and away she galloped down the back farm lanes to disturb them in their late afternoon grazing time only to be shepherded and sent through open gates and barn doors to stanchions for milking. I remembered Uncle Lew's workhorse Bob, too, and days in winter when the car would not start. And I remembered going "Up Home" to have dinner with my grandmother, Uncle Joe and Aunt Emma on Second Street.

It was the 1943 diary—far more inclusive than the post-war one—that always drew me back, always stirred my interest in what my relatives called the *war*. Mom wrote detailed accounts about every-day life, many of them about the availability of almost all products and services. On March 29, 1943 rationing of retail goods began. Two days later, with the fickle early spring temperature reaching seventy-six degrees, people rushed to town to buy whatever they could. Proprietors of Kroger's, Byerly's, Brady's, Scranton's and Tom and Pat's grocery stores dealt with the ire of valued customers who had arrived too late or cut in line to buy rationed items. Six pounds of sugar required eleven stamps. Often twelve to fifteen gallons of gasoline had to be forfeited simply because a calendar month had passed, during which time there had not been enough money to pay for fuel, as essential as it was. New tires and many other automobile parts were in such short supply that they rarely became available; a set of recapped tires at Roy Odell's in town was considered a good deal at $12.00! Consumer goods, farm produce, livestock, services and commodities which were still available varied from pre-war, Depression Era prices to selling for a far higher retail amount; everything depended upon what was needed in the war effort and the availability of labor. Mom noted that during the summer Dad purchased 10 ('nice") pigs, for example, for $100.00; neighbor Jim Caldwell bought a cow for slaughter from my dad for $150.00. In what was to become the coldest winter on record, a ton of hard coal from Stewart's Elevator cost $13.49. (Hard coal required constant stoking in the furnace to heat our sizeable farmhouse on Rickett Road; thereafter when fuel was needed Stewart's was able to change their delivery to two tons of easier to burn "Pocahontas" soft coal). By July 10, even with coupons, *"everything is scarce—chicken feed, no beef, no sugar, no butter, no coconut, no syrup."*

Mom's entries were not limited to the availability of consumer items, limitation of traditional services, higher prices and rationing books. She also wrote about visitors, farm tasks, illnesses and church. Auntie Ruth called Mom one morning in the spring to announce that Dad's eccentric farmer cousin, Louise Hackney, was visiting from Mt. Morris and should be expected soon. *"Taking care of an early lamb in the house,"* she wrote one day and *"little Carolyn has chicken pox."* Rev. Shoup received a raise; at $2,000 per year his was the highest salary ever. The church organist, Lena Musch, would now be paid $4.00 instead of $2.50 per Sunday. She and her sister sang duets at St. George Church for funerals. She did not even neglect the life of Detroit socialites: *"The Free Press had pictures and a large write-up on Josephine Ford's wedding."* There were asides, too, meant to be very private. Was little Eddie going to have a sibling? She wrote March 6 that she and Dad *"had callers from Judge Lyons about adoption."*

A great many of Mom's entries revealed how a middle-aged mother coped with a toddler, what she did in her leisure time and her duties as a housewife. She wrote that Eddie, my year old brother, *"will soon be walking and gets a thrill out of life and can play with the simplest things,"* this in spite of misguided toddler activities like eating candles, falling down the basement steps and drinking toilet water. She was a talented seamstress; in March she made a blue muslin dress *"with a square neckline finished with new pinking shears,"* and *"pajamas for the Red Cross."* She struggled with the long, cold winter, still managing to do household chores like washing and boiling eighteen diapers. Those jobs also included washing the bedroom, kitchen and dining room door curtains, cleaning the upstairs clothes closet, washing the kitchen woodwork and windows, making an apple pie and ironing the bedroom curtains! She made out and sent a check for the income tax March 13—$2.28 for 1942. One day alone, in late May, she *"broke the Sabbath by mowing the lawn after doing the usual odd jobs"* the day before.

Mom was an avid book, magazine and *Detroit Free Press* reader. Often she wrote in her diary about newsworthy *Free Press* stories. On my brother's first birthday Jan. 29 she briefly noted that FDR and Churchill had met on a battlefield in North Africa; on Feb. 26 there was a disturbing entry noting that two troop ships had been sunk. One of them was the *Dorchester*, with 674 deaths one of the largest loss of lives at sea in World War II. She subscribed to and read *Life Magazine* and *Woman's Day* from cover to cover. Among the books she finished in a few short days from her Book of the Month Club were *We Took to the Woods, Our Hearts Were Young and Gay, Big Family* ("can hardly put it down!"), *How Green is my Valley, Winter's Tales, Combined Operations* and *Look to the Mountain.* She also listened religiously to the news on WJR in Detroit and addresses by prominent politicians or military figures, such as famed flying ace Eddie Rickenbacker's account of his B-17 crash and survival in the Pacific in October 1942. She never missed *News of Importance* or commentaries by H. V. Kaltenborn and Edward R. Murrow, whose broadcasts originated from the European Front. During the day while ironing or cleaning, she always tuned in to entertainment programs like the ever-popular soap opera. *Ma Perkins, One Man's Family* and *The Romance of Helen Trent* were her favorites and evenings she and Dad never missed the hilarious *Fibber McGee and Molly* or the misadventures of *Henry Aldrich.*

Her extended family was more important than ever in those years and she spent as much time as possible in town with her mother, my aunt and her bachelor brother Joe when he was home from tending Westin Brothers Grocery Store in Fowlerville. In spite of Mom's busy schedule, she still made time for shopping trips to Ann Arbor or J. L. Hudson's in Detroit with Aunt Emma occasionally. In March she wrote almost with guilt about "buying a black coat with a silver fox collar," at Hudson's. My aunt, Mom and Dad enjoyed the occasional night out watching movies that cheered all Americans up in those difficult times as well. She and Aunt Emma saw Ronald Coleman and Greer Garson in *Random Harvest* at Detroit's United Artists Theater in March. The long list of Hollywood "flicks" both noted in their diaries included *Late Honeymoon* with Cary Grant and Ginger Rogers; *Winter Tie*, with Sonya Henie; *Blossom Time*; *Lady of Burlesque*, starring Barbara Stanwyck; *Hit Parade of 1943*; *Here We Go Again*, starring Edgar Bergen and Fibber McGee and Molly and *The Constant Nymph* with Charles Bergen, Alexis Smith and Joan Fontaine.

Because Livingston County was predominantly rural, Washington, Lansing and Howell kept close track of crop and livestock production and who was actively engaged in farming. Enforcers of agricultural provisions of laws were advised to pay particular attention to small farmers, especially new township residents who had relocated from Detroit. In Green Oak, our long-time neighbor Frank Meyer and my father, not called to service because of their age and lifetime occupation as farmers, served on the township's agricultural quota board. They knocked on doors for weeks on end after county quotas were released, informing neighbors what their crop and livestock production needed to be for a quarter or half year to remain exempt from draft status.

My father had little idle time in those years according to my mother's wartime daybook. Then again, farmers never did. Not only was he inundated with his duties on government war boards but there was one of the three rural Green Oak schools to deal with. Dad and Frank Meyer were directors of the local two-room frame schoolhouse for many years and during the *war* they were required to meet far more frequently with representatives of government education boards than usual. Fuel had to be purchased for heating the drafty old wooden structure, concerns from parents and teachers dealt with, upkeep of the building seen to and proper books kept for the Michigan Board of Education. My mother and other neighbors generously assisted Frank and Dad but there always seemed to be unforeseen things to worry about. Hiring, paying and providing a good ear for teachers was just another part of the job. Miss Dusenberg, one of the school's two teachers, knocked at the back porch door one blustery morning in March to announce that vandals had broken into the school and, among other things, strewn beer bottles on the floor. Better security was needed at once. Sheriff Kennedy was notified but the same thing happened with far more vandalism April 17. Fowlerville native Mrs. Bernice Chappel, teacher of the Kindergarten through third grade classes, was hired soon after Miss Dusenberg resigned that term. Mrs. Chappel was the mother of a young son, Kenneth, and with her husband in the military, her reasonable requests from time to time for cost of living raises were rarely turned down.

Though Dad was on Green Oak's farm quota board he was not exempt from wartime production demands himself. Nor was he exempted from providing a living for his family in times when farm incomes failed to keep up with expenses and essential fuel and feed became scarcer by the month. Crops had to be planted and harvested at the right time, milk produced at pre-war levels and livestock tended to. Quotas were not waived because of bad weather or lack of manpower, either. With a blizzard striking Southeast Michigan blocking roads and temperatures plummeting to ten below zero Jan. 20, it was necessary to send the usual three cans of milk to town on Brighton Township resident Henry Ross's sleigh. Uncle Louie Weber had stored it in his barn for many years, an unforeseen stroke of luck that harsh wartime winter, as Maud, one of our faithful workhorses, was dutifully recruited for service. By spring following that memorable winter, there was little time left for any jobs that could be put off until later. On April 10 he and his brother husked corn, yielding six or seven hundred bushels that were loaded on a wagon and drawn to the corn crib; three days later he was helping his neighbor, Ivan Coupar, husk corn on the old Maltby farm, a half mile away, then owned by George Fink, President of Great Lakes Steel Corporation. Ten days later Dad helped Charlie Priestley shear forty sheep and soon after he plowed fifteen acres for corn. He planted early potatoes April 27, got eight acres of oats sown May 4 and three weeks later plowed for silage corn until 10 PM! The field corn was planted June 4 and ten days later found him sowing silage corn seed, with haying and planting late potatoes coming later in the week. And what of June 21?

Harvesting grain, putting up hay for fodder, preparation of fields for sowing winter wheat and a host of other jobs made a farmer's life in the hot summer months a busy one. Busy and always dangerous. June, July, August and September were peak months for farmers' visits to doctors to be treated for such ailments as broken legs or arms, heat strokes or machinery injuries. After the death of Brighton's beloved Dr. Singer April 15 and with Dr. Duncan Cameron serving in the army, victims of accidents could only be treated in town in the office of one of only four doctors still practicing—Niles Clark, Archie MacGregor, W.O. Rice and Olin Wilkinson.

Dad had known numerous victims of farm accidents, the closest to him his Uncle Henry Weber, the victim of a binder severing most of the fingers on his right hand. Knowing the consequences of the loss of income for his family if an accident were to occur, he had always been cautious around wayward livestock and malfunctioning machinery. He was ever deliberate in his decisions about how and when to use farm implements—and just plain lucky, considering the number of incidents of farm accidents in mid-century Livingston County. Nothing could have prevented a close call in 1942, however, when he narrowly escaped having his right arm severed from his body.

Corn husking took place late in the fall after all the field corn had been shocked, dried and drawn into our large barn from the fields. The twine-bound shocks were pitched on the barn floor between hay mows and piled high next to our McCormack-Deering husker–shredder, which had seen far better days on my grandfather's, Uncle Louie's and our farm. The stocks of corn were crammed into the large feeder in the rear of the machine, where its large, sharp blades were always a threat. Inevitably, the husker, like a host of other hay and grain cutting implements, would break down. Either the long belt attached to the operating wheel of the tractor, anchored in neutral by a sturdy stake on the steep incline leading to our large barn, would fly off the wheel or the husker's conveyer belt would get twisted, causing the delivery chute to be clogged. That is what happened in mid-November just after Dad's fortieth birthday.

Uncle Louie, whose farm was only a mile north on Rickett Road, and Dad always were close and had teamed up on farm work since their youth. Louie usually worked with machinery; operating and maintaining his or my dad's John Deere tractor for haying, corn reaping, husking and feed grinding were his normal jobs. He was on-hand that day when Dad reached into the husker chute, tugged at an offending corn stalk and almost instantaneously found his arm bloodied. It was stuck on the shredder's nasty conveyer chopping block, its blades racing to chop off one of his limbs! Never in his life did he shout louder than in that moment to his brother to stop the tractor's power wheel. And just as he realized he was about to lose his arm to the savage gargantuan, his arm and the corn stalk were disengaged from the feeder! Uncle Louie rushed Dad to Mellus Hospital where Archie MacGregor, like a master tailor, stitched his patient up with the outstanding medical expertise that was his trademark, laboring for hours to prevent amputation and infection.

The hard physical labor of the spring and early summer following Dad's accident took its toll. Arthritis plagued him to the point that there were days when he could only do daily chores, like feeding and milking cows. Young Burl Cain was called upon to help him with routine work, like hauling more shocked field corn into the barn that had been neglected in the fall and rolling plowed ground for silage corn. By June 21 he could do little farm work. Small things like changes in the weather exacerbated his pain; he actually felt a jolt in his arm when the telephone pole just outside our house was struck by lightning. On June 24 my mom's wisdom finally prevailed: "Seek a doctor or let your arm worsen, perhaps even debilitate you for life!" He agreed to see Dr. MacGregor and at last found some relief from a shot and pills that seemed bigger than the ones he had routinely used to worm the horses! On July 8, 10 and 11 he saw the new osteopath in town, Dr. W. O. Rice, for chiropractic treatments that ushered in the first stage of his ultimate recovery. Close call. But no one had ever said that life on a farm would be easy, particularly in the middle of an all-out war that required everyone on the *home front* to pull his or her weight.

The front is right here at home, in our daily lives (and) in our daily tasks.

Ray Carmack   *Mary Hitdlebaugh*

CHAPTER THREE

Stardust   **March 1941**

> *Beside a garden wall when stars are bright you are in my arms*
> *The nightingale tells his fairy tale, a paradise where roses bloom*
> *though I dream in vain in my heart it will remain*
> *My stardust melody, the memory of a love's refrain.*
> — "Stardust," Hoagie Carmichael

"HURRY, TEX!" a little girl shouted excitedly. "He's coming down the stairs!"

A kindergartner from Miss Oyer's class was desperately trying to get her friend's attention from a vantage point at the north end of the high school's first floor hallway. She was standing tip-toed next to the door of a converted classroom that would have to make do that year until more space for an elementary school were found. The outfit she wore was straight out of J. L. Hudson's children's spring showcase— Buster Brown shoes, lace white socks, satin hair ribbon and pastel blue dress tied at the bodice. Her friend was also smartly dressed because her mother insisted that she look young lady-like, down to the hair style that had been much in fashion for over five years. Acting young lady-like, though, was just not enough incentive for a five-year-old to keep her dress clean, shoes unscuffed and Shirley Temple ringlets perfectly in place.

It was a Friday afternoon and the two girls made excuses to come out of the school room closest to the staircase of B.H.S. precisely when the senior stomp was under way. They already had crushes on the boys of the class of 1941 and knew the exact time their teacher would stop reading *Little Black Sambo* and ask the children to get their wraps in the adjacent cloakroom. "Hurry! You'll miss him!" the little girl in the blue dress yelled one more time.

Tex hugged the four year old boy sitting next to her for story time and said good-bye. He was African-American, the son of one of the many newcomers in the Brighton area doing defense department projects at the General Motors Proving Grounds. On her way out she gave another hug to her friend Barbara Ulman who lived just across from the high school. Barbara was a Massachusetts transplant whose father was also employed at G.M., a researcher from M.I.T. "Tex" was the hero of the cowboy adventure show on *WJR* Carol Pelkey and her best friend listened to every day after school. When Carolyn Weber showed up at the Pelkey home on Second Street wearing an overly large western hat that looked more like a *sombrero* than a cowboy hat one Saturday afternoon, Carol came up with the romantic name of a hero of the West for her sidekick. Not to be outdone, Carolyn christened her friend "Dusty," another of their heroes. Carol's parents didn't mind the girls re-inventing themselves, nor did Aunt Ruthie and Uncle Lew Weber. The names stuck—in the band, bumping into each other at the locker they shared at B.H.S and in their formals with Larry Oliver and Jim Meeks at the J-Hop. The two buddies kept those nicknames whenever they saw each other for the rest of their lives.

"Dusty" was talking about Ray Carmack, the younger son of the owner of the Grand Theater. Ray was voted the most popular boy and class president at Brighton High School that year. Despite their young age, Tex and Dusty swooned like sixteen-year-olds when they looked into his flirtatious brown eyes. His handsome face was accentuated by thick, ebony black eyebrows, dimpled and sparsely freckled cheeks and a widow's peak cropping down ever so slightly just to the left of the part in his wavy hair. In fact, had he not been so modest, he could easily have been the latest Hollywood heart-throb and on one of the posters in his dad's theater lobby—and his personality matched his good looks! He played football, got good grades and tooted the clarinet in the band. When Tommy Leith, Bob Lietzau, Chuck Brady

Carolyn Weber's and Carol Pelkey's Kindergarten Class, 1942
(Kneeling, Middle Row Left)

and Don Juipe raced down the stairs from the second floor after study hall in the assembly room, anxious to pair up with their sweethearts, Ray was always with them and always stood out.

Mary Margaret Hitdlebaugh had her eyes on Ray like the rest of the girls in town, but Ray had his eyes on her, too. Mary was a slim brunette who stood out in a crowd just like Ray. Don and Tommy noticed her the day her older brother Kenny picked her up from school after the family moved to Brighton from Ionia following their father's death. "She's a good-looker, all right," Ray told his friends as they pursued Mary and Kenny down School Hill. "And she sure looks swell in her bobby sox and that dress!"

Mary liked Don Juipe's cocky, self-assured manner and Tommy Leith's wavy hair and winning smile but Ray won out. The rest of the school year the two were inseparable—at school dances, at the Federated Church and Sunday school, even the Grand Theater where Walt Carmack gave Mary a job selling tickets and candy bars. When the rush before the main feature was over, Mary made her way to the seats below the projection booth where Ray worked to join her friends. From below the tiny cubicle the group of girls tormented him, throwing popcorn kernels and wadded up candy wrappers at the small window in the booth. Ray feigned disgust and anger but the thought of doing some serious necking moments afterward did not keep him mad for long.

After graduation, training as a file clerk in Detroit and transfer a few months later to the aircraft plant at Willow Run, Ray told both

Mary and his parents that he was better off choosing for himself which service to enter than letting the "Old Man's Draft Board" decide his future. His father grimaced when he heard that Lt. Harold Leitz had convinced both his older son Ted and Ray to join the army air corps. He knew no branch of service could shield them, but somehow the danger of being crew members aboard a B-24 bomber in the Pacific or Western Europe seemed to be a bad alternative. On Oct 21 his younger son, sixty-nine inches tall and weighing one hundred forty-six pounds, swore his allegiance to the United States and to defend it for the "duration of the war plus six months."

Tailgunner Ray Carmack

Nov 1943

The thin young woman thought nothing could match last winter's record cold as she stepped onto the train platform in Ann Arbor. The damp fall night chilled every bone in her body. Could it only have been four weeks since she boarded the same train to take her to the west coast? She should still have been reveling in the balmy California climate in the small house at 375 Mission Blvd. Should she be thankful or angry? The Brighton years were the best times of her life and she would be there again—a job at the Grand, living at home and keeping her mother from worrying about Kenny, Leonard and Keith.

A soldier in uniform, smoking a cigarette and carrying a beat up brown leather suitcase, reminded her that the world conflict was never very far away from home. He paused beside her and offered to help carry the luggage she had bought in October at Crowley's Department Store. Both pieces were lavender, her favorite color, and still smelled like the small room in Riverside Ray had rented for her. They were bulging with the wardrobe she and her mother hastily put together before her departure. She politely declined, but only as the G.I. tipped his cap and walked away was she aware that Ray was once again far away—twenty-five hundred miles to the west—and that realization was worse than the cold she felt in the dimness of Ann Arbor's lights on a wartime night.

Mary Margaret took out the picture she carried in her purse of Ray in uniform, shot on a bright summer day the same year, precisely where she was standing outside of the depot. That pose of Sgt. Ray Carmack, known to his superiors then as 16149074, interrupted her reverie. He was caught with a broad smile on his face—obviously forced—anxious to report for radio school in South Dakota but torn between two worlds. His air force training had taken him to so many places after he enlisted that Mary had trouble remembering them all or the reason he was there—Sheppard Falls in Harlington, Texas; Pocatello Army Air Force Base and Gowen Field in Idaho; Sioux Falls Army Base in South Dakota. She only knew that she was in love with him and proud of him wherever duty in that irreconcilable setting took him. Going home to Brighton was the only option she had now; she would make it work.

Ray's excellent training at the Ford Apprentice School in Detroit honed his interest in all things aeronautic and allowed him to advance in army air corps ranks quickly, finally to sergeant and graduation as a radio gunner on a Consolidated Heavy Liberator. For all he knew, he would be flying in a bomber he had seen on the production line at Willow Run where he worked! He loved the corps and wrote to his parents on Nov 17 that he planned to train as a pilot after the war: *"Filled out papers the other day for Officers Training School...the exam was easy. (This is a military secret, by the way.)"*

His scores on the O.T.S. mock test were, in fact, so high that 2nd Lts. Koeppel and Dock, his pilot and navigator, told him he would be foolish if he did not follow through with his plans. Not everything was that easy. In the same letter he reported that he was working very hard and flying high altitude missions every day. Then, almost as a postscript, he referenced a mishap that Mary and his parents thought he took too lightly:

> *"Crew made the March Field paper as we had our plane stand on its nose after we landed, and were parking it. The front wheel came unlocked and stood right on its nose. Nobody was hurt or anything as we were almost stopped. We sure had a time trying to get its tail down, but we did it ok."*

Apprehensive that he would be getting his overseas orders any day, Ray sent Mary Margaret money for a train ticket to Riverside the last week in October. Two days after arriving, Mary and he were married—the same day Ray received a good conduct medal. The short ceremony was at the Mission Inn, just a short distance from the apartment Ray had rented on Mission Blvd. The inn, already seventy years old, was built in the Spanish mission style and its storied past included stays by Presidents, movie stars and noted athletes. Given the couple's financial circumstances, it was no champagne and caviar affair. But Mary could not have been any happier, standing in the inn's courtyard with her new husband.

The honeymoon consisted of walking to town after the ceremony with friends, snuggling up together while listening to the radio that evening and gorging themselves with the homemade candy Mary brought from Brighton. It was cold outside on that first day of November but inside their cramped apartment on Mission Blvd it was toasty warm. The memory of that evening—two teenagers who fell in love walking down School Hill, now a couple—touched Mary's heart as long as she could remember. She never forgot the image of Ray getting up from the sagging studio couch where they were embracing, walking to the radio broadcasting more static than anything else, and tuning it to the March Field base station. It was playing *their* song, Hoagie Carmichael's *Stardust*:

> *Sometimes I wonder why I spend the lonely nights dreaming of a song,*
> *The melody haunts my reverie and I am once again with you*
> *When our love was new and each kiss an inspiration*
> *But that was long ago, now my consolation is in the stardust of a song.*

Their first morning together featured a special wedding breakfast. Mary confessed in a letter to the Carmack's three days later that it consisted of French toast made with "two borrowed eggs" and two oranges her new husband got in town. She also wrote that Ray "looked and felt 'swell'." One evening they went to the show and saw Robert Cummings and Olivia DeHavilland in "Princess O'Rourke"—"*a night out with my honey,*" as Ray wrote to his parents breaking the news about being married. Mary's wedding present to Ray was a pair of wide-striped red and blue "pjs" to keep him warm. Ray had already presented Mary with an eighteen-carat gold locket bearing a picture of the two taken in Brighton. A present for both of them was discovering Ray's name on a list Nov. 15 promoting him to staff sergeant.

They had hardly been married a few days when Ray came down with a bad case of the flu, sending him to the hospital. Once there, his illness was diagnosed not as the flu but a burst appendix, requiring surgery. Mary puzzled about that for days afterward. A blessing in disguise? Ironically, she was able to see more of her new husband there than if he had been well and on duty! Making the best of it, she ventured out every afternoon with some of the other military wives whose husbands were also ill, joining Ray during visiting hours in the evening.

Nov. 26th was the day Ray and Mary Margaret reluctantly decided she would return to Michigan, accompanied by the wife of one of Ray's friends. "There will be a ten hour wait in Albuquerque again and I will have to sit on a bench with a terminal filled with G.I.s while you will be in the air with your buddies between here and San Francisco," she told Ray tearfully at L.A.'s Union Station. "I will be sitting on a hard bench filled with the memories I feel I don't even own yet. We stole them for a few days when we were together in Riverside—but I *promise* I will not forget them for the rest of my life."

As Ray struggled to remember the events of late November, December and early January a few weeks later, nothing stood out like saying good-bye to Mary at Union Station and their prolonged embrace. He had never been more certain of anything in his life. He was in love with her, all right; she was not just the high school girl that all the boys in the B.H.S. class of '41 had their eyes on. Being hundreds of miles away from Mary for most of his military service had drawn them closer than ever to each other. A continent and a war five thousand miles away would not change things.

It was not until the train was out of sight that day that he remembered a quote he had memorized only a few years earlier by Blaise Pascal in Hildreth Clark's literature class at B.H.S., a quote so beautiful and profound that Miss Clark read it in French before assigning an essay to her class on it:

"Le coeur a ses raisons que la raison ne connâit point."

"The heart has its reasons that reason does not know." Ray loved Mary from the bottom of his heart; she was his soul mate now but he was not asking himself the reason why.

The B-24 Flying Fortress Bomber

CHAPTER FOUR

The Diary **Old Buckenham, England Feb 1944**

> *"Oh, I have slipped the surly bonds of earth/ And danced the skies*
> *on laughter-silvered wings/ Sunward I've climbed, and joined*
> *the tumbling mirth/ Of sun-split clouds — and done a hundred*
> *things/ You have not dreamed of — wheeled and soared and swung..."*
>
> "High Flight," John Gillespie Magee Jr.
> (Courtesy The Liberator Men of Old Buc, Andy Low and Lloyd Prang, Eds.)

RAY'S DIARY WAS BEGINNING TO SMELL MUSTY from the English winter. Old Buckenham was dark and dreary even at mid-day. He had made up his mind. After the war he and Mary would move to a sunnier climate to start their family—California, hopefully—maybe even Riverside. He thought he could attend O.T.S. somewhere in California, for sure. Maybe his dad would lend him enough money to put a down payment on one of the bright two bedroom bungaloes he had seen near March Field. And there was talk that the Old Man was determined to get Congress to pass a bill to help returning veterans get financial aid for housing and education after the *war*.

My Record of Service was tiny enough to fit into Ray's shirt pocket. It was a standard issue for every soldier, with an I.D. page, a section to record highlights of service and a part for names of buddies. There was enough room to write about events in soldiers' lives and even attach pictures of sweethearts, friends, or small *Life* Magazine pictures of matinee queens like Betty Grable. The daybook part of Ray's diary had but a few entries. Whenever there was a spare moment, writing to Mary took priority. But December and January were happy times in his military career and he wanted to remember them all his life, if only by a minimal amount of scribbling in his sometimes illegible longhand.

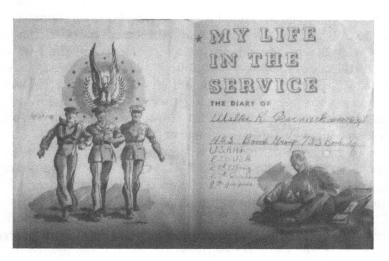

Ray had recorded the ten names of every member of Crew 32 – 42 -64460 that was organized at Gowan Field in August in it: Master Sgt. Vern Gill, Crew Chief; 2nd Lt. Paul E. Koeppel, Pilot; 2nd Lt. Dixon Griffith, Co-Pilot; 2nd Lt. Marvin L. Dock, Navigator; 2nd Lt. Edward V. Chovancak, Bombardier; Technical Sgt. Rufus Emmons, Engineer; Staff Sgt. James R. Farris, Engineer; Staff Sgt. James J. Corban, Engineer; Staff Sgt. Wayne T. Lillibridge, Armorer Gunner; Staff Sgt. Walton T. Seed, Armorer Gunner. His best buddies were Lilibridge, Emmons and Corban, probably because they were good at lifting everyone's spirits and had special skills that he admired.

Emmons held the same rank as Ray and his nickname was the "Piggy Bank Kid." He was a *first rate engineer and ball gunner whose favorite pastime was flirting with N.C.O. waitresses…Any time you want something, just yell 'Limey' and he'll come running!* Ray joked. Corban, the top turret gunner and 2nd engineer, was a married man and answered to the name "Old Father." Lillibridge, "Puttle" to his crew-mates, was a tail gunner who had studied to be a radio man at Tyndale Field in Florida, graduating in the same class as 1930s box office star Clark Gable. His favorite sport was picking on engineers! He had taken a few art classes before the war and enjoyed making caricatures of everyone in the crew, often to their displeasure.

――――――――――

Ray was so much on edge when he returned from Union Station in L.A. without Mary that he almost took a swing at Limey and Puttle when they kidded him about being alone in bed that night. But his anger was short-lived and he played practical jokes on them that might belong to the record books. Corban, the other married man in his circle of friends who hated being away from his wife and was another victim of the jocularity, was his able ally. Then, before he and "Old Father" could plot any further, the anticipation of both echelons of the 453rd leaving for overseas diverted them. The air echelon, to which they belonged, left March Field as planned Dec. 2. The first part of their cross-continent odyssey, however, took them north to Hamilton Field in San Francisco, there to remain for most of the month. *"Our crew got our airplane today, a B-24, #11-42-4460,"* Ray wrote on the 14th, though he made no mention of the crew christening it *Shack Rabbit* with generous splashes of champagne. He also neglected to mention that Lillibridge had painted the ship's name below the nose in bold cursive letters and sketched a whimsical giant hare with protruding teeth next to it, anchored by a run-down "hog" cabin and outhouse.

On Dec 23 the 733rd air squadron left for Palm Springs, a five-and-one-half hour flight, spending Christmas there and getting some long deserved passes. Four days later it was farewell to the sunny West Coast, bound for cold and muddy Midland, Texas, a four hour trip. Flying east again, "Shack Rabbit" landed in Tennessee at year's end. *"Spent New Year's Eve in Memphis at the Red Cross canteen playing ping pong and pool… no passes!"* he wrote a few weeks later in Old Buckenham, forgetting to mention the trauma of noisy off-base revelers waking him up from his dream in a sweat. It was a dream he did not want to end, in bed next to Mary back at March Field, the din of B-24 bombers overhead.

Shack Rabbit was Ray's crew's pride and joy but its real test was yet to come. Transatlantic flights were precarious at any time, not to mention in wartime with German aircraft lurking over the high seas. Making things more precarious, *Shack Rabbit* could not get armor plated until it reached England. But as dangerous as it was, its voyage was safer than many had suspected it would be. *"First hop out of the States,"* Ray wrote Jan 9, *"flew to Trinidad, British West Indies, landed at 10:47 A.M., 9½ hour trip."* The next two days found the crew flying further south to Belem and Natal, Brazil. *"Had our first good meal here since leaving the States,"*

1:15 A.M.," he recorded Jan 11. The following day the crew *"pulled a 50 hour inspection on the ship and put all Shack Rabbit in shape...'spected to pull out at midnite but 'no soap'."*

At 0435 amt, (American Military Time) January 14, *Shack Rabbit* finally pulled out. Its destination was Dakar, West Africa, across one of the shortest spans of the Atlantic between the western and eastern hemispheres. It was a flawless ten-and-one-half hour trip. The next day the crew landed in Morocco, North Africa, where American, British and Free French forces had battled valiantly to prepare for the 1943 invasion of southern Europe. Marakesh, Ray noted, was a six-and-one-half hour flight from Dakar, again a flight perfectly executed. Then, two days later, Crew 32 headed for England, headquarters of the European Theater of combat, from which point strategic missions were planned in the heart of Nazi occupied territory and Germany.

On Jan. 17 at 0930, amt, *Shack Rabbit* landed in Prestwick, Scotland, diverted from southeastern England due to bad weather. It was to be ten days before that Scottish January allowed the ship to leave. There was anticipation that the weather was cooperating at least three times, and *Shack Rabbit* was airborne more than once. Everyone was uneasy, for there were rumors that an all-out bombing campaign had been put on hold because the nasty Anglo-Gaelic weather was not cooperating. Needing the manpower in the south, part of Crew 32 was ordered out of Scotland. *"Seed, Lillebridge, Emmons, Corban and Lt. Chovancak went to final destination in England by train,"* Ray wrote on the twentieth. *"Sure hated to see the boys going without us."* Three days later and certain that the weather had cleared, *Shack Rabbit* took off, circled the field ready to leave but returned eighty minutes later. A third flight was aborted, *"the roughest flight I have ever been on,"* according to Ray's diary, *"so we stick around here a little longer, I guess!"*

Ray's diary entry Jan. 27 was decidedly more upbeat:

> *"Finally getting out of Scotland. Took off at 3 P.M. and landed at 5 P.M. Got together with the crew again."*

For once, the sun shone brightly over the patchwork of fields surrounding Old Buckenham, England. Ray's first impression was positive. *"Love the countryside when the weather is nice,"* he later wrote to Mary. *"The base is enormous...Sure was good seeing Old Glory flying at headquarters when we landed."*

USAAF Station 144 was built as a home for the 453rd that had been activated at Wendover Field, Utah the first of June. It mushroomed almost overnight in 1943 at the site of a strategic Royal Air Force base two miles south of Attleborough in Norfolk. Green and gold fields of wheat, barley and hay surrounded it with what resembled medieval stone crofters' cottages dotting the landscape. Two earthen bastions for defense carved out of the ground to the northwest and southeast were evidence of the Roman occupation of Britain two thousand years before. The Park and Castle Farms—freely held land since the time of Harald Blue Tooth—lay immediately to the south. Quaint old Anglo-Saxon and Norman names like Puddledock, Burgh Commons and Sherrards Green added to its historical charm.

On Feb 5, 1944 the Union Jack was lowered and replaced by the Stars and Stripes. The Fourth Army, of which the 453rd was a part stateside, now became a component of the Eighth Army and called Station 144 one of its homes. It was to fly 259 missions in Europe, concluding 6,655 sorties, dropping 15,804 tons of bombs yet losing only 58 aircraft! The fame of the 733rd, Ray's Squadron, was sealed with the completion of 82 consecutive missions later in the war without a loss. Commanded by Col. Joseph A. Miller, Hollywood film star Jimmy Stewart was to become its Group Executive Officer in March.

Though unique in many respects because of the East Anglian terrain and proximity to the village, 144's spider-like design resembled many of the four score Allied Air Corps bases in Britain. Almost in the middle of the base was the 453rd's headquarters, immediately to the south of the hospital. On the western perimeter were the areas or "sites" where close to fifty Nissen crew huts were clustered, with the WAAF quarters and mess hall just to the east. On the northeastern margin were the bomb storage areas and firing butts. An enormous delta-shaped tarmac occupied the south and south central part of the base with three concrete runways forming an inner triangle servicing more than fifty combat-ready B-24s.

Ray couldn't help but be amused by the clever, endearing and pugnacious names chosen for those awesome B-24s; he thought *Shack Rabbit* was one of the best, even though Piggy Bank and Puddle had not asked his opinion when she was christened. At times, he regretted never getting a chance to suggest *Mary Margaret* to his crew, though he would likely have been outvoted. His Brighton buddy, Keith Baldwin, and fellow airmen called their B-29 bomber the *Old-Bitch-U-Airy Bess*. The colorful names of planes he saw at Old Buckenham were just as inventive, some ingenious! In his squadron were the *Ken-O-Kay, Flack Hack, Whiskey Jingles, Flying Bull, Golden Gaboon, Lil Nemo* and *Gypsy*

Queen. Some had seductive women painted on them, like the *Never Mrs.* The 722nd, 734th and 735th had the *Crow's Nest* (commanded by Lt. Crow!), *Paper Doll, Pretty Penny* and *Round Trip.* More often than not, it was the prerogative of the pilot or co-pilot to suggest their sweethearts' names for their ships—they had gotten their way on the four planes parked next to *Shack Rabbit:* the *Linda Lou, Ruth Marie, Lillie Belle* and *Ginnie.*

There was another reason for Ray's diary entry Jan 27 to sound upbeat. *"...Also received first mail!"* he wrote, completing one more page of *My Life in the Service.* He smiled at the corporal who was struggling with the names of Chovancak and Lillibridge. "Koeppel," the newly arrived pilot, was an impossibility for him to pronounce. "Carman!" the enlisted soldier shouted after a few moments of hesitation, at which point Ray snatched a letter out of his clutched fist that he imagined still smelled of Mary's perfume, a gift from Frances Carmack the day she left for California. Mary wrote that her life seemed as normal as it would ever be again, six weeks after returning from Riverside. How many letters had she received from Ray so far? Five, at last count, she thought; from the west coast, then Florida. Ray checked his diary entry from Florida. *"Wrote Mary for the first time in one 'heckuva' while,"* he had written the seventh of January. *"Darn nice weather here."* It was from Morrison Field in West Palm Beach, his last correspondence composed stateside.

Ray's mind wandered. In sixth grade Miss Shannon had moved him away from the window facing Irvin Brown's house on School Hill because he had a penchant for daydreaming—a part of his personality Mary found endearing. His unfinished letter was already five pages long but he was feasting now on good memories of high school days—it made him forget the dismal Old Buckenham weather and mud, at least. But suddenly Chief Gill interrupted his cozy session of thinking about Mary; there was routine ground work with the crew to do and, more importantly, Chief had ordered him to review every note from radio gunner school he had taken in Sioux Falls.

The orders were unsettling. Something was imminent. Emmons, Lillibridge and Corban felt it too. "Hey, Limey," Ray shouted at Piggy Bank as the crew settled in for the night in their dingy, cramped Nissen hut. "What the hell is going on anyway? You've been here longer than I have. What have you heard?"

"Who knows?" Emmons shouted back. "I only know that we didn't bring *Shack Rabbit* over here to get stuck in this quagmire all the time. Be patient for one damn time, Carmie."

Ray had managed to finish his letter to Mary but he was still not caught up writing everything in his journal about events stateside. He decided to put that off one more time but vowed to write every night about the day's events at Old Buck before turning in from now on. On Jan. 30th he wrote only two sentences but there was an indication that something was indeed about to happen:

> *"Took our ship to Modification Center today with skeleton crew. Shack Rabbit to get some Armor Plating."*

Crew 32 did not have a moment to relax after plating *Shack Rabbit*. Limey had no time to tell the non-com waitresses how beautiful they were. "Old Father" rarely talked about his wife and Puttle didn't bother to tease the engineers. No one in the crew expected that a new month would find them so busy flying their ship, inspecting it from nose to tail with a fine toothed comb and endlessly loading and unloading bombs from storage. There was no time now for letter writing or keeping journals up to date. The men were taking Piggy Bank's comment about not keeping *Shack Rabbit* stuck in the mud seriously.

In February, when the weather had lifted somewhat, the 8th Air Force initiated eleven all-out attack and destroy missions over occupied Nazi territory in Western Europe and the heartland of Germany, ultimately striking Berlin. "A secret front before the invasion of Europe," Hitler's Minister of Armaments and War Production, Albert Speer, later asserted. The missions were designed to destroy Nazi production of submarine, tank and airplane engine factories—key elements in the *Luftwaffe's* devastating blows in the Battle of Britain. By many accounts, including that of Eric Hammel in his work *Road to Big Week*, it ushered in one of the most critical eras of the *war*—successful daylight bombing of the European continent. And, indisputably, it made the Normandy D-Day invasion possible.

Ray was fatigued beyond belief Feb 11 after *Shack Rabbit's* first combat mission but he could not sleep. There were too many bad dream outbursts from crew members and his thoughts kept him in the skies over France. From then on, four operational days of February colored his entries in *My Record of Service* with the stark realities of war and dark overtones. He opened his foot locker, reached for the mildewed pages of his journal and began writing:

> *Feb 11, No. 1 Operational*
> *"Shack Rabbit" received his first flack late today – a piece of flack*
> *went through the leading edge of the wing between engines 3 and 4.*
> *Was only -24 (degrees) at 15,000 (feet) today. Target – Abbeville,*
> *France. [Take off - 0745 Landed 1200] 12/500# (bombs) / (loaded*
> *at) 4:14.*

The next few days were no different. He had promised to write often to Mary and his parents but they would worry needlessly so he resolved to wait a week when there would be a long overdue two day pass to catch up on Brighton letters. Instead he added a few lines to his journal. France, he wrote, was still targeted:

> *"Feb 12, 1944 - Flew 1½ hours today and came back. Didn't fly in*
> *Shack Rabbit as he is still being repaired from flack holes received*
> *in France.*
>
> *Feb 13, 1944 - No. 2 Operational - Took off at 12:55 today.*
> *Carrying a full load of 500# bombs. We hit the target. Landed at*
> *1640 in good shape. Ran into heavy flack but no damage. Target –*
> *15 mi. North of Abbeville France. 3:40/*
>
> *Feb 15, 1944 - No. 3 Operational - Took off at 1040 today loaded*
> *with 12 500# bombs - The flack was quite light and the target*
> *visible. Seen some pretty good hits. Landed at 1525. Target the*
> *same area as 2nd mission. 505/" "*

The long rumored pass to London five days later was relaxing, if not what one might call enjoyable. The bombing raids, though very productive, had put everyone on edge. He wrote two letters to Brighton, one to Mary and one to his parents, and abbreviated entries in his journal covering *Feb 20 – 21: "Went on a 2 day pass to London and had a fairly nice time..."*

The air offensive on the continent turned into a fiery inferno for thousands the fourth week in February. Big Week, or Operation Argument, had begun. Ray disguised the danger he and the crew faced in his Feb 23 entry, his fourth Liberator attack: *"Was in a pretty bad raid,"* he wrote. *"Most of the bombs were incendiary bombs."* He was not yet privy to casualty reports: the bombing run resulted in the loss of a great many of the 453rd's aircraft and 322 men.

His writing revealed other facts that jolted his entire crew. Back in Old Buckenham, the insomnia plaguing him returned. But writing, he discovered, was calming. It was a soldier's tonic, not just a diversion:

> *"Another crew used Shack Rabbit while we were gone and brought him back shot up some more. Lt. Ingram reported missing – one of 733rd ('s) best pilots."*

Shack Rabbit was Crew 32's pride and joy. Everyone felt ownership of it in one way or another, from the painting below the nose to the unique tiny acrostics hidden below the turret. Ray thought right away about its emergence outside a hangar back in Henry Ford's Willow Run. It was a tough blow. Who knew how soon the ship would be in the air again? And the loss of Ingram's aircraft, the *Ginnie*, had brought tears to everyone's eyes. Aircraft 42-64138 was on mission 9 of the 453rd, targeting an *ME 110* airplane assembly plant in Gotha, Germany. Commander Ingram and his crew were not listed as *KIA*, the shorthand acronym the war department conceived for file clerks, that bitterly tragic alphabetical poison newspaper readers stateside dreaded seeing. *Ginnie* was officially part of an *MACR*, another series of letters that wore out thousands of black typewriter ribbons struck by elite or pica letters at bases from Anchorage to Monte Casino. For the present, at least, there was still hope. Ingram and his crew were part of a "Missing Aircraft Report," a common form file clerks at USAAF Station 144 were soon to pull far too often.

Thirteen-year-olds from Old Buckenham and nearby villages made it their business to keep a daily record of the number of B-24s from the Second Combat Bomb and Bombardment Wings that soared into the gray skies over East Anglia on their missions that February of 1944. They knew if they were a Model H, J, L or M. They knew which fighters from bases on the coast would accompany them. They could tell precisely which aircraft had sustained damage because of the erratic *rat-tat-tats*, grinding of gears and metal shearing sounds they heard. They learned to recognize flight and mission patterns. And they kept tallies of aircraft leaving and returning, knowing instinctively if one of the Heavy Liberators were missing. Of the latter, they had counted thirty-five by Feb 24.

Ray's description of that fifth day of "Big Week" was the most detailed of any:

"No. 4 - Operational - We took off at 0945 on our fourth raid.
Loaded with 52 incendiary bombs for a Me 110 plant in Germany.
We dropped our bombs ok and ran into some FW 190 fighters,
they didn't stay long – One slug a few inches from our gas tank!
Landed at 1600 / 6:45 Roughest Mission so far. Flack was accurate
& light."

On the evening of the 24th every entry—mostly from December and January—in Ray's diary was up-to-date. He was sorry that there were no more blank pages. It was a pleasant routine now, even if the events of the last few days he wrote about were difficult—no, painful—to describe. Chief Gill informed his crew one last time before turning in how proud he was of them. They had performed brilliantly, even in their new ship. It was also called *Shack Rabbit*, an older Liberator and the third ship, they had been told, with the same name. (Later they learned that one had been downed in the North Sea.) Chief also congratulated everyone that they were due now to receive their fourth Battle Star and European Theater of Operations Ribbon for exceptional service in line of duty.

"Farris still not flying?" Piggy Bank asked.

"Heard that he and Griffith won't be flying with us until at least the first week in March," Ray answered.

The first engineer had been grounded since Feb 13. Corban, the other engineer, was reading the latest edition of 144's base newsletter. He had heard that the women of the Aero Club planned a get-together for airmen from Pennsylvania after the big leap year day party and he was searching for details. "Old Father" laid the newsletter on top of the latest issue of *Stars and Stripes* which he had slung down on the floor next to his cot and interrupted Ray's and Emmons's conversation.

"I heard he is going for Tech Sergeant like you two," Corban said.

"Yeah?" Piggy Bank answered. I'm glad me and Ray will have another techy among us! Have to admit that I'll be glad when the original crew is back together."

"I will, too," Ray agreed. "But Lt. Baker is a first-rate co-pilot."

"And Hauser's a darn good waist gunner to have down by you guys," Corban conceded. "We'll need everyone giving two hundred percent tomorrow."

Chow and briefing came before sun-up in the early morning hours of 25th February. The stars in the sky close to the North Sea over East Anglia that day were blurred by clouds but they obstinately struggled to shine through them. It was a far earlier reveille than usual but Mission Eleven of Operation Argument demanded it. It would be daylight by the time they reached *Wehrmacht XIII*, the German military zone where multiple sorties targeting aircraft engine factories at Furth were planned.

"This one will be to honor Ingram and the boys..." Ray shouted at Lt. Koeppel, handsome and always smartly dressed in his A-2 flight jacket with stand-up collar. He was already in the lighted cockpit of the Flying Fortress next to Barrette Baker pointing at charts, weather reports and a myriad of memos Major Smith and Captain Kanaga had passed on to them. In the middle of his sentence, shivering and pumped with adrenaline, he remembered that his flying goggles had been misplaced after Operational 4 and he ran to retrieve them from the Nissen hut at the opposite end of 144. Out of breath, he grabbed them from under his cot, re-fastened his drab olive B-2 gunner's cap and took a few steps to the door before glancing back at his own little open cubicle. Then he saw his journal—so small you could easily lose it had the cover not stood out with its gold-embossed shield surrounded by oak leaves and topped by the spread-out wings of an American eagle. For Ray it had come to signify at once hope, promise and reaffirmation of his life in the corps. It was open to the page with Mary's picture at Riverside. He remembered sitting next to her the night she arrived there, two days before their wedding, arms around each other and Ray reading selections from Antoine de St. Exuperay's brilliantly fanciful *Little Prince*, a birthday gift from his sister Marlene. Glancing outside at the stars that were twinkling dimly in the misty sky above Old Buc he smiled broadly, recalling four lines from the book that had made a lasting impression:

> *In one of the stars I shall be living.*
> *In one of them I shall be laughing.*
> *And so it will be as if all the stars were laughing*
> *when you look at the sky at night.*

"And so it will be..." Ray thought. "And so it will be."

Revs. John McLukas and Ernest Crocker, accompanied by a military honor guard and members of the Jesse Cooley Post 235 of the American Legion, lead the burial procession of a Brighton soldier to his final resting place in the Village Cemetery, c. 1945.
(Courtesy Brighton Area Centennial Booklet, 1967)

CHAPTER FIVE

The Ken-O-Kay is Down   **March 1944**

> *For these men are lately drawn from the ways of peace. They fight not for the lust of conquest. They fight to end conquest. They fight to liberate. They fight to let justice arise, and tolerance and good will among all Thy people. They yearn but for the end of battle, for their return to the haven of home."*
> —Franklin D. Roosevelt
> Radio Address to the Nation, D-Day Invasion, June 6, 1944

REV. ERNEST C. CROCKER of the Wesleyan Methodist Church did not approve of dancing, smoking, drinking and a few other vices he believed inhibited people from practicing their Christian faith. St. Paul made this very clear in scripture, though perhaps the exact vices the

Wesleyan Church's leadership talked about were not all enumerated in the Bible. Crocker was not the only Brighton minister with such beliefs. Rev. John McLukas of the Methodist Church on Grand River certainly concurred and Mr. Hugh Crouch at the Federated Church was, after all, the spiritual leader of Presbyterians *and* Baptists. They staunchly opposed the same habits Crocker and McLukas condemned.

Attending movies was a gray area in the realm of Christian ethics that a great many people debated those days. After all, hadn't Americans always been told that an informed electorate was essential for a democracy to survive? Along with radio and the newspapers, newsreel coverage of the *war* at the Grand was one of the most important sources of war news in Brighton in those days And one could still be opposed to watching "objectionable" films by being selective about the films people went to. Rev. Crocker had said as much to Walt Carmack every time he met him at the high school on his rounds in Brighton Heights or patrolling Washington Street. Walt believed that the best tact in dealing with clergymen was never to be argumentative. "Perhaps you have a point, Ernest," or "I will give it some thought," was his usual response if the subject came up. He liked all the Protestant clergymen in town, especially the Wesleyan preacher. His style was not unlike that of the ministers he was used to back home in Tennessee. Besides, he was one of the most decent men he had ever known.

Ernest Crocker loved people and people loved him. He visited parishioners—and a great many non-Wesleyans like the Carmack's— regularly who were in need of counsel. His main goal was people's welfare, spiritual or otherwise, and people in town loved him the more for it. Crocker had visited Walt and his wife at their home on East Street many times just to chat, but the real reason was his deep concern for Ted and Ray, both overseas by then. "Care if I offer a prayer?" he would ask Walt. "Not at all," Walt responded, more comfortable than anyone knew with the spiritual approach of the Tennessee preachers he knew Crocker embodied. The owner of the Grand always felt a little better after the Wesleyan minister left.

On St. Patrick's Day 1944 Rev. Crocker confined his pastoral calls to town. He had used up his quota of gasoline ration coupons and did not want to go into the countryside anyway. Though he worried that he was neglecting his flock, many of the township roads were so muddy from the early thaw that it was impossible to drive on them. There was a heavy downpour on the fifteenth that did not let up for hours, making them even worse. Throughout Green Oak, Genoa and Brighton Townships farmers who still had teams were called on regularly to assist less sensible neighbors who had ventured out in their automobiles. Heading east down Main, Ernest saw a state trooper he did not recognize with two military police saluting the flag at the Roll of Honor. It was not uncommon to see military personnel there but it was unusual to see a trooper from the post at Grand River and U.S. 23 accompanying them. In all likelihood they were with the M.P.s to help them negotiate one of the country roads around town.

The three men left just as the heavens opened up again. Crocker's instincts by now had told him that something was not right. They drove slowly and deliberately northwest on Grand River, turning right at St. Paul, then left at East Street. Even that town street was full of gargantuan potholes and mud puddles that threatened to stop the strange procession of a trooper's Chevrolet, two Harley-Davidson motorcycles, and a '33 Black Ford driven by the Wesleyan preacher. Strange, Crocker thought. Where can they be headed?

Up the street they went, slowing as they approached Flint Road. And there they stopped. Good God! Crocker thought. It cannot be. It cannot be!

The day Rev. Crocker stood at Carmack's front door Mary Margaret was taking tea with Frances before going to the Grand to get things set up for the early feature. "Old Acquaintance" with Betty Davis had been such a hit the middle of February that Walt had decided to show it until the weekend. It was always cozy at the Carmack home, especially on a dark rainy day. Frances Morgan Carmack was a refined, gracious woman whose ease with people always made them welcome. Patrons who went to the Grand to see a show were always acknowledged with a sincere smile and asked how they were doing. She was a good match for her business minded, serious husband who patrolled the aisles of his movie house with a flashlight like a hawk, ready to put an end to any behavior he considered too risqué.

In spite of the soggy earth, some of Frances's daffodils and crocuses had begun to peek out of the planter beside the house and that brought a smile to Mary's face. How long was it since she had heard from Ray? The last letter dated the 24th of February arrived on the seventh—that would make it ten days. If her reckoning of the lapses in delivery of military mail were correct, she would be hearing today. Apart from Ray's usual sentimentality, it would be like the three she had received after the West Palm Beach letter, a very apparent malaise about them that one sensed between the lines. *"Flew our fourth mission today,"* he wrote, *"our roughest so far...Some new crew members and Shack Rabbit being repaired...missing our ship."*

Frances noticed Crocker first and was delighted. Walt will be disappointed he missed him, she thought. His visits lift us up! Rev. Mr. Crouch, her own minister, was an exemplary Christian whom she deeply respected, though he had faced numerous challenges lately at the Federated Church, not the least of which was the fire that left only the shell of the re-decorated church standing. Yes! The Wesleyan preacher was always just what the doctor ordered. He was frank, optimistic, and he did not drone on like some of the other ministers she knew. "Fill the kettle again, would you darling?" she asked Mary. Then both women spotted the other men.

Interlopers. Dread. Hearts stopped beating. A sickening panic.

"I am afraid these gentlemen have some terribly bad news, Mrs. Carmack." Crocker realized after he said "Mrs. Carmack" that he should be addressing two women named Carmack and he was disturbed.

The M.P.s who stood beside Ernest clumsily unbuttoned their muddy green slickers but did not shed them, despite a lull in rain. The one who had the more compassionate looking face of the two ventured to utter his well-rehearsed lines but struggled when he saw the expression of the two women standing before him. "I have...I have..." he finally muttered in the high falsetto voice that sounded like a teenage boy whose voice was changing..."I have the unfortunate duty of advising you that your husband—your son—is missing in action. Please accept my sincerest...wish... hope..." He stopped before he could finish his sentence, for he knew that this was not accepted military protocol. But he continued. "My hope is that your loved one will *not* have become a casualty." Then he handed the younger of the two women a telegram similar to the three he had already delivered that dismal day.

"I *cannot* read it, Rev. Crocker," Mary Margaret told Ernest with an expressionless face. "Please tell me what it says."

Ernest prayed then summoned all the courage his faith had gifted him with as he complied with Mary's request and opened the blurred envelope. He forsook the Sunday morning style of his Wesleyan preacher training, switching instead to the comforting pastoral style that made him so genuine:

> *Missing Aircraft Report*
> *26th February 1944*
>
> *Eighth Army Air Force Hqtrs, 453rd Bombing Group*
> *733rd Squadron*
>
> *Missing in Action:*
> *Sgt Walter R. Carmack*
> *Next of Kin:*
> *Mary M. Carmack, Wife, Brighton, Michigan*

Across town, at the north end of Second Street, my aunt treated herself to the candy bar my brother had given her earlier in the day and reached for her neglected daybook for 1943-44. She had not written in it in a long time; her latest Book of the Month Club selection, *Thirty Seconds Over Tokyo,* was far too good to put down. It was a busy day at the bank again and she had spent two hours after work on the second floor with the women of the American Auxiliary Red Cross sterilizing, cutting and wrapping cloth to dress wounds. She was exhausted but proud of the women's accomplishments; a record three thousand bandages from April of 1943 still stood! She wrote hastily but deliberately in the italicized style she had developed working as a teller and dozens of other jobs at the bank for so many years:

> "...the bank is paying six percent on common stock... weather bad again...Gil's V-Mail from Italy took less than twelve days to arrive...my income tax return made out and sent in..."

She paused a few moments to dip the point of her fountain pen into the bottom of a nearly empty ink bottle then hastily added a postscript and yet another. Her last entry that seventeenth of March had begun in her prosaic, matter-of-fact daybook style but now it almost seemed poetic:

> "...Heard that Ray Carmack ("Flying Fortress") is missing. Has been since Feb. 25th. He was married last November to Mary Margaret Hidtlebaugh. This is Brighton's first foreign case of sorrow...

...prayed for comfort for the Carmack's. This afternoon's rainbow over the Mill Pond beautiful, God-sent...this night's sky never lovelier."

Summer, 1944

Mary Margaret Carmack held out hope throughout the spring and summer of 1944 after that terrible day in March that somehow her husband would still be alive. In a prisoner of war camp? Hiding with another flyer? A case of mistaken identity? Hadn't the MP inferred as much in March when he handed her the telegram that Ray was missing in action? Walt and Frances Carmack at the Grand consoled her as best they could every day when she arrived for work. Her mother did too, relieved that no such news had arrived about her three sons in service. Then, on the first Sunday in September, she knew what the mission of the MPs and state trooper was this time just as Ray's parents picked her up to go to the Federated Church. They had made their rounds in Brighton thirteen times already, each one bearing a similar telegram from the adjutant general, military decorum strictly observed:

"Mrs. Mary M. Carmack, Brighton, Michigan. The Secretary of War asks that I assure you of his deep regret in the death of your husband, Sergeant Walter R. Carmack, who was previously reported missing in action; report received in the War Department establishes the fact that your husband's death occurred twenty-five February over Germany. Letter follows.
James Ulio the Adjutant General."

Mary's soul was shaken that third day of September. She was left with only cold, hard facts: Ray Carmack of the 453rd Bomb Group, Eighth Army, 2nd Combat and Bombardment Wing, was shot down 25 Feb at 01:15 in inclement weather over Nuremberg Germany. Aircraft #42-52307, later identified as the *Ken-O-Kay*, was returning from a mission to Furth. Nine other crew members were killed in action. It was Tech. Sgt. Carmack's fifth B-24 Operation Argument bombing mission.

Capt. H. C. Leitz was one of Brighton's unheralded war heroes. After exemplary duty in the army air corps in Europe, Leitz vowed

Capt H. C. Leitz,
U.S. Army Air Corps

Captain Harold C. Leitz

to discover where the B.H.S. friend he talked into joining the corps in 1942 was laid to rest. He secured as many Operation Argument documents as he could, finally uncovering the same Missing Aircraft Report Mary Carmack received in March 1944. Successive reports on bombing missions of the 733rd revealed that the *Ken-O-Kay* had exploded near Nuremberg, after which the German government identified and interred the remains of three members of Crew 32. Returning to Brighton in July 1946, Leitz learned from the Army Graves Commission that those remains, in turn, had been moved to a U.S. military cemetery near Metz, France, some twenty-five miles west of the German border. Through tireless efforts, the captain then arranged for the radio gunner's body to be brought home from its resting place a continent away in St. Avold, France, to be interred in the newly dedicated Brighton Hills Cemetery.

Late in 1948, Harold Leitz told Mary and the Carmack's that he had received word that Ray's remains would reach Brighton any day. In February, an honor guard presented them with a flag in their home on East Street. The re-interment was scheduled for family and friends a week later, the day most of the country celebrated the birth of Abraham Lincoln. The cemetery was hauntingly beautiful that day. American flags were blowing gently in the subdued wind, coloring the gray February skyline. To the north were the hills of Brighton Township, through which the Flint Road meandered, to the west the serene stone markers of Fairview Cemetery overlooking the Millpond.

After the ceremony was finished, the pomp and precision drills of the Jesse E. Cooley Post 235 of the American Legion completed and a three-gun salute fired, Mary Margaret remained at the new grave. The crowd of close friends and family dispersed as Don Juipe, Ray's best friend in high school whom Mary had married in late 1946, was off having a smoke. Mary Margaret was alone for once with her memories, standing next to the bronze grave marker Carmack's had asked Emil Keehn, the town undertaker, to order. If there ever is closure in war, she at last had a measure of it, almost five years to the day after Ray was killed. That setting made it easier to forget dealing with Don's nightmares and the hurt caused by the Carmack's not consulting her about the bronze plate over Ray's body. She was less hurt that Ray had had so little time to tend to personal matters after they were married and before he flew overseas that he had neglected to change the beneficiaries on his policy; she had not collected any money from it as Ray's parents had.

Grave markers and insurance policies didn't really matter at that moment. Ray's parents still embraced Mary as a daughter and made it very apparent to everyone who gathered at their home before the ceremony that day. She looked down again at Ray's new resting place in the earth, thankful that he was *home* where she was. Then she glanced up at the threatening clouds for a moment, struggling to make sense of the rest of her thoughts. Ray's remains are *here* at least. Except for two crew members in graves in France, seven others were who knew where? Where was "Old Father," whose son was growing up in Pennsylvania never knowing his dad? Where was "Piggy Bank," who would never flirt with beautiful NCO waitresses again or California girls? What about the *Ken-O-Kay*, in a rubble heap in Germany somewhere? And Ray's beloved *Shack Rabbit*, with Lillebridge's hilarious rendition of a hare and run-down outbuilding below its nose? It was in Soviet occupied territory, blown up over East Berlin two weeks after Ray was killed.

The far-too-short Riverside chapter in Mary Margaret Carmack's life was finished now. It was time to begin a new one as Mrs. Don Juipe.

Emma Westin, 1943

CHAPTER SIX

Baby Boom 1944

"Tryggare kan ingen vara, Än Guds lilla barnaskara..."
("Children of the heav'nly Father, Safely in His bosom gather...")
—Swedish Children's Hymn, Caroline Sandell-Berg

IN THE DARK DAYS OF WORLD WAR II, I have no doubt that my Aunt Emma Westin's kindness and thoughtfulness toward soldiers far from home brought them much joy and encouragement. But that could also be said of her relationship with many people on the home front. My aunt was generous to a fault, she gave expecting nothing in return, inspired and brightened the lives of everyone she knew. Her friendly smile greeted customers at the bank even if she did not know them, listened with caring to their concerns, offered her help and time freely. When she became gravely ill just before the *war* began, Dr. Duncan Cameron—a friend, not just doctor to the Weber and Westin

Families—sent her immediately to Howell for tests. For her family it was an alarming few days and resulted in surgery for what turned out to be a large but benign tumor. Her room in the turn-of-the-century McPherson Hospital where Duncan conducted surgery was flooded for days with flowers and well-wishers, sentiments which continued as she recovered at home on Second Street.

Emma's joy was spoiling her four nephews, treating herself to an O'Henry chocolate bar after work and teaching small tots in Sunday school at St. George Lutheran Church. In addition to routine, every day occurrences at the bank and news about friends and family, almost every week she wrote about the antics and sayings of the two and three-year-olds in her class. Young Cathy Bosworth asked her if the church were her house. "You live down the street, don't you?" she added. Later, as the class marched around the church basement she said "We're happy, aren't we?" Sara Cameron, daughter of Duncan Cameron who was serving as an army doctor in London, said "I want to sit on you today!" *"Just too cute!"* she wrote about three-year-old Larry Moore, who lived next to the parsonage. He ran into the church during services after Sunday school, sat down in the second pew from the front then darted to Emma, who was sitting in the choir loft. When she rose to sing he did too!

Perhaps because my aunt never married or had children, perhaps because it was just in her nature, she loved kids! It seemed only natural then for her to record the births of babies in her daybook that she heard about long before others in town. Late in 1943, Emma wrote about Dan Kellogg's and Phyllis Anderson's births and on Dec. 14 *"Eleanor Davis had a baby boy (James) at midnight." "Ruth Bauer Herbst had a daughter — Karen Marie — January 14,"* she noted. Not quite on time for leap day, Emma added to her diary *"Donald Herbst has a baby boy (Larry) born Feb. 28."* Her boss, Roy Newcomb, welcomed another grandson into the world May 23 — *"Henrietta Pearsall had a baby (Dennis) boy at 4:30 — 6 lbs., 6 oz, — she went to the hospital at 10:30 the night before."* On June 9 Ruth Ludtke, a family and church friend of long-standing, presented a baby sister to Emma's goddaughter, Joyce. She visited Ruth and baby Joan Marie in the hospital June 12 — *"gave her a rattle and $1.00,"* she wrote.

Nationally, the number of births during the Depression waned due to the hardest economic times in generations but by the early 1940s that was changing. Young husbands going off to war? Young husbands returning from war? It seemed that having babies in wartime was setting a new trend; census figures are all one needs to discern the connection. They reveal indeed that a great many of the births my aunt wrote about in Brighton were sons or daughters of soldiers. These included Paul Davis, Wendell Benear, Tom Wahl, Jack Halpin, Frank Verellen, James Cain, Don Carney, Leo Sprague, Jim Caldwell, Marshall Cooper, Bob Kirchbaum, Willis Kluck, Kirby Hall, Lewis Potter and Charles Case.

In addition to an increase in the number of babies born in the early 1940s, another fact stands out. Few babies were born at home or at the old McPherson Hospital in Howell. Most '43 and '44 infants, at least, came into the world in Mellus Hospital in Brighton, all delivered by Mellus's resident doctor, Archibald McGregor, assisted by his long-time R.N., Lucretia G. Smith. Suzanne Marie Campbell, born March 20 was one of them, the first African-American born there.

The Campbell's lived out U.S. 23 between Spencer and Buno Roads in a settlement known as "Brighton Gardens." Berney Walker Smith, chief usher at virtually all of Detroit's fashionable country clubs, founder of the Urban League in 1916 and friend of Henry Ford II, the Stroh Family and a long list of influential city leaders, established Brighton Gardens as a cluster of cottages and homes in 1920, summer lake retreats for his friends. In 1943 Smith's daughter, Ina Jane, became the first African-American graduate of Brighton High School.

Ina Jane Smith (Ezell), B.H.S. '43
(Courtesy Wayman Ezell)

Was it for a better or *safer* life that the Smith and Campbell families moved to Brighton? Wartime brought out mostly the best in a nation but bad things happened as well. My mother did not fail to record both the good and bad in her diary throughout the war. Not every entry was about civilian restrictions, farming or little Eddie's antics. Some are soul-searching commentaries, descriptions of events that rocked the core of her belief in justice and the good in humanity. On the first day of summer 1943 she wrote that *"rioting has been going on* (in Detroit) *between Negroes and whites."*

Despite the heroic efforts of African-Americans and whites throughout the nation—even President Roosevelt's wife—to fight for equal rights for people of color, little progress had been made by wartime. The South remained segregated *de jure* and the North largely segregated *de facto*. This latter brand of segregation plagued the nation's fourth largest city, Detroit, with its population of 350,000 in 1942. Its African-American population grew exponentially in the first half of the twentieth century, reaching over fourteen per cent by the beginning of the war. People seeking better housing, jobs and education migrated to the city that was the leading producer of automobiles in the nation. But the urgent need for public housing to accommodate new workers in burgeoning Detroit who were engaged in the defense industry in 1942 provoked a crisis. As the number of African-Americans in Detroit grew, so too did the racism they encountered.

One prelude to the racial crisis in Detroit my mother referenced occurred sixteen months previously. A new housing project located in a white neighborhood at Nevada and Fenelon for African-Americans, named for Sojourner Truth, a hero in the Underground Railroad, provoked confrontation with whites in late February 1942. Supported by the USHA and a Detroit housing authority, the 200-unit development was the scene of wide-scale protests between whites and blacks before eventually being integrated. Forty people were injured, 220 arrested and 109 held for trial after Detroit Mayor Jeffries eventually called in over one thousand city and state police and sixteen hundred National Guardsmen to keep the peace. Just before the riots broke out that my mother wrote about, there were more race-based incidents. Whites at a Packard Motor Car Company assembly line boycotted the plant June 3 - 6 after three African-Americans received promotions to work next to them. They shouted racial epithets and horrendous remarks while picketing outside, some actions instigated by transplanted white southerners whose numbers had also grown before and during the war. Ultimately resolved through efforts by the UAW – CIO, much of the boycott's blame was attributed to the Ku Klux Klan.

On June 20, gangs of whites and African-American youths clashed on Belle Isle. Rumors spread like wild fire in both white and African-American communities and the fighting spread to the city proper.

Looting took place in businesses in the poor section of the city called Paradise Valley, cars were burned, and large numbers of African-Americans were assaulted outside of places like the Roxy Theater on Woodward and while leaving streetcars. Federal troops restored order to the city after three days but the toll was devastating—thirty-four people killed, six hundred injured, eighteen hundred arrested, between seventy-five and eighty-five percent of whom were African-American.

Risking one's life to serve one's country in wartime would not seem to justify the kind of racism reflected in the civilian world at the time of the Detroit riots but that was not the case. African-Americans were widely discriminated against in the military as well, with few attaining high ranks. This despite the fact that a larger percentage per capita than whites were drafted and served in the war. People scoffed on hearing that entirely African-American crews in Tuskegee, Alabama had been formed in the Army Air Corps; ace pilots in the armed forces, it was thought, were entirely Caucasian. Yet the Tuskegee Airmen of the 332nd Fighting Group proved them wrong. Tuskegee Airmen performed valiantly throughout the war flying fighter planes escorting bombing missions. Their discipline was legendary, never breaking ranks in their red-tailed P 39s, P-40s, P-47s and the legendary P-51 Mustangs. By war's end, they had not sustained a single loss!

It was to be another four years before President Harry S. Truman boldly desegregated the military, of which the Tuskegee Airmen were a part. And not until nine years after the war did the United States Supreme Court affirm that one of the things the nation had fought against in World War II, racism, was unconstitutional in *Brown vs. the Board of Education*. Not until ten years after that landmark decision did President Lyndon B. Johnson get Congress to fight institutionalized racism by passing law after law that mightily strengthened the Bill of Rights. *

Apparently my parents had time to think about other pursuits than working on the farm, wartime duties, raising Eddie or keeping house in early 1944. My aunt wrote on April 1 that *"Ed had supper up home* (the Westin home on Second Street)..."*Anna not feeling well so didn't come."* By June 5 she had broken the news to the family that she was *expecting*. There was no exclamation mark or rhetorical comment after that entry because that was both the Weber and Westin way of reacting to or acting upon such news. In my imagination I see grandmothers, aunts, uncles, cousins and friends drinking a bit too much, hugging, and doing whatever was the equivalent of high-fiving in the 1940s. News of my impending birth was just no big deal, despite the dynamics in the family. After all, when Mom announced she was pregnant three years before, *that* was the big news—a baby after initiating adoption proceedings *and* after twelve and one half years of marriage. I was, however, expected to look the part of a model Gerber baby food infant: *"Anna shopping with Jennie* (her sister) *in Detroit at Hudson's; bought several things for the new baby including a layette,"* my aunt wrote later in the month of June.

Mom's pregnancy, going on forty years of age, was a difficult one and Archie McGregor was summoned a great many times that summer and early fall to treat her. Despite the risks, I was born on Monday, October 16, the first brown-eyed boy in the very Swedish Westin family in generations, weighing over nine pounds. My mother noted a few of her maternal observations about me in my baby book three months after my birth. *"As a newborn, Paul smiled and laughed easily. He had a formula of cow's milk, water and syrup and at four weeks started drinking orange juice and natola...Paul does not like his playpen and walker but enjoys creeping everywhere. He has very little hair (almost bald) and is beginning to show a temper!"*

Had it not been for Dr. McGregor's extraordinary skill as a physician that fall day my mother would likely not have made it through my birth. For months on end, her movements were restricted and she was ordered to stay in bed as much as possible. The chubby, cherubic child with no hair was sent to the Carlson home on Frazho Road in Roseville to be taken care of by its godmother, my mom's older sister, Jennie, and her husband, Uncle Gust. Back home on Rickett Road, Anna Weber's strength had been totally sapped and the family was deeply concerned. Not until eight months after my birth did her recovery begin. By then Dr. McGregor had diagnosed the cause of her long post-natal illness, performing surgery at Mellus Hospital.

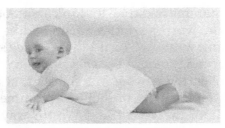

Baby Paul Westin Weber

At the end of February 1944, my aunt wrote that St. George's popular minister, George Shoup, who had led the church to unprecedented growth, received a call to Defiance, Ohio. Worship services were always well attended during his pastorate at St. George; two hundred were present for worship on Easter, many of whom were service men in uniform. Shoup was outgoing and much loved by town folk as well as parishioners, often delivering stirring, patriotic invocations and addresses at community events. The previous September he had brought tears to the eyes of everyone at the dedication of the town's *Roll of Honor* when he recounted how a black veil descended over the area at the end of December 1942 when one of the first Brighton war deaths, Edward Sarosky's, killed in the Philippines on the eve of Christmas, was reported. The Lutheran clergyman also worked for ecumenical unity in wartime. Despite the difference in their faiths, in February Shoup consoled his Catholic friend Martin Lavan, the colorful Irish town lawyer. Lavan's daughter, nine-year-old Mary Elizabeth, had just died of spinal meningitis following a long illness after a bicycle accident.

Shoup broke down when he announced his call and equivocated for almost two weeks. In March, the church council met in a special session to draft a resolution asking him to stay. But Defiance stood up to its name. Their call committee did not back down, upping Shoup's salary and terms of call in early April. Acting with dispatch, the leadership of the district to which St. George belonged used theology and diplomacy to persuade the congregation to allow their minister to be honorably discharged from his call. Defiance's persistence had won out.

One year before its centenary in April 1945, St. George issued a call to Ohio native Paul Geiger, a young bachelor serving a parish in Woodland, Michigan. Just three years out of seminary, Geiger brought along his mother Sophie—a saint of the church if there ever was one—to keep house for him in the two-story, seventy-five year old parsonage just off Fourth and Main that by then had seen far better days. His thirteen-year ministry saw continued congregational growth and, most importantly, filled the spiritual leadership role a church during wartime desperately needed. One of the first duties of the new minister at St. George Church in 1944 was to counsel the family of Roy Thomas, whose son was killed only two weeks before his arrival. Engaged for just a few months, Aviation Cadet Roy Thomas Jr. was solo training in an aircraft at Corpus Christi Texas, going for his wings in the U.S. Navy Flying Forces when his aircraft went down. The funeral, with full military honors, was on April 26. Thomas's casket was draped by the flag and surrounded by seven naval guards who fired a three-gun salute following the service.

Navy Cadet Roy Thomas Jr., 1944

Rev. Geiger was installed June 25—a noteworthy occasion for St. George with guest ministers attending from throughout the Michigan and Ohio Districts of the American Lutheran Church. It was an ecumenical occasion as well. Among others, Mr. Hugh Crouch of the Federated Church (whose church had finally been rebuilt) and Fathers Pearson and Kissane of the Episcopalian and Catholic Churches brought greetings from their respective parishes. A long service? Father Kissane, who had been a friend of George Shoup, must have thought so. The following day he was chatting with my Aunt Emma, as was his usual custom when he went to the bank. "That man (acclaimed Detroit minister Rev. Yochman of St. Paul the Apostle church) preached too long!" he said. Diplomatic as ever, Emma's response was "I liked the sermon!" Not surprisingly, it wasn't long before mothers, aunts, cousins, sisters and grandmothers at St. George were gossiping, dreaming up matches for the good looking, single town parson. One of them succeeded, our neighbor Emma Wagenknecht. In 1945, Rev. Geiger and Una Wagenknecht exchanged wedding vows at St. George.

A few days before the third anniversary of the bombing of Pearl Harbor I was baptized, my mother still very ill, her fragile condition hard to ignore. My aunt and uncle seemed pleased that some wisps of platinum white hair were at last springing up on my head and gave me a silver brush and comb set to celebrate. My Grandmother Westin insisted that I was just "too cute." After taking the news of my mother's pregnancy stoically, the family was coming around after all. My godparents, accustomed by then to my baby routines, were relieved that I slept through the entire sacrament in my aunt's arms, even when the cold water hit my head. During that period of my life it didn't appear that much of anything bothered me; getting enough to eat and napping through my babyhood were my chief goals in infancy.

Eddie was totally indifferent to all the fuss made over me that day. He resented the fact that at three months I could not yet play big boy games with him or share my candy bars as I was later instructed to do. He thought the best part of Sunday morning was rough-housing with Donnie Burt Appleton in Aunt Emma's Sunday school class anyway. During the long, drawn-out Lutheran service after Sunday school they sat together in the balcony close to the belfry, where my father often took him to keep from acting out, sitting beside the fascinating old bachelors who talked or snored during the sermon. The stairway there before and after the service teemed with kids pushing and shoving each other, Mecca for children if there ever was one.

All in all, that eighth week of my infancy was a good one. Church seemed a good place to be! Loud music, rituals and long preaching did not seem to faze me as they did many grown-ups and my routine of getting fed and sleeping was not interrupted. Eddie was not quite sure the intruder in his world should stay but he would come around.

---

* Some information about the Detroit riots was taken from June 1943 news articles in the Detroit Free Press and Wikipedia; Wikipedia was also used for certain information about the Tuskegee Bombers.

My godparents, Jennie
and Gust Carlson

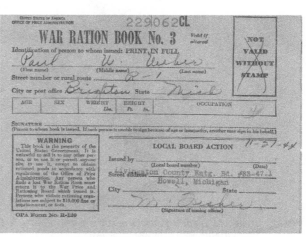

Paul Weber's Wartime Ration Book, 1944

Baby and Toddler Pictures of Classmates, 1944 – 1946. Left to Right, Top to Bottom: Suzanne Campbell, Deanna Dixon, David Denkhaus, Joann Ludtke, Ruth Worall, Larry Herbst, Jim Davis, Dale Cooper, Karen Herbst

President Franklin Delano Roosevelt

CHAPTER SEVEN

The Victory Edition   **August 1945**

> *No man outlives the grief of war, Though he outlives its wreck:*
> *Upon the memory a scar, Through all his years will ache.*
> *Hope will revive when horrors cease, And dreaming dread be stilled;*
> *But there shall dwell within his peace, A sadness un-annulled.*
> *Upon his world shall hang a sign, Which summer cannot hide,*
> *The permanence of the young men, Who are not by his side.*
> —William Soutar, "The Expectant Silence"

ED WAS ONLY THREE but he swore all his life he remembered hearing Dad shout out "Ray Lanning must be home from the *war.*" It was mid-day and someone he couldn't see in a '39 Ford raced down Rickett Road the same way Ray used to when he went to town to see Jean Leith.

The *war* had ended. One could not help but hear talk of it from the late 40s into the 50s around Brighton—anywhere on Main Street, in school, at family gatherings or in church. On a workbench in the dark, damp basement of our Rickett Road house, a yellowing special edition of the *Detroit Free Press* with headlines in huge letters attracted my attention even before I could read. ***"U.S. Turns Terrible Power of Atomic Bomb on Japan,"*** it proclaimed. I didn't know what the *war* was, just that it was terrible. It was only a few years later when the short period of post-war peace was interrupted by another war— this time called a "conflict"— that I was able to understand just how terrible *that* war was and discern the difference between *that* war, in which so many of our family and neighbors had fought, and *another* one. History too soon repeated.

My mother was always interested in politics, government and international affairs. Often at social gatherings I remember her holding her own in debates about a wide variety of topics, from the latest trip a President was taking, how unions and big business were clashing yet again about strikes and wages and how our allies were reacting to the latest Soviet threat. Even before I was born, I am confident that she could hold her own discussing the latest war news too—how the Allied front was advancing, how discord between General Eisenhower and Bernard Montgomery was undermining the war effort and how the frailness of President Roosevelt was interfering with his job as Commander-in-Chief.

One such occasion was a family gathering at the Carlson home in Roseville in March 1943 that Mom wrote about in her diary. After dinner, there was a heated discussion among family members about the latest news, each uncle or aunt sharing opinions on the progress of the war. The Carlson's, with two sons in the military, were ardent FDR supporters. They quickly voiced their opinion that President Roosevelt would have things finished within a year. The rest of the Westin's, like the Weber's, were never fans of Democrats or the President and disagreed often about his leadership. Yet they too believed that inside of a year peace would be restored. Mom withheld her pronouncement about a timeline for the war until she had had time enough to think about all the news articles, editorials and political columns she had read lately in the *Free Press* and the radio commentaries she had listened to. Finally, she spoke her mind.

"Knight (the *Free Press* publisher) thinks the war will be protracted until after the Italian invasion, freeing Stalingrad and Leningrad and the continental invasion from the west," she asserted without reservation. She paused for a reaction from her storekeeper brothers Carl and Joe, who, despite their misgivings about FDR's leadership, concurred with my godparents about an early end to the war. Then Mom invoked the name of Marjorie Avery, one of her favorite columnists. The former Woman's Page editor of the *Free Press* had become a war correspondent and was soon a rising star in journalism. Before long the feisty, good-looking 1921 U. of M. graduate nicknamed "Dot" was cabling news home every day about the course of hostilities in a column called

"London Diary." By war's end, she had distinguished herself and won national accolades for the *Free Press*. "The signature 'By Marjorie Avery,'" the *Free Press* reported, "has come to mean graphic, colorful on-the-spot war reporting." In just over a year after Mom brought her name up in Roseville, she was on the scene in Normandy and soon after that one of the first reporters crossing the Rhine River Bridge at Remagen. Ahead of her times by decades, she wrote in the *Free Press* just before leaving her position as editor of the Women's Page "Women need to go and get man-sized jobs...If more women participated in the responsibilities of our democracy, our war world might be a happier place for all."

"Marjorie Avery agrees with Knight," Mom said before resting her case. "There will be two invasions...the *war* won't end before that happens...I believe that we won't see the end of the *war* for another two years, about the time I turn 40."

––––––––––––––––––

Indeed the war in Europe could not be won, as Knight and Avery suggested, until two invasions of Europe had been mounted. The September after the discussion in Roseville my godparents were much relieved when their son survived a successful invasion of both Sicily and Italy. But though Hitler's friend and ally, Italy's *duce*, was ultimately deposed, bloody fighting in the south of Europe continued. Not until eight months later was there another decisive military action, the long-awaited invasion of occupied Western Europe at Normandy. Military strategists, commanded by Supreme Allied Commander Gen. Dwight D. Eisenhower, had planned *Operation Overlord* for months, waiting until any number of conditions would make it possible. Among the most important were prolonged, clear weather for air squadrons to protect the infantry and artillery, a full moon for light, and catching the Germans temporarily off guard. That historic combined sea, air and infantry assault known as "D-Day" was an overwhelming success. After five days, 7,000 Allied ships had delivered 326,547 troops, 54,186 vehicles, and 104,428 tons of supplies onto five of Normandy's beaches, ultimately allowing Allied troops to push forward to the heart of Germany. Throughout Europe, from Nazi extermination camps in Poland, devastated cities in the Soviet Union and the outermost reaches of the British Isles to the *Nordkapp* of Norway, people listening to sequestered radios in attics or wireless sets in living rooms rejoiced. French resistance workers hugged Free French troops they had not seen since their evacuation from the continent at Dunkirk four years earlier. The French capital, the *City of Lights*, was freed. American G.I.s drank Bordeaux wine and danced on the *Champs Élysée* with French women shouting *Vive la France! Vive la liberté!*

People standing in line to cash checks at the Brighton State Bank could not hear Emma Westin behind the teller's cage when she greeted them at mid-morning that Tuesday, June 6th. At 10 o'clock, she wrote in her diary, the fire siren sounded for sixty seconds. Brighton residents were ecstatic! More than a few pints of beer were downed at the Brighton Hotel on First and Main and the few bars that dotted East and West Grand River. High school students about to begin summer vacation atop School Hill hugged each other then jumped into beat up jalopies to join others who were honking horns, screeching tires and hurrying to join a parade down Main.

The war *was* being won! After the prolonged sieges of Stalingrad and Leningrad, Stalin's Red Army was finally recovering and driving German troops from the western Soviet Union, once the "bread basket" Hitler bragged about conquering. From there the diminishing *Wehrmacht* retreated to the west to defend the homeland. Through the Ukraine and occupied Poland the Soviets marched, crossing the Vistula then on toward Prussia, the bastion of German military power for centuries. Early in 1945 they neared Berlin itself, reaching the strategic Oder River. At the same time occupied countries in Western Europe were slowly being liberated and Allied troops ever so slowly conquering port cities along the English Channel. Through the summer of 1944 and into the autumn, troops on the continent could at last be strengthened by a never-ending flow of war materiel and man power.

Despite the elation in Brighton and the nation, people used to a steady diet of disturbing news were disappointed that after the victory at Normandy no end in the fighting in Europe was in sight. What is more, *Operation Overlord* and the war by then had taken a horrendous toll. It had already become the most destructive in world history, the twentieth century's bloodiest. Then, as winter set in on the European continent, Hitler shockingly began a surprise offensive, his army augmented by troops that had withdrawn from the Eastern Front. It was the German *Fuehrer's* last-ditch attempt to thwart the advance of the enemy, now over a million strong. Known in history books as the "Battle of the Bulge," the Allies prevailed but paid a terrible price— almost 90,000 casualties alone in December and January, a bitter blow, victory so close yet so remote.

*Cemetery at Omaha Beach of Allied Fighters killed in
Operation Overlord, Normandy, France*

To this arctic maelstrom many of Brighton's finest young men and women were sent. One was Frederick Singer, Eric and Elva Singer's second son. Eric's small, false-fronted printing shop—later a nineteenth century anachronism standing as it did across from Bob Leland's modern new drug store—was located on the southeast corner of West and Main Streets, just up from Don Leith's ice business. Eric was so active in town affairs, so loved by the people of Brighton that he ought to have received a yearly good citizen award after returning from the trenches of France in 1918. There was no civic endeavor of which he was not a part. Among other things, he served as chief of the volunteer fire department, was a justice of the peace and selflessly mentored young athletes at Brighton High School for over two decades.

In the 1930s Eric and Elva moved to a Victorian house at the bottom of "Piety Hill" on East Grand River, just below Mellus Hospital. The Singers' new home was a quaint, cream colored, two-story frame house with gingerbread ornamentation around its front porch befitting the artistic talents of its new owners. One could almost envision Norman Rockwell setting up his easel in the front lawn painting a cover for the *Saturday Evening Post*. There Eric and Elva raised their family of three sons and two daughters—Robert, Doris, Frederick, Priscilla and Daniel. Frederick Nicholas, their second son, was a bespectacled All-American looking boy who just two months after his eighteenth birthday enlisted in the army. Inducted at Fort Sheridan in Illinois, he boarded a troop train bound for the Deep South, where he did his basic training in the sweltering summer sun of Camp Wheeler,

Georgia. Assigned to Company B of the 2nd Infantry's 5th Division, he was sent to Europe in January 1945, where the 5th had been holed up at Eisenborn Ridge in the German Ardennes Offensive during the Battle of the Bulge.

After recouping their losses in that German assault, the 1st and 12th American Armies, joined by the 21st British and 101st American airborne divisions, crossed German soil for a second time. There were no more surprise offensives after that; the Nazi's *Siegfried Line* of defense was breeched for the last time. Tragically, however, it was too late for thousands of Allied soldiers who battled German defenses close to the *Rhine*. Frederick Nicholas Singer was killed March 15, soon after the 2nd Infantry seized the city of Gmund, across the *Ahr* River from Luxembourg.

Too familiar now with the picturesque church, cemetery, City Hall and Millpond which defined the town, the two mounted MPs who were sent to Brighton with the news of Pvt. 1st Class Singer's death no longer needed a state trooper to escort them. They rounded Grand River where it curved sharply to the northwest and headed for the turn-of-the century home with two stories at the bottom of the hill, next to the Federated Church and down the hill from the Georgian red brick hospital. Eric and Elva greeted the men warmly, thanked them for their service to their country and sat down on the front porch swing, the telegram from Adjutant General Ulio in Elva's hands. They wished to be alone for a few minutes, just the two of them, to mourn the death of their son, About the same time, nine thousand miles away in the Netherlands East Indies, Army Air Corpsman Robert Singer, serving in the 13th Air Force, thanked a chaplain bearing the same message from the War Department. "Fred thought we could have a reunion with the rest of our buddies from high school when we got home," he said in a soft voice to the chaplain wearing rimless glasses like his brother's who delivered the message. "Guess it just wasn't meant to be."

My mother's prediction about celebrating the end of the war on her fortieth birthday was on target. One *war*, at least.

Two weeks before Singer's death, President Roosevelt addressed a joint session of the Congress of the United States. Looking haggard and weak after his fourteen thousand mile round trip to Yalta in the Crimea to confer with Allied leaders, the President apologized for speaking from his wheel chair on his dais in the well of the House chamber of the Capitol. His speech and delivery were classic FDR, optimistic about the impending end of the war yet zealous about achieving goals not yet reached—establishment of the United Nations and a stable political future for nations in post-war Europe. As eloquently as ever Roosevelt spoke passionately about his mission of bringing about an unconditional surrender of the enemy:

> "...We know that it was Hitler's hope—and the German warlords'—that we would not agree—that some slight crack might appear in the solid wall of Allied unity, a crack that would give him and his fellow gangsters one last hope of escaping their just doom...but Hitler has failed."

Always respectful of the President's physical limitations, the nation's press and members of the media tried hard not to overdramatize FDR's frailty that day. In the waning months of the war, Roosevelt's body was worn out and he was failing. A trip to the Little White House in Warm Springs, Georgia, would do him worlds of good, he reckoned. His usual entourage of close advisors, physicians, servants, and his daughter, Anna, would be there to keep his spirits up. Lucy Mercer Rutherford, the President's lifetime friend with whom he had once had an affair, would also be there, spirited in by his Delano cousin and confidante, Daisy Suckley. Conveniently, Mrs. Roosevelt would be elsewhere leading her own life, carrying out her own agenda as the First Lady.

The nation's thirty-second President died on the twelfth of April in that place he loved, the victim of a stroke. In the living room where he spent many a leisurely hour dictating memoranda and conversing with intimates was the unfinished portrait Lucy Rutherford had commissioned her friend Elizabeth Shoumatoff to paint. Her subject was dressed impeccably, as usual, wore the cape for which he had become famous and held a holder with a cigarette. It was the portrait of a heroic figure that put duty to country first, a national legend that had ignored traditional obligations to his patrician class in favor of improving the lot of ordinary men and women. Roosevelt did not live long enough to watch news footage of Red Army soldiers and American G.I.s embracing at the Elbe River, an event that presaged the end of the Third Reich. Nor did he live to hear about Hitler's suicide five days later, the German High Command's surrender in a fortnight, and the euphoria that lifted a nation tired of war.

It would be up to someone else to attend to the unfinished business of ending the war in the Pacific Theater. Eleanor Roosevelt broke the news of her husband's death to Vice President Harry S. Truman in the White House at 5:30 P.M. The shocked thirty-third President of the United States asked Roosevelt's widow what he could do to help.

"Is there anything we can do for *you*?" Mrs. Roosevelt responded. "For you are the one in trouble now."

A world away, and with a new Commander-in Chief, fierce fighting continued. Operation Ichigo late in 1944 had made the Japanese defeat of the Nationalists in China look imminent. But despite this success, in the Pacific Theater of Operations the Japanese were at last very vulnerable. In Southeast Asia there were Allied victories in Indochina and General Douglas MacArthur, Operations Commander in Asia, was on the verge of liberating the Philippines. President Roosevelt's island stepping-stone war strategy to expel Japanese troops in the Pacific was also succeeding; the Allies were inching their way to the Japanese mainland, close enough for bombers to attack it.

In Kunming China, at the northern terminus of the Burma Road, Chug Smith was safely ensconced in the spring of 1945. He read *Stars and Stripes* whenever he had the chance, learning that the War Department was at last deploying more personnel *and* faster and bigger fighters and bombers to the Pacific. With more and more enemy bases abandoned, it would finally be possible to engage in regular barrages of the Japanese mainland by air instead of conducting the occasional bombing foray. Chug listened closely, too, to military banter every time one of his pilot friends asked him to join the crew on a routine mountain-hopping run to Burma.

"Won't be long now," one of them told Chug in mid-summer. 1945. "Can't say anything more. But get your guitar packed. You will be playing it stateside by fall."

One month later Dave Hecht was making plans for Chug to meet his sister for a date in Chicago. The war was indeed over and Chug was pasting more pictures on the black pages of his photo album. There were pictures of MP friends on motorcycles; Shorty Wong was on every page and there were Chinese families from Kweilin that he never heard from after Operation Ichigo. There were volumes of pictures of bombers from the 14th with awesome paintings of open-mouthed sharks going for the kill. There were other kinds of pictures, too, many that his pilot and non-com friends had given him—Gen. Wedemeyer conferring with Chiang Kai-shek in his Chunking headquarters, General MacArthur in the Philippines, and many shots of General

Chennault. They were the good memory pictures. But interspersed among them were the not-so-good memory pictures: severed heads of Chinese children from the slaughter at Kweilin, crowds at chaotic train stations evacuating the city, sad faces of doomed civilians.

The largest picture of all was not from China. One of his military press photographer friends had managed to give him a copy of one of the horrendous photos of devastation taken on the Japanese mainland in mid-summer that he had managed to secure. In an Aug 7, 1945 special edition of the *Detroit Free Press*, Ernest Barcella of the UPI reported

> *"the most terrifying engine of destruction ever devised by man —*
> *an atomic bomb — carrying the explosive force of more than 20,000*
> *tons of TNT— was turned loose against Japan Sunday..."*

In another report from the *Free Press's* wire service, there was a column with the headlines **"Home Isles Hit by Raid from Ryukus 100 Mustang Fighters Visit Tokyo Area."** The lead sentence was:

> "Japan learned Monday that total destruction awaited her
> homeland if she chose to prolong the Pacific war."

President Truman, faced with the military challenge of a giant leap to the last islands in Roosevelt's offensive strategy—an invasion of the Japanese mainland itself—opted to use a nuclear weapon for the first time in history at the beginning of August. His advisors had warned him that the enemy would not surrender even if thousands of Allied soldiers landed on the homeland, resulting in a massive bloodbath. They were not wrong about "surrender," though military strategists have debated the number of possible Allied casualties for seven decades. The *Free Press* special edition headlines Aug. 15 proclaimed

World War Is Over: Japanese Emperor Bows.

Back in Brighton at last, former MP Chug Smith was glad to be home. He enjoyed civilian life again—his wide circle of friends, his family, his fast cars. Like most Americans, he was confident about the future—a new job, the newest model cars from Detroit, maybe even building a new house for his mother. And one thing was sure: if he ever had a daughter he would name her Kweilin after the place where he had spent over a year and made scores of friends. Never one to dwell on the past, there was nonetheless more time than he wished for the occasional unsettling thought—about India, Burma, Kunming, and, above all, Kweilin.

Soon after his return, Ruthie Weber organized her brother's China pictures. She found a black photograph album at Leland's Drug Store, bought a new fountain pen and white ink, and in her neat, flowery hand labeled every picture Chug had taken while in service. "Who was the other MP?" she asked. "Where was the train station with the masses of people? Who was Shorty Wong?"

Dead silence. There was an uncharacteristic puzzled, sad look on Chug's face. "I'll tell you another time," he said.

Chug never let his war experiences get the better of him. He was one of the lucky ones who came home healthy—in mind, body and soul. Yet, like tens of thousands of other war veterans, he was disturbed by what he had experienced in China. Even more upsetting was the war's aftermath—Chiang Kai-shek and the Nationalists' retreat in China, the Soviet threat in Eastern Europe, and news releases of Hitler's extermination camps. The *Detroit Free Press* featured an article on July 3, 1944 about a Swiss report that 1,715,000 civilians had been killed in Eastern Europe, a number that turned out to be far smaller than the documented 6,000,000 Jews alone who were killed. Like many other ex-G.I.s, Chug was dumbfounded by what had happened. He thought nothing could be more shocking than the stories he heard in China about the slaughter of innocents in Kweilin. But when the *Free Press* published pictures of Soviet and Allied troops freeing concentration camp victims it made another sickening impression. Everyone in his family and circle of friends heard him laud General Eisenhower and other commanders more than once for marching German villagers to infamous camps like Dachau, Buchenwald and Bergen-Belsen to make them view the horrendous remains of death camps that sometimes were only a short ways away from their homes.

At the G.M. Proving Grounds Chug learned more. There he got to know one of the chief mechanical engineers, Joe Ulman, the civil defense patrolman Walt Carmack assigned to Chug's mother's neighborhood whose daughter was one of his niece Carolyn's school friends. Joe heard stories that the news media could not even release from the Jewish rescue committees of which he was a part. One report was about Danish Red Cross representatives being duped touring Theresienberg, the Nazi's "model" camp. In reality, it was merely a stop along the way for thousands who later died at Auschwitz and other extermination camps. Then there were stories about how the State Department shamelessly heard about atrocities but claimed to be "powerless" to prevent them or President Roosevelt's inaction due to military priorities. Another unfathomable report was about the *MS St Louis*, a German ocean liner whose Jewish refugee passengers were denied visas to enter Cuba, Canada or the United States and who returned to Europe only to face the horrors of Nazi extermination. Years elapsed before Americans like Joe Ulman could even consider how his world would ever be the same.

Sadly, the scene at Carmack's front door on Flint Road in March 1944 was to be repeated far too often. Twenty families—the Sarosky's, the Morlan's, the Singer's, among others—all mourned the deaths of fallen husbands, fathers and sons. In small towns dotting the Michigan peninsula there came without ceasing war department telegrams, curt notifications from Adjutant General James Ulio that he had never even seen, assembled by aides working around the clock to notify *next of kin*. For far too many, there was no closure, no body to inter in Brighton Hills Memorial Gardens, no tattered uniforms or medals for bravery, not even torn pages of *My Life in Service*. But thousands of miles away, throughout the European and Pacific Theaters of War, there were military cemeteries, stone markers over precisely plotted gravesites, flags of uniform size flying over the remains of maimed bodies.

Corp. Don Juipe

William Richmond was a young man with an engaging personality, an excellent musician whom Elsa Marten, B.H.S.'s first band director, chose as her drum major. With one eardrum removed, Brighton G.I. William Richmond seemed to be an unlikely candidate for a Red Arrow Division scout, which he became to honor his friend Robert Morlan, killed in action in the *war* shortly after Pearl Harbor. Like Ray Carmack, Bill was a newlywed. His sister's best friend, Winnie, would seem to have been a better choice but it was Winnie's sister, Josephine, he fell in love with. Short and with fine features, Josephine was two and one half years older than Bill. No one quite knew the reason but Bill's mother, Florence, and Josephine never became close. That did not make Bill's parting for Luzon in the Philippines after basic training as amicable as it should have been when he stopped by the house on Rickett Road to say goodbye with his wife that last year of the *war*.

Late in the winter of 1945, just beyond the railroad crossing on Rickett Road south of town, mounted MPs and a state trooper accompanying them were spotted by passengers on a *Pere Marquette* train. One of the MPs sped ahead of the other and was intent on reaching the Richmond house as quickly as possible, for he knew the fallen soldier. Fred and Florence Richmond had heard Bill speak often of that tall MP. He entered their small house first, slamming the screened porch door behind him and breaking the ice by explaining to Florence that he and Bill were good friends. Were they friends at Fort Knox, Florence thought afterward, where Bill's sister, Evelyn, and Winnie Crout had delivered his '37 Plymouth after he joined the service?

As she saw the men arriving, fearing the worst, Florence had sent her son Bobby—five years old and the mirror image of his brother Bill—over to Carolyn Weber's house across the street so he would be pre-occupied. Only after a short interchange did the MP hand Fred Richmond the grim telegram. Bobby saw his father cry for the first time that day when he ran home from the Weber's. The impersonal message from Adjutant General Ulio started out the same way as the one Mary Margaret Carmack had received in September:

> "...William Frederick Richmond's death occurred on March 3 in the Philippines..."

The Richmond's and my Uncle Louie and Aunt Ruthie were not only neighbors but good friends. After his farm chores were done in the evening, my uncle cleaned up, shaved and—though it was the middle of the week—put on his best tweed herring bone suit so he and Ruthie could go across the road and be of some comfort to Bill's parents. Bill's widow, they noticed, was conspicuously absent that twilight hour. She had chosen to stay with her parents and Winnie at their home in Brighton after hearing the devastating news.

Ironically, the Richmond's later learned that Bill died in the same part of the world as his friend Robert Morlan. He was killed by Japanese machine gun fire crossing a God-forsaken ridge while scouting for the 3rd Army. In 1950, with the help of the Graves Commission, Josephine had the body of Pvt. William Richmond laid to rest at Westlawn Memorial Gardens, a military cemetery in Plymouth, twenty miles from Brighton. Five years after her husband's death, she had still not become close to her husband's family.

Reconciliation does not come speedily for nations, families or individuals, sometimes not at all in the aftermath of war. It eluded the *Nisei* for decades, that group of people of Japanese ancestry that had been assimilated into American culture and lived and worked in their adopted country for decades. But when the war started, they were treated as enemies of the state. Japanese-Americans became targets of U.S. propaganda, demonized as the "enemy within our borders" in

Dec. 1941. In Hawaii, white businessmen acted judiciously and quickly to prevent well over 120,000 of the *Nisei* population from being interned following the hysteria after the bombing of Pearl Harbor. The situation was much different on the mainland, however. Most of the Japanese-Americans living on the West Coast of the United States, 62% of whom were American citizens, were forcibly removed to internment camps, their homes and property seized. On Feb 19, 1942, President Roosevelt signed Executive Order 9066 authorizing the War Department to direct 112,000 *Nisei* to what were euphemistically called "reception centers." Not until forty-six years later was action taken by Congress to address these events and reparations paid to families of victims interned.*

Reconciliation for soldiers-turned-civilians sometimes comes slowly and at great cost as well. Mary Margaret Carmack's second husband—Don Juipe—struggled mightily to find peace of mind after the war. He thought it would all be different, easier. The bloodshed he witnessed caring for shell-shocked buddies in some of the fiercest fighting of the war during the Battles of Leyte and Guadalcanal was beyond description but probably the worst occurred from mid-September to the end of the month in 1944. During that period, Corporal Don Juipe operated a crane under artillery and mortar fire by the Japanese while floating on a barge off a coral reef on Peleliu Island. His heroism there in unloading critical materials during battle earned him a letter of commendation from Maj General W.H. Rupetus for his "astute professional skills:"

> "...His courage, initiative, and devotion to duty during this critical period were on (of) an inspiring nature and were in keeping with the highest traditions of the United States Naval Service." **

After becoming a civilian in 1946 and marrying Mary Margaret, his conflict from within over the war memories he could not rid himself of continued, even in Mary's calming presence in the peace and quiet of the house on Walnut Street in Brighton that they shared.

For Cousin Harry Herbst, G. I. memory overload was similar, though less threatening, than Don's. Harry enlisted in the army in April 1941 knowing that he or his brother would sooner or later be drafted with war looming. Only one brother, according to the Old Man's Draft regulations, could help manage the family farm on Bauer and Brighton Roads. Harry never forgot the images from his service in the army in the Philippines. There were stories from friends about terrible treatment in Japanese prisoner of war camps, about the infamous Bataan Death March and Battle of the Philippines, about starvation and civilian atrocities, some of which he experienced himself. They were far worse than the recurring bouts of tropical illnesses and complications from battle wounds he sustained late in 1942. Harry was a hero to kids at our family reunions with full stomachs who were soaking wet after a dip in Bishop or Lime Lake and begged to hear him tell about the *war*. They loved his hilarious, dry sense of humor combined with his gritty voice. Little did they know that Cousin Harry's nervous laugh and eye twitch betrayed the pathos of his and so many other veterans' experiences in the hellacious jungle campaigns in the Pacific.

Would the world be the same after the surrender of Germany and Japan in 1945? After the atomic bomb was dropped and after the murder of millions in European concentration camps and displacement of thousands of American civilians in our own country? After hundreds of thousands of casualties of American soldiers? The editor of the *Brighton Argus* believed it would, that a different, though kinder world had emerged. With this belief, my parents' 1924 school classmate, Frank Seger, penned these words in his inimitable way in the paper's Victory Edition, August 22:

> *"The war is over and we are truly thankful. Now as the din of battle fades, we pledge anew to the accomplishment in fact of an enduring peace...We join our fellow Americans in celebrating this righteous victory and promise to play our part in creating a bright and happy future...for our country and the world."*

Information about Marjory Avery, the closing days of World War II, the Holocaust and Japanese American internment taken in part from Wikipedia and the Detroit Free Press, 1944 -45.

**U.S. Marine Corps Headquarters, First Marine Division, Fleet Marine Force, San Francisco, California, Oct 4, 1944 (courtesy Joe and Donna Chasteen)*

Frederick Singer   Bill Richmond

Our Farmhouse in Winter, 6910 Rickett Road

CHAPTER EIGHT

Maltby and Rickett   Fall 1949

> *"That is the land of lost content,*
> *I see it shining plain,*
> *The happy highways where I went*
> *cannot come again."*
> —"A Shropshire Lad," A.E. Housman

NOT UNTIL LONG AFTER I LIVED THERE did I realize that my early years were spent in one of the most beautiful parts of the nation. Several millennia ago, receding glaciers blessed the future inhabitants of my mitten peninsula with a landscape and bodies of water so appealing that one would be hard pressed to come up with a finer, more idyllic place. No accident, really, that a long ago committee charged with creating a motto for the State of Michigan came up with *"Si Quaeris Peninsulam Amoenam Circumspice,"* ("If you seek a pleasant peninsula, look around you.") I still look around and I still see pleasant vistas. But even now, not one can compare to the stretch of gently rolling, forested hills between Ann Arbor and my hometown, through which a body of water lazily flows that the French and Native Americans called the *River Huron*.

Ann Arbor is where I studied after high school and the *Huron* is where in our boyhood Eddie and I met neighborhood kids like the

Wunderlich's, Duke Williams, the Lanning brothers and Billy Sawyer to swim. That swimming hole and the fields surrounding it have as much or more richness in my imagination as the beautiful places I have traveled to in my lifetime, including the red gorges and canyons of the American West or the German *Vogelsberg* from which my ancestors emigrated. Only eighteen miles north of Ann Arbor and a mile to the west lies the intersection of two county roads called Maltby and Rickett. A person I do not remember once referred to that area as *Green Oak Plains*. As a child I did not know if he was talking about the lay of the land where I lived or the serene place where many of the township's early pioneers were buried. For me now that is inconsequential. What matters is that I spent the formative years of my life on a farm in "Green Oak Plains" and that is where my earliest memories were made.

My parents moved into our Old Colonial two-story frame house on the west side of Rickett Road between Lee and Maltby Roads as newlyweds in 1929. I have often wondered if the colorful history of Green Oak Township or that stately home itself was responsible for the keen interest my parents and I always shared in their history. During the Black Hawk War with Native Americans in the early 1830s, the original settlers of the township were advised to leave for areas protected by the army. When peace was restored, the earliest settler, Stephen Lee, returned to Green Oak. Isaac Smith Sr. followed Lee after that to his farm on the Huron River south of Silver Lake. In 1850, Smith's son—Isaac Smith Jr., a drover—bought eighty acres of land two miles south of Brighton village, a quarter of a mile north of Maltby on Rickett. On it he built a one-story house, to which a two-story wing was later added. He situated it on a small knoll facing east and planted pine, black walnut and maple trees near it to shield it from the wind. Like many homes of tradesman and prosperous farmers of the era, its new wing was Federalist in style, with wide vertical end cornices and pediments placed above the second story horizontal lintels.

Shortly before my mom and dad were married, my grandfather and uncle helped Dad remodel the house my parents were to raise Eddie and me in. It had withstood fires, cyclones, and three quarters of a century of other weather events. There were huge leaks in the roof, much of the clapboard siding was decaying and woodchucks had dug boroughs everywhere in the earthen part of the basement floor. On the first floor, Brighton contractor S.L. Simpson replaced the open front porch with a sunroom. He them transformed the old parlor into a modern living room with new windows, a new stairway to the second story and French doors opening to the dining room. A trap door was installed on the landing of the living room stairs to conserve heat in winter. He also built a modern kitchen and installed a bathroom that adjoined the downstairs bedroom. Master painter and plasterer Floyd Borst oversaw the decorating and built an attractive fireplace and hearth in the living room.

When finished in the late 1920s, that attractive white house with green shutters, beautiful front, back and side lawns and an English rock garden on a hill between the barns and house must have seemed like Shangri-la to my newlywed mother! Twenty years later the house became a cavernous place to play for two young boys who were familiar with every square inch of its twelve rooms! There were so many nooks and crannies to explore and hide in that we never ran out of new haunts for our friends. Upstairs there were four bedrooms and a large attic full of antique furniture and beds—even dresser drawers stuffed with letters and cards sent in Victorian times to the children of the family that lived there!

Edwin Weber and Anna Westin, 1929

My parents inherited the 153-acre farm where Eddie and I were raised from my grandfather, Con Weber, who owned two more sizeable farms almost adjacent to ours. Native Americans must have found our land, so close to the *Huron*, as ideal a spot for hunting as settlers did in the middle of the nineteenth century for farming. For many years, with his eagle eyes, Dad found dozens of arrowheads of all shapes and sizes in our fields when he was plowing, dragging and planting.

Eddie and I were allowed to play with them and show them to friends when we were old enough. We made up stories about the hunters who had fashioned them, about their exploits and hunting trips far to the north and south of the *Huron* and the kind of game they hunted. Every time we played in one of the twenty or thirty acre fields along Maltby, Rickett or Lee Roads we imagined those braves long ago shooting arrows at deer or rabbits for an evening meal.

Our farm could indeed have prompted someone to talk about "Green Oak Plains." Save for a low-lying spot behind our house, the land was perfectly flat. It was divided into ten, twenty and thirty-acre fields that were fenced in, all with gates and lanes well rutted with wagon and tractor tracks leading to them. My dad planted crops of corn, beans, wheat, oats and hay and rotated them from year to year to enrich the soil. My grandfather had insisted that after so many years of neglect, many fields required heavy fertilization with lime, an effort that paid off almost immediately. Before long, the farm produced outstanding stands of alfalfa, clover and timothy that were much admired in our corner of Green Oak Township. Not all fields were used for crops, though. Some were reserved as pasture land for horses, Dad's herd of Milking Shorthorn and Holstein cattle and, in later years, sheep. My brother and I were allowed at a very early age to roam around those fields by ourselves with Dad's faithful dog, Jip, but were always cautioned to watch out for protective cattle with young calves or fast galloping horses that might suddenly decide to chase us. Never were we allowed to venture as far back as the ten-acre field furthest to the west adjoining my Uncle Carlos's or the Cline farms. That field was next to marshy land and two small but deep lakes and was teeming with rattlesnakes.

Dad always said that among his fondest memories was plowing one hot spring day and seeing Eddie approaching through the fresh furrows with a jar of water. There was very little water left in the Mason jar he carried and most of it was muddied yet he sipped some to see the proud look on my brother's face. Those plowed fields were a wonderland for little boys to play in. I was usually covered from head to toe with rich black loam when I returned to our house after finding the perfect furrows to explore, ideal places to search for earth worms. I loved those farm fields and the slimy creatures I discovered angling in them! And I loved the clean, fresh smell of the black dirt that provided a living for my parents. I was always fascinated as well watching my dad driving our green and yellow John Deere "C" tractor back and forth from one end of a field to the other, always careful not to disturb any wild life lurking there. Often I was so content being with my dad in that pastoral setting that I fell asleep daydreaming, watching flocks of killdeer search for food.

Mom, Eddie, Paul and Dad, 1947. An outing at the Detroit Zoo.

In summer that John Deere tractor was usually parked outside in back of our barns, most often the "big barn." To a five-year-old, the big barn seemed enormous, probably because it actually was. It was wooden, hip roofed, 100 X 30 feet and built over a walled stone foundation. The ground floor was divided into horse stalls in front facing the road, a medium sized cow barn with stanchions in the middle and a large open earthen area for cattle, horses or sheep in the rear. On either side of the barn there were stairs with trap doors to the second floor. Its cavernous storage area, no less than 30 feet high, had oak floors, a granary with a walkway and four bins topped by a feed storage loft, elevated hay and straw platforms on either side and main hay and straw lofts extending the entire length of the barn. A pulley track for delivering loose hay ran half way across this area. Accessing this was a ladder that also led to three ventilation windows at the roofline. Two large doors on tracks on the ground level led to a fenced-in barnyard. This area was bordered by a "little barn," corn crib, chicken coop and a livestock watering trough. Gates from the barnyard led to a small field and the main farm lane.

Our barn was another excellent place for our friends and us to play! Dad closely monitored any of our friends who may have accidentally strayed into a dangerous part of it. There were always cattle that might kick to be wary of or even a wayward bull. He always welcomed our pals but strictly forbade anyone to smoke in or near the barns. We made forts to defend in the hay and straw mows and hatched plans for our next place to play hide and seek. (As we grew older, it was a place for older boys to have rendezvous with their girlfriends!) The cinder block milk house, which housed a large cooler and can cleaning station, was just steps away from the front of the barn. It was always open to friends for conversations about the best-looking girl in school or teachers that were particularly annoying.

Two Weber brothers, 1946

The seasons at Rickett and Maltby brought their unique demands, always requiring different planning, always immediate attention. In the spring, all crops except winter wheat were sown. Preparing the soil and planting that crop took place in the fall. As the weather turned cold and with the first light snowfall, the green sprouted wheat would have made the perfect subject for a landscape painter on our farm. Fields with one or two towering leaf-less burr oak trees—home to cardinals and other birds foraging for food in the stubble of nearby cornfields— stood in stark contrast to those green-carpeted fields dusted lightly with snow The rest of the fields had to be tilled properly in spring to prepare for planting. Unless already prepared and lying fallow over winter, they were plowed and prepped with a harrow or spring-tooth drag then flattened with a roller. From time to time it was necessary to fertilize the soil as well but normally proper crop rotation or manure from the barnyard provided fields with enough renourishment. By the time the last crops, Great Northern beans, were planted in June, it was time for a new cycle of farm work to begin, cultivating corn.

The summer season was understandably the busiest. Haying often began in late spring, depending on rainfall, and lasted into late summer. Two cuttings were normal in order to supply enough hay for the livestock once pasture grazing was stopped, cows alone consuming two to two-and-one-half tons during the winter. Haying time required all hands on deck and was hot, laborious and monotonous. It was cut using a mower with a five to six feet horizontal arm with blades attached and powered by a special drive installed on the back of the tractor. After a period for drying, the hay was deposited into rows with a side delivery rake, allowed to dry yet again and finally loaded onto wagons.

Eddie, Paul and Dad on a hay wagon drawn by Maud and Queenie and overseen by our shepherd dog, Jip, c. 1947

Paul (left) and Eddie (right) on Maud and Queenie, 1946

Until Eddie and I were in the upper elementary grades, when baling was the usual haying method, it was common to use a top heavy, cumbersome relic from the early part of the twentieth century called a hay loader. Loose hay, cut and dried in rows, was lifted mechanically on a conveyor to its top and deposited on a wagon hitched behind it. The wagon was fitted with slings made of wooden slats and rope, lying vertically across the wagon. New slings had to be lain successively on top of spread out hay until the wagon was full. It was then drawn into the barn beside the loft, the layered hay compressed in slings, attached to a pulley system and dropped into a mow.

A McCormack corn reaper was used for harvesting field corn, though that took place in early fall when at least the weather was cooler. After the corn stalks were cut, they were bound in shocks and left to dry. As winter approached, when there were fewer field chores to do, they were drawn into the barn and husked and shredded mechanically. Silage corn required a somewhat different harvest technique. Entire shocks of corn were fed into a "silo filler" machine set up next to our cement tower tile silo, shredded and transported to the top in a conveyer, then layered by two or three men with pitchforks inside. An inside chute next to the silo structure provided a ladder access to it.

Wheat and oats grew well on our farm, wheat produced primarily for the wholesale market and oats used for livestock feed. Harvesting those grains took place from mid to late summer and remains one of my most vivid farm memories. Threshing could only take place when Mr. Kellogg from Brighton could work Dad into his busy schedule. His enormous thresher was pulled with great care and difficulty down the road from town where Kellogg's lived or from its last job site. Then it made its way down our driveway and through the barnyard, where wide openings in two fences had been made to allow the thresher to halt at the gigantic pile of grain shocks next to the little barn. The din of the gargantuan thresher, powered earlier in the century by steam and later by gasoline, could be heard all the way from Lee Road to Maltby and beyond and the chaff and dust cloud it created enormous.

Threshing was essential on the farm and among the hottest and most laborious summer tasks, requiring no less than six neighbors and my uncle to help. One team dealt with untethering and pitching stacked oats and wheat shocks into the thresher's huge hoppers. From there a bladed separator sent flailing grain and straw to the appropriate conveyors. Another team then bagged and tied the grain, throwing it on a wagon to be drawn to the barn floor closest to the granary. Gathering straw from piles beside the thresher had to be properly managed, too. It was either pitched onto piles inside the nearby barn or on top of tall stacks for later use in livestock stables.

No less than eight hungry men had to be fed on threshing day and that task fell on my mother's shoulders. It was a big undertaking, some threshing days occurring more than once during the summer. My grandmothers, Auntie Ruth or Mom's closest friend, Emma Lietzau, were always Mom's stalwart helpers. Getting men to help with threshing was never a problem at the Weber farm since neighbors knew the reputation my mother and Dad's mother and aunt before her had for serving the best food anywhere in Green Oak! Men who showed up at her table included Honas Musch and his son, Jonathan; Dad's good friends Herman Nevereth and Frank Meyer; Uncle Louie; Everett Holcomb—Uncle Carlos's tenant farmer; Steve Mullaney—our neighbor to the west, A.T. Cline's, tenant farmer; Ivan Coupar and Jim Cowie—George Fink's tenant farmers and our Maltby Road neighbor, Jim Caldwell.

Chairs and two or three wooden tables with leafs were brought outside and positioned in the shade so the hard working men could cool off and rest under two lofty maple trees. To accommodate men by then barely recognizable because of sweat, chaff and dust there was a copper laundry tub filled with steaming hot water. On a table next to it were four bars of Lava and Fels Naptha soap and several starched white cotton roller towels that were usually in our washroom. The meal Mom prepared had to be enough for at least ten men, always enough for second helpings. Normally roast beef, mashed potatoes and gravy, summer vegetables from the garden, cabbage salad or a fresh leaf lettuce salad with a sweet-sour milk dressing and homemade soda biscuits or rolls was the fare for the day. No less than four fruit or custard pies had to be baked for dessert with coffee.

The advent of the hay/straw baler and combine machine in the late 1940s and early 50s marked the end of the vertical hay loading and threshing eras. Dad usually managed to get Mr. Blem for the baling job. It was interesting to see him coming down Rickett Road after hauling his baler 8 miles with his Jeep from North Brighton then through the back lanes to an alfalfa, timothy or clover field. That Jeep was also occasionally used for the baling process instead of a tractor. As always, timing and scheduling were all important. Blem had his own farm harvests to deal with and had to coordinate those with jobs for farmers who sometimes lived quite far away. Hay bales were loaded onto wagons and, like the loose hay in slings, stacked in the barn lofts before rain threatened.

The wheat and oat harvest involved less coordination since our neighbor, Chester Sak, owned his own New Holland combine. Chester and Dad always got on well together and he never hesitated when Dad asked him to work for him; he worked efficiently and quickly, usually harvesting a large field in less than a day. Down Maltby Road where he lived Chester made his way east with the cumbersome tractor and harvester, directly to one of our fields or lanes. Dad had to see to it that by combining day he had collected enough cloth bags and twine for bagging and the tractor and wagon were ready for service after all the summer jobs. When Chester's combine bin was full, he had to be ready to drive his tractor and wagon next to it to fill as many grain bags as it took to empty the bin.

Dad in his prize wheat field, 1955

Chester Sak combining wheat, 1955

With time, outdated pieces of farm equipment like the hay loader, riding hay mower and dump hay rake were unceremoniously parked in the burdock and other tall weeds behind our barn. There they stood for years, rusting but fun relics for kids to play on, places where we could stretch our imaginations inventing new wonders of the Space Age.

That line up of outdated farm equipment made a perfect setting for growing up. Adding to the enjoyment were the farm animals and pets that we raised and played with. As long as I can remember, horses were a part of our lives, from the workhorses like Queenie and Maud that Dad kept even after owning tractors to riding horses that both Eddie and I were drawn to. At only seven, my brother was challenged by our first non-workhorse, a feisty black pony that had a mind of his own named Flash.

Dad's friend Paul DeLuca, owner of Deluca's Sweet Shop in town, bought the three-year-old Welsh pony for his two daughters, Carolina and Josephine. Flash was kept temporarily in a shed in the back of his shop, where several of Mr. DeLuca's daring younger customers were challenged to ride him but failed. The young pony would have nothing to do with any human whose goal was something other than feeding or bedding him! One day young Josephine, undeterred by reports of unsuccessful attempts to break Flash, tried her hand at riding him. She saddled and mounted him but she, too, was forced to give up when Flash decided to wallow in a newly dug grave with her on top in the Village Cemetery! She ran home in tears while Flash roamed around the graveyard contentedly grazing on grass until he was ready to wander back to the DeLuca shed.

Finally, an exasperated Mr. DeLuca asked Dad if he could stable Flash in our barn. Years later my mother told the story of how only a day after getting him, Eddie determined to ride him. In his mind, a pony was simply a smaller version of the riding horses Uncle Louie had on his farm that he had ridden many times. Rising at the crack of dawn and without telling anyone, my adventure-loving brother saddled the recalcitrant pony up and rode him with ease outside of the barn and down the lanes of our fields! After that, Carolina and Josephine were able to ride the "pony from hell" anywhere they chose to!

Our animals were memorable and their names aptly chosen. Flash was comparable to a lightning strike and Lady-Be-Good, a saddle horse Uncle Louie kept for our Uncle Carlos that we frequently rode, a proper gentle lady. As Eddie became more interested in riding, Dad and Uncle Louie purchased a beautifully marked Arabian horse for him in Northville. That horse was named Ranger and always kept us guessing which field or neighborhood our gelding had roamed to after breaking out of his stall! About the same time, Eddie chose to exhibit a Milking Shorthorn heifer for our 4-H club at the county fair. Her name was "Daisy" and she won first prize at the fair in Fowlerville that year, the only roan yearling shown in an arena dominated by prize-winning black and white Holstein cattle.

Left to Right, Top: Paul and Eddie with Flash, 1950.
Middle: *Paul with a Shorthorn heifer, 1952; Friend Martha Werner with a Shorthorn yearling, 1954.* **Bottom:** *Boots and Johnny, 1955.*

Like Eddie, I enjoyed having pets and livestock and had fun naming them. I called a Jersey cow Dad bought from our family friend, Bill Lietzau, "Dolly Dimples" and her stanchion mates "Monabelle" and "Myrtle." I chose a male name, "Johnny," for the pet ewe lamb our neighbor Frank Meyer game me a couple of years later. I bottle fed Johnny, whose mother chose not to nurse her at birth, and she followed me everywhere I went. Johnny never forgot her upbringing. A few years later, after building up my herd, Johnny, invariably would inch her way through a sea of wool to greet me in the sheep pen whenever I appeared.

Though not a very original name, my mixed-breed spaniel with white paws, acquired about the same time as Johnny, was called "Boots." Boots, too, followed me everywhere on the farm and had one of the most unique personalities of any dog I have ever owned. She had a shiny, curly coat of fur and was every bit as loving as my pet lamb. She loved wandering down nearby roads and lanes looking for companions and adventure and often neighbors discovered easy-to-mouth articles of clothing that had fallen from my mother's clothesline in their back lawns that Boots had run away with. Eddie searched for hours everywhere for his scarlet red baseball cap before a Little League game one afternoon, only to discover it neatly buried across the road in a pile of leaves! If she came up missing, we could count on her being across the road in a tiny house in the woods that belonged to our neighbors. They welcomed her daily into their house for an afternoon nap on their comfortable rug and even allowed me to let her nurse puppies there.

Our parents filled Maltby and Rickett with incredible memories. There was stability balanced with firmness, a free spirit tempered by behavior parameters, work responsibilities mixed with ample leisure. Neither Eddie nor I realized how hard our parents worked to provide a living for us or even to hold on to our property when we were growing up. They never fretted in front of us about scraping up enough money for the yearly payment to the National Land Bank or to cover a small loan from the Plymouth State Bank. I later realized that like many farm families after World War II, we lived on such a small budget that Dad rushed downtown on the first of the month to cash the milk check sent by the Detroit Creamery as Mom decided which bills had the highest priority to pay. Though money was not always available, she inevitably found a way to make the best of a situation. Dad worked hard to keep the farm going, an enterprise that required his attention seven days a week from sun-up to sundown. If he worried that out of nowhere a milk inspector from the creamery or state would suddenly appear who could possibly shut down his dairy operation, we never knew about it.

Those remarkable Maltby and Rickett days remain in my memory to cherish.. I have returned many times to that special place near the *River Huron* just a stone's throw away from the federal highway numbered twenty-three and each time seems like a pilgrimage of sorts. No barns, corncribs or twenty-acre fields accessed by winding farm lanes exist anymore, nor do any giant white pine and burr oak trees. But a Federalist-style house with five bedrooms on a small knoll facing Rickett, brightened each day by the rising morning sun, is still there to greet me. Built when Abraham Lincoln was practicing law in Illinois, it remains the stately home I remember, beautifully preserved and now a landmark. Within its walls, I still see two boys playing and arguing about turning out lights at bedtime. I still see an unheated washroom in winter, my father standing at a sink, cleaning up after chores for dinner and my mother lighting the pilot light and burners of her gas stove to fry pork chops and potatoes for supper. And, more than anything, I still feel the love that was always present there.

Eddie, Dad and Paul in our back yard, Father's Day, 1951

The Old Millpond Dam, c. 1945. (Looking East at Main and West Sts.)
(Brighton Homecoming- from the Pages of Time, **Brighton Fire Dept., 1961)**

CHAPTER NINE

My Town   **1948-49**

"Memory is the diary that we all
carry about with us."
—Oscar Wilde

HOME IS NEVER VERY FAR AWAY.

Admit it or not, where we are from most often defines who we are: it colors how we embrace life, how willing we are to deal with both the good and bad turns life takes, how we accept ourselves and others, how we reject failure. No matter how far away we live, if we are truthful with ourselves, memory always beckons us back to the place we used to call home.

I was raised in a small family, associated with a small circle of friends and lived in a relatively small neighborhood. And I am from a small town, a place where memories were remarkable. That town coasted into the middle of the twentieth century unchanged, for the most part. It was a quaint village with a scenic church overlooking a millpond, the city and fire hall just below it anchoring stores on both sides of its main street. No less than six churches competed for peoples' souls and were places for fellowship if you were not gathered for social activities on friends' front porches or living rooms.

In the town proper or on its outskirts were a bowling alley and motion-picture theatre, two law offices, a furniture store, four car dealerships, a small implement store, flower shop, funeral home, two drugstores, three soda fountains, five restaurants and six grocery stores. As in most small towns throughout mid-century America, there were also blacksmith and shoe repair shops, a bank, post office, feed store and mill, bars, an elevator/lumber yard, a printing shop, two dry goods stores and the Masonic, Eastern Star, Rebecca and Veterans Halls. More than the usual number of hardware establishments, plumbing and electrical contractor stores, shoe and clothing stores, barbershops, beauty salons, the town newspaper, a beer garden and hotel added to this commercial lineup. Not a small number of gas stations, where one could easily make it through the week by purchasing one dollar's worth of gas, dotted both sides of Grand River, my town's main thoroughfare.

"Town" and "home" were indistinguishable to me in the first few years of my life. Going "downtown" was a ritual for most families at least once a week. Very unostentatious cars, mostly gray or black and dusty from gravel roads in the country, parked parallel on streets abutting sidewalk curbs. A penny or two deposited into meters covered two hours of parking at the most, zealously overseen by the town cop. It was likely you would see someone you knew from Brighton or the vicinity—perhaps even someone you wanted to avoid—strolling down Main Street or Grand River. More often than not, my parents would stop to chat with them—women laden with grocery bags and purses and men with small toddlers clinging firmly to their daddy's hands. No one was what one could properly call a stranger on Main Street in those days; and seldom, if ever, did things happen that people were not made aware of within a very short time.

———

For as long as I can remember, making the two-mile trip to town was a Saturday evening ritual. It was the regular run to buy the *Detroit Free Press* at DeLuca's Sweet Shop because the 10 cent Sunday edition, though published that day, was not delivered with the mail. Eddie and I were allowed to stay up later than usual that night instead of going to bed as soon as it got dark, a strictly enforced custom in our home that I particularly disliked. Before we left for town, my mother required all of us to get ready for church in the morning by taking a bath, putting on "town" clothes and wearing the freshly laundered shirts and pants she laid out for us on our beds. Eddie was the more mature older sibling because he had nothing against dunking his head in the hot bathtub water to have his hair washed. I always protested to no avail both the dunking and the liberal amount of Ivory soap I was asked to use that burned my eyes. But we could set off for town and go to church the next day. My mother had completed her obligatory duties.

Down Rickett Road we drove, past the Glen Griffin and Frank Meyer farms, finally driving into Uncle Louie and Auntie Ruth's driveway. There Eddie climbed out, content to spend a couple of hours playing with our cousin, Carolyn, and her neighbor, Bobby Richmond, instead of going to town and meeting all the adults Dad and Mom would see. Dad's preferred parking place had changed little since going to town in his father's buggy in the first decade of the century. There was a large livery barn next to the Eastern House hotel on the northeast corner of Main and Grand River that his father, Con Weber, had patronized for years when going to Brighton after moving to the farm where Dad was born on the southwest shore of Lime Lake. With the advent of automobiles in the late teens and 1920s the family began parking across from where the Eastern House stood, on Main just west of its intersection with Grand River. After Mom and Dad were married there was no need to change old habits. Dad usually found a spot to park in front of Tom and Pat's Grocery Store, Robert's Shoe Store, the D & C store, Bob Leland's drugstore, Grace Rickett's dry goods store or Paul Deluca's Sweet Shop. Unless the number of summer visitors to the lakes increased more than usual during the summer there was no need to venture any further. That would be toward West Street in front of George Woodward's Plumbing Shop, Trevor Rickett's Jewelry or Phil Baetcke's law office. As I look back on this, Dad and Mom were as much creatures of habit as anyone, but then again the same could be said for almost everyone in and around Brighton in those days.

Going to my town was not always a Saturday evening event. In fact, it was not unusual for my parents to go shopping or do other errands there on week days. While Eddie preferred to stay home and play with kids in the neighborhood, I tagged along with both or one of my parents. At an early age, I grew accustomed to strolling into businesses, mostly the ones on West Main closest to Grand River where we parked. I knew the owners and they knew me. A friendly smile and tap on my shoulders always greeted me and sometimes there was even candy, a balloon or some trinket that made the store appealing. Mom or Dad always saw to it that they held my hand firmly when approaching Leland's Drug Store, which fronted both Main and Grand River—a little too close to traffic to be completely safe if I walked on my own. Larry Cooke, Bob Leland's pharmacist, was always in that store with a smile that had won customers' affection year after year. Until the day I moved away from Brighton and for years afterward, Larry worked for the same employer, long after the store relocated to the corner of Main and West Streets. "How ya doin' today, son," Mr. Larry would say to me as soon as I walked in. There were times, however, when even Mr. Larry's salutation would make me put on my most sober face, much the same as when it was necessary to see Dr. McGregor at Mellus Hospital. Those were the times when I had some childhood illness and Mr. Larry had prepared medicine I knew I would hate. The smell and taste of it made me almost more ill than the sickness for which it was prescribed.

The most intriguing business by far in that section of Main was the small D & C dime store two doors away. I will never forget the smell of Dad's favorite treat roasting—Spanish peanuts, salted and placed in a large bin, ready to be bagged for the next hungry customer for only five cents! Mrs. Smith from Brighton Gardens worked at the D & C for as long as I can remember and for as long as I remember she topped that delicious paper bag of peanuts with more than the amount one nickel could buy. She also knew my favorite kind of chocolate bar—Three Muskateers—and never neglected to wink at Mom or Dad with a grin as she handed one to me on days when the milk check had just been cashed. No visit to the D & C would be complete without checking out the latest new toys in stock and the courteous stop at the counter where Ken Chappel, the manager, was working. Dad had known Mr. Chappel's wife, Bernice, since he hired her at the Holden School, and I was about to have her as my kindergarten teacher. It brought a smile to my parents' face when he said "Bernice likes Paul very much and she is looking forward to having him in kindergarten."

At my age, nothing was more boring than stepping into Grace Rickett's dry goods shop—long owned by Mrs. Boylan—next door. My mother was a fine seamstress and it was always one of her favorite haunts. There was nothing of interest to me there nor did I find the clientele particularly interesting—older women like the Stricker sisters from church—all in hats, pacing up and down the creaky wooden floors examining the newest synthetic or cotton fabrics and searching for the perfect pair of shears or notions for a new project. In an age when threads, yarns, needles and patterns were every bit as important as the dry goods the store stocked, Rickett's was one of Brighton's most bustling businesses, even competing as it did with the ever popular Strick's Dept. Store across town. Dad always came to my rescue in those days by stepping next door to visit his friend Paul DeLuca in his sweet shop. He sat me down on one of the stools at the soda fountain even though I was not big enough to reach the counter top and we waited for almost an hour for Mom to do her browsing. About that time Paul and Dad remarked about Grace Rickett's brother, Trevor, walking to his sister's store from his jewelry shop next to DeLuca's— never failing as he had done for decades to return to his store to check if it were locked properly. Mom would eventually appear with a parcel from Rickett's and a large bag of groceries from Tom and Pat's market. For once she had managed to evade Dad and me and do her shopping without worrying about me bumping into or knocking over one of Ella Sharkey's neat displays of canned fruit and vegetables!

On rare occasions on our treks to town it might have been necessary to park across Main in front of Rolison's Hardware, Marshal Cooper's Jewelry and Virginia Hartman's beauty shop, Wendell Squire's Electric Shop, Voortogian's Shoe Repair or as far away as Eric Singer's Print Shop. Claude Rolison, a leading civic figure in Brighton and Livingston County, had been in the hardware business since early in the century and Dad often called at the store just to visit with his old school chum, Claude's son Meryl. It was a sizeable store, almost fortress-like in appearance with its shiny, reddish-brown block exterior, its display windows always alluring and artistically decorated. I associated the smell of new merchandise—basketballs, sporting equipment, bicycles, bicycle tires and kitchen items of every description—with Rolison's more than any store in Brighton as a kid. Rolison's also carried the perfect gifts for Mother's Day, Father's Day, birthdays or holidays. One Christmas when spending money was scarce both Auntie Ruth and my mom bought a treasured holiday keepsake there—individual figurines with elves and children in red and green holiday togs bearing the letters N, O, E and L. The ceramic "what not" section was by no means my brother's favorite part of a store full of sporting goods but one cold winter day he found himself there out of necessity. His favorite location for practicing basketball after making Bob Sacranton's seventh grade team was the dining room, the same place where Mom proudly displayed her porcelain items. He managed to smash no less than two bone china English coffee cups and saucers one afternoon dribbling the ball around the dining room table, a misfortune that required Dad to take him to town to purchase the only bone china tea cup set Meryl Rolison's mother had on display—and that one not English made. Mom complimented Eddie for his choice. That very special porcelain cup, with a Japanese geisha girl's portrait on the bottom visible when held up to the light, was Mom's favorite what not display item thereafter!

Wendell Squire was also Dad's old school chum and his wife, Helen, was a member of our church. His electrical equipment and appliance store was one of a handful in Brighton that had not been modernized, the interior of the old building making the modern, late 1940s appliances he displayed look anachronistic. "Squee" Squire was Dad's electrician of choice. Farm building maintenance often required him to make a trip to town to book Wendell for a job or to make an essential wiring purchase. Aram Vartoogian, nextdoor to Wendell, was the outgoing Armenian-born proprietor of the town's only cobbler shop. Dad always enjoyed visiting with him, probably because his old world ways and accent reminded him of Nick Tipu, the hired hand on his dad's Grand River farm growing up. Aram's shoe repair services were indispensable for a family that could not always afford to buy new shoes across the street at Robert's Clothing when holes appeared in thin soles! Vartoogian was interesting to watch at work, a skilled craftsman whose inventory of leather, shoe strings, straps and polishes never failed to capture my fancy.

I always thought that Eric Singer's Main Street print shop, just to the north and steps away from Don Leith's ice business on West Street, had been in town since the beginning of time. The small, false-fronted wooden building was weather beaten and gray. It seemed to me even as I grew up that a more proper setting for it would have been on a street somewhere in the Wild West, stagecoaches passing in front of it or thirsty cowboys slamming the swinging doors of a saloon across a rutted, dusty street! In the window there was always a sign with the words *Notary Public*, for Eric was the town's justice of the peace, its chief judicial officer. Singer was always quick to greet customers in his leather, ink-spotted apron, in later years ably assisted by his daughter Priscilla's husband, Don Lueker. Dad or Mom always spoke with Eric if they saw him standing in the door and I do not think there was a resident of Brighton that they held in higher regard. He was known as one of the fairest men around, his wife Elva and children much loved.

Dad drove further than that small block of stores on either side of Main between Grand River and West Streets less frequently. Those trips would usually take us to one of five destinations: the Brighton State Bank, Alfred Stewart's Flour, Feed and Coal Store, Ratz's Hardware and one of two grocery stores. Of the five, the bank was most often visited. Standing on the southwest bank of the Millpond at Main, the two-story brick building I first remember had not yet expanded to include the one story mid-century modern wing on its west side. It had a unique quality to it because it was always busy, always teeming with blue collar workers, business-people, housewives, professional people—people from town and miles around. I loved it more than almost any other store or business for two reasons. Before going inside in the summer we could feed the Mallard ducks at the Millpond that swam toward us quacking contentedly knowing there was food to be had. On banking days, Dad or Mom always produced a crust or two of stale bread from our kitchen breadbox for me to feed them. As I remember those "duck days" of summer, it never occurred to me that my parents were probably equally as gleeful watching those hungry, brazen ducks snatch my tidbits of bread as I was! Another draw at the bank was Aunt Emma, who had worked there over twenty years. Immediately upon entering, she was the first to greet us with a hug and smile, always in stylish, well-appointed business attire, her hair in a bun, prematurely turning gray but beautifully done up and with exquisitely chosen make up on. I delighted in the candy bar she kept for our visits and even was allowed to look in my very own green savings account book that she had started for me. Often as my Mom or Dad were engaging in grown up conversation with my aunt I glanced beyond the teller's cubicle where she stood. I knew little about financial matters but I tried to imagine how much money Aunt Emma's bank must have! You could almost smell stacks of currency, U.S. Treasury bonds and checks, accounting books, paper for coin rolls, and volumes of manuals relating to commerce that were either in book cases behind swinging wooden gates and railings or upstairs in the mammoth bookkeeping department.

Usually on a Saturday morning in the winter Dad would make a run to Al Stewart's feed store and mill on Main at the alley across from Strick's to have corn ground. If there was not enough oats in the granary or if the haylofts were looking meager, field corn still on the cob had to be ground for fodder to pile on top of silage corn. There was always enough room in our green Chevy for Eddie and me to ride along, both of us looking forward to that trip to Stewart's. We were instructed to put our fingers in our ears when the corn grinder in the mill in back was cranked up and tie the hankies Mom had sent along over our faces. Dad shouted at us before the whole process began, keeping us in the alley out of traffic, well away from the grinder and milling area.

The narrow, deep false-fronted frame store had stood the test of time well and Stewart's had a thriving business, even after Al Stewart died and his daughter, Mary Mathias, and son Al helped run it. They delivered coal throughout Brighton and the rural areas surrounding it in addition to selling farm feed items, flour, seed and fertilizer. The bookkeeper and sales assistant, Al Stewart's wife Fern, reminded me of Aunt Emma—one of the sweetest persons in town, always eager to help, always friendly and outgoing. Though Fern dealt primarily with farmers in overalls and heavy work boots, she was always the well-dressed, fashion savvy businessperson. She was often hard to spot because she sat at an enormous roll-top desk used by the Stewarts and mill owners before them for a good many years. Large ledger books, worn and dog-eared from daily usage, took up most of the desk space. Occasionally Mom would stroll into Stewart's to chat with Fern if she had errands on the other side of town. She loved going through Fern's inventory of "better" flour sacks. Since Stewart's main business besides coal was milling grain, there were never less than a hundred empty bags piled on counters in front and in the back of the store. Their coarser feed bags for grain harvesting lasted for years and used time and time again but the flowery, cotton cloth print bags used for seeds made fine fabric for women to make any number of household items— pillow cases and girls' dresses, primarily. Mom was patient enough to endure the intermittent din of the leviathan grinders in back and dust blowing everywhere to discover four or five bags perfect for material for dresses to send to Lutheran missionary fields and Social Services, the Red Cross or even play dresses for children of friends.

Sometimes my mother preferred to shop at one of two grocery stores on West Main with franchises in Michigan, Kroger's or Byerly's. The stores stood side by side from the beginning of the 1940s between Brighton's old post office and Strick's Store on the north side of Main. Mom tended to shop regularly at Kroger's, run for many years by Harold McMacken, but also frequently looked for bargains at Byerly's, which continued to do a robust business on West Main after Kroger's closed in 1950. Upon entering, customers at both stores gave clerks shopping lists that were filled quickly and efficiently. It was fascinating as a boy to watch how they sped into action doing their job! Large inventories were stacked on shelves reaching as high as the ceiling, making it necessary for clerks to use ladders on tracks to reach items such as cereal or canned goods. If a ladder were not available, agile assistants who were shorter in stature used a long hooked pole to latch onto boxes or cans that they could easily catch. Equally as intriguing was the large meat counter in the store. Chet Paquette, always outgoing and well known throughout Brighton, was Kroger's affable butcher, moving across Main in the new decade to join Lawrence Oliver at Stop and Shop, Brighton's first supermarket, when it opened. He custom cut any amount of meat my mom required, from pork chops for supper to the large pot roast we normally had after church on Sunday. The huge rounds of cheese at those stores always captured my attention too, even if the aroma was not always pleasing. Sales assistants cut sections of Cheddar, Edam, Gouda or Swiss with precision using large, sharp knives then wrapped the slices in paper, tying packages with a string cut from a ball suspended from the ceiling.

Ratz's Hardware, across the street at Main and Hyne, always seemed to me to be a throw-back to the turn of the century. Or earlier. Like Rolison's, it was another of the businesses in town owned by the same family for a long time. Ratz's was also one of the businesses with a family connection. Dad's mother's uncle, John Becker, opened the business in partnership with Henry Pipp not long after town lots were platted in the Smith-McPherson addition to Brighton on what is today's West Main Street in the early 1870s. Pipp, in fact, carved these words in old German script underneath a wooden counter as he finished construction of the building just before the business opened:

"I, Henry Pipp, a simple man, wrote these words in the year of our Lord One Thousand Eighteen Hundred Seventy and Three..."

George Ratz, the owner and another of Dad's relatives, inherited the store from his father, who bought the store from Pipp and Becker later in the century. The sturdily built, false-fronted store had high wooden counters, a drop-down gate for access to the broad aisle running from the front door to the back and shelves on either side reaching to the ceiling. Even though the store itself seemed caught up in tradition and the past, George Ratz had a thriving business. This was due to George's work ethic and the assistance of Dean Sellman, his adopted son. Dean was courteous, outgoing and always available to wait on customers. If you wanted quality paint, Dean was the go-to man in Brighton. On the Ratz Hardware sign outside of the store, a bright colored globe splattered with paint—the traditional Sherwin-Williams logo—always fascinated me. The paint counter at the back of the store had every color imaginable; if you couldn't find an exact match for something, Dean would mix it for you or special order it. The store also carried hardware items for construction or repairs and metal containers filled with nails, washers and screws of every size and shape took up ample space on shelves. Larger construction materials, such as electrical wiring, shingles, glass, tar or lumber, were available in a storage room behind the store.

West Main looking east from Hyne Street, 1948. Ratz Hardware anchors the south side of the block, Kroger's and Byerly's just across the street. (Courtesy Carol McMacken, "From Settlement to City")

Main Street of my town is indeed never very far away and always beckons me back. I still see Chuck Uber standing behind his soda fountain making a *Uber's Special* ice cream sundae for a customer who is already licking his lips. Wendell Squire is still in his gray work shirt and pants at the front of his electrical shop tinkering with the connections to the twelve-inch black and white Motorola television set in the window. Aunt Emma reaches behind the teller's cage at the Brighton State Bank for an O'Henry candy bar for me and Fern Stewart writes an entry for five feed bags sold to my mother in her ledger. Main Street Brighton at age five with false-fronted stores, creaky wooden floors, water splashing everywhere as it cascades over the

Millpond dam and parking meters that take only pennies and nickels are images I will never forget. Entries indelibly written on the pages of a mid-century diary that I can never forget.

Grand River looking south from Main, 1945
(**Brighton Homecoming-From the Pages of Time**, Brighton Fire Dept., 1961)

West Main Street looking east at the C & O R.R. crossing, mid-1950s,
"Peanut" Cline's store bldg. left, the Hyne Elevator and Brady's store building, right.
(Brighton Homecoming—from the Pages of Time, B.F.D., 1961)

CHAPTER TEN

First and Main   April 26, 1949

> *manslaughter: "the unlawful killing of a*
> *human being without express or implied*
> *malice."*   *robbery: "the action of taking*
> *property unlawfully from a person or*
> *place by force or threat."*

"PEANUT" CLINE'S WAS A MEN'S CLOTHING STORE located at
the northeast corner of First and Main. The store had not changed
for decades, the same false-fronted two-story frame building across
from the Brighton Hotel where my grandfather lodged in the early
1890s. Outside, facing First Street, was a rickety stairway leading to an
upstairs apartment that the store owner, Earl Smith, rented out. It was
a business my dad frequented often with Eddie and me because young
boys grow quickly and young farm boys needed denim togs that were
well made and serviceable.

I could never understand why Cline had been given the name
"Peanut" until much later in life, when I learned that he rarely cooked
for himself and his diet consisted mainly of cold food, peanuts being
one of his staples. Cline was slightly eccentric, eighty-three years old
and lived in the back of the dark, musty store. The old man must have

had some way of detecting if a customer entered, since by the time the patron reached the front of the store Cline met him there. A red-hot stovepipe with an elbow leading to a coal or wood burning heater extended across the ceiling for the entire length of the store, causing many a customer to remark that with Cline's huge inventory of cotton clothing, his establishment was an inferno waiting to happen! That inventory, though not remarkable by its variety or even color, was adequate enough to meet the needs of working men and their children in the area. Gray, tan or brown; large, medium, or small—those were about the only questions Peanut asked his clients when they said they were in need of an article of clothing. He carried overalls, coats, jackets, work shoes, boots, caps, socks and shoestrings—even the one piece, old-fashioned thigh length BVD underwear, long favored by my father.

On the Peanut Cline shopping trip I remember best, Eddie was old enough to climb on top of a counter top, where he was fitted with new shoes. At my age, though, Dad still had to pick me up and plop me down on the expansive wooden surface, once all the odd sizes of denim products were removed to make room for me. "That size is perfect for Eddie now but you will be back inside of six months at the rate he is growing," Peanut said. "And the youngster here seems to need a bit more space in those overalls to fit him," he added, referencing my chubby build. "You have a budding football blocker here, Edwin," Peanut quipped, using the same name he had addressed Dad by for nearly forty years. I was content to disregard the conversation the two adults had about farming or townspeople. Instead, I peered inquisitively up and down the aisles at the multiple piles of clothing piled up on countertops everywhere in the store and at the doors nearby leading to Cline's storage and back rooms.

Karen Kirchbaum and I attended the St. George Lutheran Sunday school together. Karen was blond, had curly locks and a way about her that always made her fun to be around—even during class! She and Joann Ludtke, another member of our Sunday school class, were neighbors who lived just a block away from each other off Second Street and had the same kind of perky personalities. They loved talking so much together that Rev. Geiger at St. George placed them far apart during junior choir practice and Sunday services. The two chatterboxes never changed! Just before entering fifth grade at the new upper elementary school adjacent to the high school, their teacher conferred with the principal, Bob Scranton, and recommended that the two be separated the following year. "Karen and Joann can talk all they want at recess," Doris Smith told Zelma Beers and Evelyn Fitzgerald at a teachers meeting. "They are sweet kids and I love them. But they *can* test your patience!"

Karen was always inclined to explore places in town she had not been to—even at five years old—if Joann were not available for a play date. Often she could be found as far away as Ore Creek spearing fish or staring into the Federated Church basement windows just below the hospital on Grand River wishing she too could be in school there. Straying that far away from home was fun yet safe, especially because it was just a stone's throw from her dad's tool and die shop across from Adolph Martin's blacksmith shop on North Street. One day at the end of April 1949, she was delighted when her mother, Kay, asked her to make one of her downtown excursions. She was instructed to go to Brady's Grocery Store on West Main for a loaf of bread. But this time Kay reminded her independent minded child to return straight home and *not* feed bread to the ducks on the Mill Pond as she often did. "Put this dime and nickel into your purse, dear; that's all you are going to need today," she told her daughter.

Always fair in their prices and a favorite of customers, Brady's business was booming. People coming from out Brighton Road who made stops only at Hyne's just across the railroad tracks did few errands elsewhere other than at their store across from the Brighton Hotel and Peanut Cline's. Many had been accustomed to shopping at Brady's for years in Chilson and their prices were comparable to Kroger's or Byerly's on that side of town. Joe Brady's wife, Haidee, was one of the town's most prominent businesspersons and a key to the store's thriving trade.

Haidee loved visiting with Karen, listening to her stories about kids in her neighborhood and accounts of Joann's and her latest adventures with their pets. She greeted her warmly as she entered the store and chatted a while after Karen brought a loaf of Wonder bread with its colorful polka dot packaging to the check-out counter. Kay had long ago told Haidee about her daughter's penchant for wandering so she placed it securely into a small paper bag after it was paid for. But as she deposited Karen's coins into the cash register, she was suddenly diverted. "Oh look!" she said. "Seems like there is an awful lot of traffic across the street...I better see what that's all about. Now off you go—straight home this time, Miss Kirchbaum!"

Henry Dammann lived in an apartment in the back of Cline's store. Eddie and I knew him from church, though sadly we were too bashful to talk to him. His pew at St. George had forever been in the balcony at the end of the stairway where Al Zimmerman sat along with Uncle Joe and another bachelor or two. Henry seemed to us kids to be well over one hundred years old, often needing a shave, though he always had a clean shirt, suit and tie on. He wore old-fashioned horn-rimmed glasses, a wide-brimmed brown fedora hat that had seen better days and always had a cane. Henry did not own a car, choosing to walk the few blocks to church every Sunday, despite his slow gait and limp. Normally if offered a ride he would decline, the kind congregant who offered it worrying like everyone else that because of his poor eyesight and limp, Henry could get run over crossing Main or one of the streets between Fourth and First. With time, however, they realized that Henry's pride was far more important than lecturing him about keeping safe.

Henry and William "Frank" Cline were close friends. Every morning Henry opened the door of his apartment to be greeted by Frank, who had a cup of coffee waiting for him. Often he came so early that he awakened Frank, whose bed was a broad countertop. Other times, if his arthritis was bothering him, Henry waited until mid-day to visit, perhaps joining Peanut for a brown bag lunch of liverwurst on rye from Brady's and an apple or banana. The two old men caught up on town gossip or how soon they thought the Democrats in Washington would be losing their political grip on the country now that Taft and Eisenhower were mounting successful rival campaigns for the '52 election. Often Cline would talk about an upcoming visit from his nephew, Austin, who taught high school in Detroit. "Austin thinks he can talk me into throwing in the towel but I ain't gonna do it!" he had told Henry in one of their latest chats. That same day he told Henry about how Earl Smith, the men's landlord, was getting rid of the handyman he had hired to do some work in the basement. "Spends more time talking to people wandering in than working, Earl says."

About the time Karen set off for Brady's that morning, Henry paid a later than usual morning visit to his friend. But instead of the usual spirited response when he shouted "Frank, you there?" there was silence. Henry shouted it again as he approached the aisle leading to the front of the store. "It's late. Must be outside talking to someone," he thought. Then he discovered him. He thought his failing eyesight was deceiving him at first, thought what he saw was another of the fuzzy images Dr. Rieckhoff in Howell had warned him about. What Henry Dammann saw, though, was no illusion.

Peanut Cline's store had indeed turned into an inferno, as it turned out. But it was a much different inferno than people had imagined.

The day before Henry Dammann made his discovery, John Prinz had driven to his brother Ted's gas station and store just east of Brighton. John owned the Fix and Drive Garage in Detroit and with him was his employee of three months, Fred Giles. In Brighton that evening, they met John's brother and an acquaintance, a carpenter and handyman who lived just north of Brighton.

"Want to join us?" John asked Giles not long before.

"Join you? For what?" Giles responded when his boss nervously made a proposal to the twenty-three-year-old Air Force veteran nicknamed "Gingles."

"Heard that old man Cline in Brighton has $20 or $30 grand hidden away in the back of his store. Could be ours…"

Giles seemed dumbfounded at first. "Rob him, you mean?" he answered John.

"That's what I mean," he fired back. "You in or not?"

Droplets of sweat covered Giles's face as he tried to comprehend the gravity of the proposition his friend was making. John Prinz grew impatient. "What do you say? Yes or no?"

After what seemed like an eternity to him, Giles spoke.

"I'm in," he said, hesitatingly. "But no weapons…No weapons or I won't have any part of it."

Brighton residents prided themselves in not being nosy. Yet being able to spot new or familiar faces in town standing leisurely outside of stores or strolling down Main was important to small town folks. It was not unusual, then, for Larry Johnson, a mechanic at the Morgan Garage on Grand River, to see Frank Cline standing in front of his store. Johnson had taken some time off to get a haircut when he spotted Cline between 11:10 and 11:30 on the morning of April 26. It was also not unusual for folks to know who drove what kind of car in town or where they usually parked. Few were unrecognizable, including those who parked in front of Strick's Store. Patrons of Strick's were mostly women and Walter Maples looked puzzled standing nearby as he saw

Ted Prinz drive away on the morning of that same day, only to park a block or two down the street. A second car not seen often on that side of town, a Plymouth, was also spotted there.

Earlier that morning John Prinz had made a test run to town, turning up with Giles in front of Cline's store. Giles was charged with checking out the store to see where the storage room and Cline's cash register were. Once inside he purchased a polo shirt—the sale the last entry in Peanut Cline's record book. Was it Giles who laid a hammer down near the front of the store that day? Or was it the handyman or Ted Prinz? Prinz had not turned up at his second job at the Brighton Recreation Center that day, telling his co-worker, Roger Jensen, that his child was sick. Instead, he went to Brighton where he waited close to the Plymouth parked near the Brighton Hotel, its keys left in the ignition. The handyman had returned to his job that day, repairing joists in the basement of the building.

Giles and John Prinz entered the building again just before noon. They had gone to Ted's house after Giles purchased the shirt, changed clothes and returned to town. Not seeing anyone stirring at Cline's, the two entered the building furtively, catching Frank off guard in the back of the store. Prinz struck him in the face and ribs, bound him at the chin with a bloodied shirt tied by two clothesline cords, dragged his body to the storage room and forced the drawer out of the store's cash register. The four accomplices then fled, meeting back at Prinz's store and gas station.

Cline was still conscious when Henry Dammann found his friend lying on the floor of the storage room. "Two men were looking to rob me ... one of them attacked me," he managed to say before Henry took the old man to his own bedroom and laid his limp body on his bed. With little hesitation, he summoned Earl Smith and his wife, Dr. Niles Clark, Brighton police officer Kenneth Graham and Sgt. George Malnar, commander of the Michigan State Police post. Clark took Cline to McPherson Hospital in Howell, where he was diagnosed with broken ribs and other injuries. But he did not survive, dying early in the morning two days later with Clark present.

The drawer from Cline's cash register was thrown by the wayside and its $60 to $70 contents stuffed in a cigar box at Prinz's house. The brothers and the handyman accomplice were apprehended the same day Cline died in Detroit, both the brothers pleading innocent to charges of manslaughter and robbery unarmed. George Charlain, the handyman, contended his innocence May 13 in Howell in Livingston County Prosecuting Attorney Erwin's office, with no arrest warrant issued. To keep him safe from the Prinz brothers he was allowed to go to Deerfield in southern Michigan, coming back of his own volition the following Monday. Giles, however, eluded arrest. Hearing about Cline's death April 28, he dyed his hair red and left for Columbus, Ohio. Detroit detectives arrested him there three weeks later, having attempted suicide twice. Nine days had passed since Sgt. Malnar had signed the complaint charging the Prinz brothers with murder and robbery unarmed and examining Ted Prinz. The latter denied any part in the crime, as did his brother when questioned by another state police officer who had entered the case, Det. Sgt. Joe Pearce.

Det. Pearce, the major investigator in the case, did not question either of the Prinz brothers after May 12, when both had secured attorneys to represent them. Ted and John Prinz were arraigned seven weeks later on charges of manslaughter and robbery unarmed, their trial set for Sept 8 in Judge Willis Lyons's circuit court in Howell. Wilfred Erwin, who had worked for the F.B.I. until 1947, was the prosecuting attorney, Don Van Winkle his assistant; Louis J Colombo of Detroit and Stanley Berriman of Howell served as the defense lawyers. Consistent with the days following their arrest, neither brother confessed to the crime, first pleading not guilty but Colombo later changing it to "standing mute." Giles, however, served as the primary witness for the prosecution, describing in detail the plan to rob Cline and John Prinz's blows to Cline's body. He also testified about helping state police find Cline's cash box at a site on Euler Rd where the accomplices had thrown it, his story substantiated by Det. Gerrard Rockledge of the Michigan State Police.

Upon examination by the defense, Pearce denied that any bribes or promises of a lesser sentence had been given to Giles, as had been alleged. Further, Charlain's wife had not been told by himself or prosecutor Erwin that murder warrants would be issued if her husband did not admit to the crime, implicating the Prinz brothers, and Charlain had not been submitted to any rough treatment. Walter Roney, a court reporter for the thirtieth judicial circuit, corroborated this story. He testified that he had been called by Pearce to headquarters in Brighton on the night of May 12 to make a stenographic account of Giles's and Charlain's statements with Prosecutor Erwin, Det. Tom Grant and Sgt. George Malnar also present. No threats or promises were made but Giles and Charlain were told that it would be better for them if they confessed—they would find out the facts anyway in examining versions of confessions in the case.

The trial lasted for almost three weeks, with fifty-one witnesses—including the parents, spouses and siblings of the accused—character witnesses, nearby onlookers the day of the crime, criminal experts and law enforcement officers. Stereotypical expressions like "come clean" and "you will get off light if you confess" were referenced in testimony for the defense. Testimonies were marked by stories that often were so intriguing—many filled with an incredible amount of pathos—that they might have appeared in national crime investigation publications or been the subject of Erle Stanley Gardner's next *Perry Mason* story. Some reached the height of the absurd. In his alibi, for example, Ted Prinz claimed he had not missed work the day of the crime because his child was sick but that his pregnant wife asked him to go to Brighton—where he claimed he was for three and one half hours—to buy oranges and lemons. He had "borrowed" Charlain's car with the keys in it because his own had broken down. Charlain, on the other hand, testified that his car was taken by John Prinz and Giles without his permission, even reporting its theft to the police! A search for the car's registration had ultimately led to his questioning at the Michigan State Police post by detectives and Prosecutor Erwin. Giles's account of his part in the murder and trial Charlain called "dirty, rotten lies!"

Another memorable incident occurring before the trial but reported in its proceedings involved a feverish attempt by James Prinz, Ted and John's brother, to interfere with Giles's confession. George Charlain and Giles had been sent to the Ingham County jail in Mason for holding as material witnesses. Early in the investigation, James Prinz smuggled a note to Giles through an inmate saying "Do you know what you are doing to my brothers?" Later, during the trial, James testified that police had searched his brother's garage in Detroit where he was working, looking with no search warrants for a Mercury convertible involved in the Cline murder.

Arguments for the defense and prosecution ended Sept. 27, at which time Judge Lyons charged the jury—only one from Brighton, Mrs. Bertell Buxton—to deliberate, advising them of five possible verdicts: guilty of murder in the first degree, guilty of murder in the second degree, guilty of manslaughter, guilty of robbery unarmed and acquittal. He advised them that all parties in a felony are equally responsible, motive was *not* an essential element in their decision but the fact that a crime had been committed was. He also instructed them that the defendants could be found guilty on the testimony of an accomplice, they could disregard any or part of a testimony they thought was false and they had to determine the credibility of witnesses in the proceedings. That both Charlain and Giles were implicated in the case was not the present question; it was, rather, the guilt or innocence of the respondents, Ted and John Prinz.

Defense attorney Colombo in his defense plea before the jury said Giles's testimony was not supported by a single witness; nothing was important to the jury deliberation except who robbed and killed Cline. The Prinz brothers had no motive to commit a crime, he asserted, and the real robber and murderer was still at large. Colombo threatened to charge Erwin with perjury because of the prosecution's questioning of witnesses and two of the accused. The prosecution reaffirmed its belief that Fred Giles's confession implicating the Prinz brothers was backed up by the testimony of witnesses. Ted Prinz's alibi about his whereabouts on the morning of the murder and robbery, it asserted, was one of the weakest stories ever heard during a trial. (Prinz had claimed that not only had he spent time in Brighton the morning of the murder running errands but had also been occupied attempting to help an anonymous person who had left car keys and a note at his store. The anonymous person instructed him to pick up and fix his broken down car at a nearby bar.)

Business boomed in the county seat during the trial and streets near the seventy-year-old Livingston County Courthouse in Howell were full of cars belonging to people who either participated in the court case or were onlookers. There was widespread coverage of the Prinz brothers' trial and its aftermath, lasting until the final sentencing of accomplices took place in 1953, more than four years after the robbery and murder. Major Detroit newspapers and both the *Brighton Argus* and *Livingston County Press* featured long articles about the crime, the trial, appeals and even a political advertisement defending the actions of Judge Willis Lyons. Perhaps the most comprehensive and best coverage was that of the *Livingston County Press*. Its stories appeared alongside local articles about engagements, social columns, school coverage and the usual weekly national news roundup, such as the death of a local woman's husband, Supreme Court Justice Wiley Rutledge. Advertisements the year of the trial included that of the Diamond Dot Market, where a beef roast or ground beef could be purchased for $.45 per pound and a round trip ticket on the Greyhound Bus Line from Howell to Tampa could be had for a bargain $37.35!

Eight days after the jury began deliberations—Mrs. Ted Prinz recently having had a child at Detroit's Saratoga Hospital—it returned with a verdict, the third possibility Judge Lyons had instructed it to consider. Guilty of manslaughter. Not surprisingly, the defendants and their families were shocked, John Prinz grimacing and uttering an obscenity at Prosecutor Erwin. Two weeks later, upon hearing Judge Lyons's sentencing of the brothers to thirteen to fifteen years in Jackson State Prison, his last words before being remanded for incarceration were "We're still innocent."

The story of the robbery and murder of an eighty-three-year-old man was not yet over, however. For Livingston County residents weary of reading about it—particularly Brighton friends of Peanut Cline—the Livingston County Press's coverage did not end five and one-half months after the crime was committed.

Based on his belief that his clients were innocent and questioning Prosecutor Erwin's moves prior to and during the trial, Defense Attorney Colombo immediately asked for a new trial, ultimately moving for an appeal before the Michigan State Supreme Court. Ted and John Prinz were granted bail upon their guilty verdict Oct. 6, their appeal taking two-and-one-half years to decide. A final request for typed transcripts of their trial to be submitted to the court rather than an expensive state certified transcript was denied almost a year to the day following their guilty verdict, their appeal for a new trial rejected by the court in Dec. 1951. On Jan. 1, 1952, Ted and John Prinz were finally remanded to the state prison in Jackson to begin serving a 13 to 15 year term for the murder and robbery of Frank Cline.

Handyman Charlain was eventually charged with being an accomplice in the murder and robbery unarmed of Cline as well, a charge he originally confessed to but retracted by the time of the Prinz trial. Because his trial could not begin until after the Prinz brothers' appeal was heard before the Michigan State Supreme Court in late 1951, he was not tried until Oct. 21, 1952. The trial was in Eric Singer's justice court in Brighton, where he was charged with murder and robbery unarmed. By then he had confessed to the crime, testifying that he had helped plan the robbery. His role, he said, was to bang on pipes in the basement of Cline's store to create a diversion. Further, he was to lend his car to Giles and John Prinz for the getaway. He testified that he and his wife, who had been questioned at length with Giles by Prosecutor Erwin, had no advance knowledge of the crime. His trial was short, the jury finding him guilty but recommending mercy because of a good prior record and having a wife and two children. He was given credit for having already been incarcerated seven months in the county detention home but ordered to start serving an additional five months in jail in January and pay trial costs of $200.

As with George Charlain, Fred Giles's case could not be tried until the Prinz brothers' appeal before the Michigan State Supreme Court was heard and decided. Information was filed at long last against him on Oct 24, 1952 charging him with three counts of murder, manslaughter and robbery unarmed, his trial also held in Judge Eric Singer's justice court in Brighton. His testimony three years earlier in the Prinz proceedings may have colored the outcome, but he was nonetheless pronounced guilty early the following summer. On June 24, 1953 Fred Giles was sentenced to eighteen months to fifteen years, but for charges of robbery unarmed. Quarantined in Jackson State Prison temporarily, he was sent to the Detroit House of Corrections for the rest of his incarceration, separated from the Prinz brothers. *

When I was only seven my parents bought my first bike—a red and white twenty-six inch Hiawatha from Gamble's, a Minneapolis-based hardware store franchise run by Brighton businessman Art Schumann. My perennial love of wandering at an early age took me on jaunts to town on hot summer days to buy ice cream from DeLuca's Sweet Shop or Uber's Drug Store on the "other" side of town. Often, and to the chagrin of my parents, I went beyond Uber's to the store my bicycle had come from just to peek in the display window at the latest Hiawatha arrivals or to be waved at by the manager's son, Bruce.

After getting my bike, Eddie, who was never one to hold back his feelings from an annoying brother, made an off-the-cuff remark about Gamble's. "You know that place is next to where Peanut Cline's store was, don't you?"

"Whose?" I said.

"You know," he answered me, as if everyone should know about "Peanut" Cline. "The store where Dad used to take us to get clothes when we were little! He got robbed and killed."

Gamble's, as it happened, opened in the building adjacent to Peanut Cline's only a year or two after the events of late April 1949.

With time, people began to forget about the story of a murder in Brighton, but with time even I had heard about it. There were no more lead stories in the *Livingston County Press* after 1955 about a crime that made people in town cringe, a crime of greed that did not turn out as the perpetrators planned. My family often talked about it as the years passed—about the old man we remembered, the musty smelling store, the robbery and murder. Of course they had heard the news first-hand, as had my brother. But I was blessed with sensitive parents who kept stories like that to themselves. They did not share them with a four and one half year-old boy who never could have processed the ghastly details—a bloodied shirt tied around the victim, an old man of 75 who had difficulties walking discovering his best friend's body, a trail of blood leading to a back storage room.

As I got older, every time I saw Henry Dammann sitting in the balcony of the church I tried as best I could not to recall the nightmare of one morning of his life in April of the next-to-last year of a nightmarish decade for the entire nation. I have thought a lot about that Main Street crime which, sadly, was not to be Brighton's last. I was stunned boarding the school bus one morning in the spring of 1955 to hear about the murder of Larry Jackson, an outgoing, handsome high school graduate the year before who had been a varsity football player his junior and senior years and was active in the dramatics club. Jackson was working as a night shift attendant May 19 at the Standard gas station on Church and Grand River when he was robbed at gunpoint and kidnapped by two brothers, Robert and Richard DuFrie. The B.H.S. graduate suffered the same fate as the Brighton merchant six years before, his body found in a ditch at the end of Rickett Road, the victim ordered by one of the brothers to leave the car and summarily shot. He was not to have the wish fulfilled that was under his picture in the 1954 school yearbook, the *Brightonian*: "Do not disturb, for I want just to lie and watch the world go by." * *

Larry Jackson

Another senseless murder rocked Brighton five years later, one felt deeply by our family. Eddie's and my friend, Bobbie Richmond, was looking for employment late in the summer of 1959. Always active in the Brighton Auxiliary Fire Department and other civic organizations, Bobbie was encouraged by his friend, State Trooper Albert "Bud" Souden, to pursue a career as a policeman. Bud had even volunteered to recommend him to the Michigan State Police if he wished. Less than three weeks later Trooper Souden, the father of a seven-month-old baby, was dead. He was attempting to question Albert Franks, who had been charged and arrested for theft at Milford's Numatics factory, when he was forcibly overcome, kidnapped, tied to a tree and shot near the small Livingston County community of Argentine. Franks was apprehended a short time later in Tennessee and returned to Livingston County by Trooper Bill Novak and his partner.

My mom was part of a judicial panel of one hundred, from which fourteen jurors were to be selected to decide the guilt or innocence of Albert Franks. It did not take defense attorney Martin Lavan long to dismiss her that March day in 1960.

"Did you know the victim or do you know anyone in the victim's family?" Lavan asked her.

"Yes," she answered softly but assertively in a way I can never forget. "Albert Souden was a friend and member of our church."

Not long after jurors were selected, Franks confessed to the murder and was sentenced to eighteen to twenty-five years in prison.* * *

Trooper Albert "Bud" Souden
(Courtesy Michigan State Police)

History has a unique way of affording us the luxury of teaching lessons about both the good and bad events of the past, events that dare not be forgotten. The "Peanut" Cline, Larry Jackson and Bud Souden stories should always be remembered, to put things in perspective and to honor the victims. What happened at First and Main, Grand River and Church Street and the small community of Argentine to this day remains among the saddest chapters in Brighton's past. Yet even out of tragedy, *Remarkable Brighton* learned to appreciate more the importance of caring and concern for others. Most of all, however, the value of a single human life.

Information about the Cline murder and trials of individuals involved in the crime were primarily drawn from articles in the Livingston County Press.
**The story of Jackson's murder was in the Livingston County Press May 28, 1955
***Coverage of the Souder murder trial was in the Livingston County Press editions of April 6 and 20, 1960.

Grandmother Amanda Sofia Westin, Paul Westin Weber and Eddie Weber,
Maltby and Rickett, Summer, 1945

CHAPTER ELEVEN

Up Home

> *We felt loved up home,*
> *We sensed belonging,*
> *We were nurtured there,*
> *And there our hearts remain.*
> —p.w.w.

EXCEPT FOR THE FIRST DAY OF OCTOBER, when I expected the obligatory birthday presents to be put ceremoniously on the foot of my youth bed instead of fifteen days later, the most important event of the year was the day the carnival came to town. That was on the Fourth of July, the same day fireworks were set off at Sloan Memorial Field. I tested my parents' patience for days, drilling them about when we would be going to the carnival in front of Mr. DeLuca's store and Aunt Emma's bank. Independence Day week took forever to arrive, and when it did, the excitement was incredible.

One special year in my early childhood, the anticipation was overwhelming! We would be riding to the carnival in a new car! Our old car had finally given up the ghost, a 1936 black two-door Chevrolet "Standard" that my parents had bought used in 1940. The old Chevy had the common features of many family cars of the period—running board, gear shift on the floor, crank up windows, folding front seats, spare tire mounted over the rear trunk and a horn. But the horn had not worked for ages, the tires were thread-bare and the battery was dead more often than not. It had been a stalwart throughout the war (my parents had brought both Eddie and me home from the hospital in it) but after eight years the old scrapyard on wheels was no longer worth keeping. One afternoon, after not starting for the better part of a week, it was hauled unceremoniously to our little barn and parked on its dirt floor, there to collect bean pods, chaff and dust for weeks. It was the perfect place for us boys to conceal ourselves when we played hide and seek with the neighbors—until Uncle Louie's mechanic neighbor, Tim Forbes, could tow it away to fix up for himself. A bargain at $100 cash!

Eddie and Paul in front of the new green Chevy, 1948

The old Chevrolet was replaced by a newer Chevrolet. I knew the moment had come for the car to arrive when I saw dust clouds from Rickett Road rising up to the north and rushed to Mom and Dad's bedroom window to get a better view. Aunt Emma and Aunt Ruth were among the only women in the family I had seen driving in those days; seeing Aunt Anna Westin from Fowlerville at the wheel of the new car pulling into our driveway was itself a novelty. Behind her was my Uncle Carl in the shiny four-door Dodge Coronet they had just bought and would be driving home. Dad had finished the farm chores early so we could leave for town as soon as my aunt and uncle had gone. Eddie and I were so excited that we climbed into the back seat of the car to admire all there was to take in, even before Mom and Dad had locked the house doors. That Chevy had been so well taken care of by my uncle and aunt's son, Charles, that it still smelled new, almost like the day it was driven off a transport truck onto the car dealership lot in Fowlerville. Finally, Dad took the wheel and before setting off for town made a test run in our long driveway, getting used to all of the fancy new features G.M. had included as standard in its 1941 model. Even a gearshift mounted on the steering column instead of the floor and a radio tuned to WJR were not to deter him from concentrating on getting us safely to town.

In my early childhood, before it moved to an empty lot next to the Chevrolet dealership outside of town, the carnival was held on Main Street. Cars were directed to park on a side street to make way for the midway, which stretched from Grand River as far as First Street. Dad took an unfamiliar route downtown, avoiding city streets and traffic by parking a few blocks from Main on North Street, near his friend, Adolph Martin's, blacksmith shop. The sounds of the carnival were almost deafening! Loud music emanated from the carousel that was always the central attraction on Main Street. The B.H.S. band was playing every march in its repertoire and carny workers shouted repetitive phrases, hawking merchandise they knew would be irresistible to every girl with her boyfriend or children begging their parents for trinkets. But probably loudest of all was the ballyhoo of side show talkers drawing people into dark tents filled with scary ghosts, crystal ball readers or freaky creatures ready to lunge at people. The closer we got to Main walking up West Street, the tighter Mom and Dad held my brother's and my hands, fearful of losing us in the crowd. "Watch your bill-fold pocket and purse," Bert Miller, the town cop, warned Mom and Dad. "Already caught a couple of roustabout pick-pockets!"

Often it was difficult to discern who enjoyed the banter of the barkers, colorful Roma, booths with tantalizing, exotic foods and rides more—my brother and I or our parents! They took their turn riding on the merry-go-round and other kiddy rides with us, even venturing onto the Ferris wheel—Mom with me, Eddie with Dad. Zany carny workers bearing monkeys stopped Dad every few minutes to ask if they could play his favorite song on their calliopes for a nickel. Unicyclists dressed as Uncle Sam wove in and out of the crowds juggling and flashing sparklers. Mom stopped a few times to buy special carnival treats for all of us that she had enjoyed since her girlhood—pink cotton candy for Eddie and me, caramel corn for her and roasted, salted peanuts for

Dad. When we begged for ice cream cones on that hot sultry evening to top everything off we were told that would have to wait. Mom reminded us that we would enjoy the homemade ice cream she had bought from Paul Deluca's that was in the freezer at home in the den all the more.

It was hard leaving the excitement of the midway but soon it was time for the second major attraction of Independence Day, the fireworks show at Sloan Memorial Field. As we drove up East Main toward the high school the traffic was so bad that Eddie fretted we would miss meeting his neighborhood friends and Uncle Lou, Auntie Ruth and our cousin Carolyn. I was too young and by that time a little too sleepy to protest anything. I knew that we would make it because Dad had promised us this year there would be no chance of our car breaking down like the year before in the middle of the throngs of people parking everywhere around school or in the large lot in back of it. True to his word, we made it in time for the show. Eddie was pacified because our uncle and aunt had saved seats for us in the bleachers next to Carolyn and her friend, Carol Pelkey, just below the P.A. booth. In front of us, some of the Rickett Road gang Eddie was looking for were sitting—Gary Griffin, Billy Sawyer and the Lanning brothers.

Representatives from the Brighton Volunteer Fire Department soon emerged from the crowds to stand at strategic spots surrounding both sides of Sloan Memorial Field to ensure the safety of the large crowd. Joining them were deputized members of the police department and scores of volunteers from the town Kiwanis and Chamber of Commerce Clubs. Huddled around members of the B.H.S. band, which was scheduled to perform after the fireworks, was a large contingent of high school age Jr. Chamber members. My aunt and uncle waved at all of them because they knew them well; they were as welcome on their farm just within the city limits as they were in their own homes and spent many hours there.

The din and movement of the crowd was broken by a loud testing noise on the P.A. system. Sitting as close as we were to the sound booth we were startled by it and the audio distortion that came from a litany of announcements. No less than three members of the town council welcomed the audience, followed by safety precautions everyone needed to heed. Finally, the fantastic Fourth of July extravaganza that kept us all on the edge of our seats began! The sky lit up brilliantly for over an hour with every imaginable color and shape, every sequence of blasts better than the last, every sound mimicking Revolutionary War rifle and cannon volleys. Transfixed after every round, I looked at Carolyn and Carol, who were sitting close to me on either side holding my hand, and exclaimed as only a soon-to-be four-year-old could,"*Booh-ti-full! Booh-ti-full!*"

Far too soon the fireworks were over. Smoke still wafted through the air atop High School Hill as Dad shouted at me "You can take your fingers out of your ears now, Paul! Now hold your brother's hand as Mom and I try to remember where we parked so we can go to your grandmother's house."

As late as it was, we had been invited *Up home* for dinner, our final stop of the evening. *Up home* was one of many places other than Rickett Road where my brother and I felt secure at a very early age, a place where some of our fondest and earliest childhood memories were made. We took it for granted that once or twice a week on trips to town we would turn left at the stop light at Grand River and Main, drive two or three blocks then turn right on First Street. A bit further there was a curve in the street to the west that would bring us to Grandma Westin's on Second Street. She or Aunt Emma would be at the door to greet us with a hug and a snack then let us play with a favorite toy. Eddie was always allowed to make a trip to Uncle Joe's "old gray barn" next to the garage, where mechanical treasures and tools filled every niche of an old, dilapidated building that had been my Grandfather Westin's haven.

"*Up home*" was a 19th century two-story farmhouse owned by my Uncle Joe where my Grandmother Westin, Aunt Emma and he lived when my uncle was not working at Westin Brothers Grocery Store in Fowlerville. A white wooden picket fence surrounded one side of the large back lawn overlooking Cross Street that could easily have shown up in front of a Victorian home in any of Norman Rockwell's paintings. The flower garden cultivated by my uncle for his mother was uniquely American yet exactly like the ones in Grandma's ancestral home, small garden plots along the *Kattegat* Sea between Sweden and Denmark in the Swedish province of *Halland*. Lilies of the valley flourished in shaded areas near the house and garage like the ones his mother picked in Sweden for her mother, walking home through a birch forest from the estate where she worked. The textured, green patches of grass on the sprawling lawn contrasted beautifully with the lofty blue spruce tree my uncle had planted and the colorful red, white and purple peonies, petunias and bleeding hearts that bloomed profusely everywhere in season.

Up Home with Aunt Emma and Eddie, 1947

Perhaps I remember *up home* so well because of the special persons who lived there and because of the love always coming from within its walls. Eddie and I were always the center of attention, very much the spoiled youngest grandchildren and nephews. After we arrived, my aunt often gave us a new toy from "Aunt" Arbor, my brother's name for the town where she often shopped on her days off. Knowing how much Eddie and I liked the treats she made for us, it would not be long before Aunt Emma, wearing her casual housework smock, disappeared into the dungeon-like basement, emerging with two cans of tuna fish for sandwiches to go with the O'Henry candy bars she always had for us. Grandma kept my toys and some of her treasured mementos from her Swedish home in a basket of wonders that she always brought out for me to play with on the dining room floor. She all but weaned me on strong percolator coffee that had been richly whitened with fresh cream, always served with one of her special Swedish pastries and two or three pieces of her favorite coffee bean candy.

I never wanted to leave *up home* when it was time to go following dinner after the adults had visited and Eddie had bided his time tinkering with one of Uncle Joe's home crafted puzzles. Often I tried to hide in the sunroom just off the dining room where my grandmother normally took her afternoon nap. I had found the perfect place to call my own there under a large wooden quilting frame covered with carpet tacks. There I stayed until I heard both my brother and dad calling my name saying it was time to go. They would walk into the sunroom, Dad taking the last puff on the R.G. Dunn cigar Uncle Joe had given him, pretending not to find me. That was Dad's way—never wanting to spoil the good times either Eddie or I were having. But Eddie did not care that I had found my own special place; he was sleepy, cross and anxious to go. "He's in the corner under the table with all the nails sticking out of the top!" he would shout at Dad, spoiling my fun. "Come on Paul," he said, the agitation in his voice clearly discernible. "We gotta go!"

The knitting, crocheting, needlepoint and other creations in that sunroom were fascinating, even for a four-year-old! They were colorful pieces of artistry that neighbors and family greatly admired, particularly the exquisite appliques for quilts. The patterns were of dahlias and other bouquets, double wedding rings, kites, decorative plates and many more of my grandmother's own design. She had made quilts for each of her five children, five grandchildren and so many nieces and nephews she had lost count. One of those heirlooms would remain with me wherever I lived later in life, always a center of conversation, always providing warmth when it was cold but, more important, warm memories.

Amanda Westin's cozy old-fashioned kitchen with a black cook stove in the center was the meeting place for a large family circle that included nieces, nephews and life-long friends, many of whom had emigrated from Sweden like my grandparents. The Swedish language was often spoken *up home*, usually with family members when Grandma did not want young ears to hear what she said. Though I was not yet four, I enjoyed hearing the beauty of its lilting, poetic phrases, even though they were punctuated with sounds that English speakers shook their heads at. There were many times when my grandmother simply wanted to teach me a few words of the language of the homeland from which she had emigrated in her early twenties. Two responses to polite questions were never spoken in English *up home*: "Thanks" was always *"Tack så mycket"* and "You're welcome" was *"Var så god."* I could never forget the distinctive Scandinavian accent with which Grandma spoke English. With time, there were words that neither my parents nor my first school teachers could coax me into saying correctly because I was not willing to! "Chair" was "shair" in my vocabulary and "chicken" was "shicken." And as I grew up, hearing the Swedish language forever brought back the vivid memory I have of the wonderful woman who spoke it. Perhaps that is why I developed an early love for the language and later in life learned to speak it.

Swedish customs, cuisine and baking traditions were also always maintained *up home*. Rarely did a day go by when some Swedish delicacy was not baked in Grandma's "workhorse" wood burning oven. Most commonly it was *kake brod*, a simple flat white bread topped with granulated sugar that my father ordered whenever he knew he would be going to Second Street. My mother, aunts and uncles, however, preferred the mainstay of most Swedish households, *limpa brod*, a sweet rye bread made with molasses and caraway seeds. Where dessert treats were concerned, Grandma Westin was unexcelled! No respectable Swedish housewife would bake any less than the essential *sju sorter*, seven varieties of cookies, to serve with four o'clock afternoon coffee for special occasions. The center of any hostess's dessert table by far were *sandkakar*, shortbread sugar cookies, and no one—not even close relatives—could duplicate Grandma's. I think it fair to say that her passion was indeed baking—any kind of baking—not just recipes passed down for generations by peasants in her homeland either. From the home where her children were raised in the coal-mining town of Wishaw in northeastern Pennsylvania she brought recipes that made her the village's finest baker. Each of her children requested her *Lady Baltimore* cake for their birthday or a holiday dessert, a luscious three layer white cake with butter cream icing and fruit and nutmeat filling. That best of the best of Amanda Westin's recipes was always served on a table spread with the finest starched linen table cloth, gold rimmed china coffee cups, saucers and dessert plates, her *pièce de résistance* cake centered on a pink flowered square *Limoges* porcelain plate.

The days after Thanksgiving *up home* were filled with the aroma of wonderful taste delights our family savored during the Advent and Christmas celebrations. Pound upon pound of butter, flour and sugar were used to bake the traditional *Sandkakar*. They were shaped into bells, wreaths, stars, angels and *jultomtar*, the Swedish Santa Claus, then preserved in the cold basement for "coffee afternoons." Santa Lucia Day, Dec 13, was the official beginning of the holiday celebration when *semlor*, white flour rolls made with cream, were served along with cardamom buns and, on special occasions, saffron buns. Limpa bread was never in short supply for pre-holiday meals nor were loaves of the ever popular *kake brod*.

The tradition that Eddie and I remembered most about our grandmother (and one later maintained by our mother, cousins, aunts and uncles) was not just her Swedish holiday baking, however. It was the almost sacred Christmas Eve feast. Less wonderful than the smell of cookies and breads coming from the Second Street kitchen oven was what many called the "odiferous" aroma of dried fish aging in large crocks in Uncle Joe's cellar. That was the dungeon-like place, he kidded, where "Moses" lived—in itself a mysterious place from which such a "unique" smell to emanate. The smell so permeated the house and was so objectionable to kids that my cousin, Charles, always quipped that as a boy of five he disliked it so much he threw his slippers in the aging fish vat to express his distaste! It would be almost anathema, however, for Scandinavians not to prepare *lutfisk*—dried, salted codfish that had been cured for a month in a lye solution—for Christmas Eve, the most revered Swedish holiday. Prepared after rehydration in a tasty *béchamel* sauce, it was the main course for the Christmas Eve buffet dinner feast after services at St. George Church. We arrived *up home* to find lights turned on in every room, candles burning, the dining room table fastidiously set with angels dancing around a *glockenspiel* and the tantalizing smell and sounds of Swedish Christmas pervading the house. Though the memories are incomparable, Eddie and I were too young, tired and anxious to open presents after the church's children's pageant to appreciate the special significance of the Eve of Christmas nor remember the accolades Grandma drew from serving that holiday evening's main course, creamed *lutfisk*.

Equally as memorable as the fish were the *smorgåsbord* main dishes served with it—roasted fresh ham and a Swedish meal staple, *kötbullar*—meatballs. They were made by mixing ground pork and beef, eggs, cream, seasonings and dried bread crumbs, forming the meat into balls, simmering them slightly and steaming those savory delights with the lid only slightly ajar until done. Side dishes included creamed pickled herring, pickled herring tidbits in wine sauce (*gaffelbiter*), *limpa* bread, pickled beets, Swedish brown beans in a sweet and sour sauce and a cheese platter. Desserts were cookies and rice pudding topped with whipping cream served with steaming cups of coffee made with an egg. A special added touch included a single almond in one of the servings of rice pudding. According to Swedish lore, the recipient of the almond was to be married in the coming year. No less than five single members of the Westin Family competed for that prize year after year—mostly to no avail—when I was very young.

Most young children rarely understand that life is fleeting. If by chance at an early age they witness someone passing away, the mystery of the cycle of life is not something that can be easily comprehended. And so it was for me when I was not yet five.

The secure, childhood *up home* days in town ended for me in early 1949. Dinner after church at St. George on Easter Sunday—that year April 17—brought over 15 family members together. Always invited on those family get-togethers was my other grandmother, my father's mother, Clara Conrad Weber. It was a brilliant, sunny day. The Dutch Elm trees lining Second Street had just started to leaf out in their light green hues and Uncle Joe's spring flowers—a rainbow array of daffodils, tulips, hyacinths and lilies—blossomed abundantly around the side and back lawns. The dining room table was set as only my grandmother could with the usual oversized starched white linen table cloth, gold rimmed china and silverware polished to perfection.

I was uncharacteristically restless that day—or so I have been told. I could not stay in my "shair,' choosing instead to act out naughtily, as if the "terrible twos" had not yet run their course. Eddie was contenting himself playing games with our older cousins as we waited for dessert but I made it my business to make my rounds repeatedly around the table chattering nonsense and very clearly embarrassing my parents. *"My little mother died tonight!"* I muttered to everyone who was courteous enough to listen to my menacing remarks. *"My little mother died tonight!"*

Why I was obsessed by the word "died" at four-and-one half I will never know. Grandmother Weber, who had heart problems, lived with us much of the time. Having suffered one or two strokes and losing a sister the previous year, did the word slip from her mouth a bit too often when my mother was not around to talk me through the meaning of it? Not helping matters were the frequent "spells" my grandmother was said to be having along with the resulting *angst* my parents experienced. I had also heard talk about "funerals" at Sunday school and church and references to the austere brick Tudor house across from church called a "funeral home." What I was saying mattered very little within a short time, for when I had ceased my scary litany my father's mother slumped in her chair, suffering from another stroke. Dr. Archie MacGregor was summoned immediately along with Uncle Louie and Uncle Carlos from East Lansing. Within the hour, Grandmother Weber passed away at the age of seventy-four.

A day or two afterward I learned firsthand what a funeral home was. From the outside it did not look much different from Erwin Hyne's Tudor brick house across the street from it or Grandmother Weber's home on East Grand River, all built by Ed Rosene in the late 1920s. Uncle Joe's beautiful garden flowers were not outside bordering the lawn; they were in the large gathering place inside in vases on stands like at St. George Church. Inside was a mysterious place—somber and dark with few windows and people with serious faces. A big bed with covers was there too. Eddie was taller than I and could see someone lying on it but not moving. "It's Grandma Weber," he whispered to me.

"She is *dead*." Dad, Mom, Eddie and I said hello to Uncle Louie and Aunt Ruth who were talking to my Uncle Carlos and Aunt Frances in the front of the big room standing next to the flowers. I had cried before after I was naughty and punished and seen Eddie and a few of my friends cry too after being scolded. But it was different seeing *grownups* like my aunts and uncles crying. And for the first time in my life, I saw my mother in tears.

My father was not crying like most of the grownups around him, looking at the death of his mother in a different way. He had heard what Eddie said and told me that Eddie was right. "Yes, Paul, it's your Grandma Weber. She is sleeping and she is in heaven." Dad wanted to make sure that I could see the peaceful look on his mother's face and lifted me up so I could view what Eddie had seen. He had slipped Grandma's glasses on her face and placed the wedding ring on her finger that Mr. Keehn had just given him. "Her soul is in heaven, just like you and Eddie say every night when you pray 'Now I lay me down to sleep...' "

Amanda Westin, Clara Augusta Weber,
Eddie and Paul. Rickett Road, 1947

I did not realize that one of the happiest times in my young life was quickly ending in the spring and summer of 1949. Other than flowers, a lot of crying and my dad lifting me up to see Grandma Weber in her bed I remember little about Clara Augusta Weber's funeral at St.

George Church a few days later. One morning at the end of May, we drove to the garden store on the corner where our neighbors, Mr. and Mrs. Kunz, lived. Fred Kunz had very few teeth, always dressed in denim coveralls and could usually be found watering geraniums in his greenhouse or cultivating fields of gladiolas or vegetables next to it with his small red Ford tractor. Dad chatted with Mr. Kunz then bought a lot of his bright red geraniums to take to Fairview Cemetery, where he planted them in the soil in front of the large granite monument marking his parents' graves. I was charged with fetching a bucket of water from the hand pump on the hillside nearby for watering them.

When Dad put on his suit to go to church that Sunday, Mom pinned a white paper flower on his lapel. I asked her why he put a white flower on that day and why hers was red. "It's because it is Memorial Day Sunday today. Remember that your Grandmother Weber died and is in heaven just like Grandfather Weber and Grandfather Westin. Dads and moms wear red or white carnations to church today. I wear a red carnation because Grandma Westin is still living. That is what we will do every year now, just like taking geraniums from Kunz's to the cemetery."

Neither Bambi, Thumper, Flower or the *Donald Duck* comic books Aunt Emma always brought to Eddie and me on her visits with Grandma Westin to Maltby and Rickett could make up for the loneliness we felt less than a month later. Aunt Emma was alone suddenly on her visits in the summer of 1949. Amanda Sofia Westin had passed away peacefully in her sleep June 30. *Up Home* was no longer and Mom, like Dad, pinned a white paper carnation on her dress on the Sunday closest to Memorial Day the next year.

"Up Home," 8721 Second Street

One of Uncle Joe's sedans, Second Street, 1943

CHAPTER TWELVE

Starlight Staircase   **1949**

> *"I love those dear hearts and gentle people,*
> *who live in my home town.*
>
> *Because those dear hearts and gentle people*
> *will never ever let you down."*
> *"I Love Those Dear Hearts and Gentle People"*
> —Sammy Fain/Bob Hilliard

I WAS FASCINATED AT AN EARLY AGE (four going on five) on trips to town by the cars I saw stopped at the traffic light on Grand River downtown and the ones parked along Main Street. Not unusual, I suspect, growing up less than forty miles from Detroit where the major industry was automobiles and with General Motors Proving Grounds so close to town. But it occurred to me once that it was Uncle Joe who was responsible for the way I fancied cars. To broaden my knowledge about them, Uncle Joe let me sit on his lap in the living room one Sunday after dinner and patiently taught me the name of virtually every car manufactured in the late 1940s. Then he showed me pictures of many of them that were advertised in the Sunday edition of the *Detroit Free Press*. To his amazement, I remembered many of the names when I was quizzed one week later:

"*Chevy, Dodge, Ford, Buick...*" I parroted back at him. I paused after *Buick* because the cars I named were all driven by my relatives or people in the neighborhood or at church. Then I continued, remembering what cars the chauffeur of our rich neighbor, Mr. George Fink, and some of the city people who showed up at our annual Conrad Family reunion drove. *"Cadillac, Hudson, Packard..."*

As time passed, I could easily spot the make and model of every car parked on Main quicker than Eddie or either of my parents. Unlike the more familiar West Street to Grand River area where Dad parked, my relatives' and neighbors' cars could usually be seem well past West Street—Uncle Lou and Aunt Ruth's four-door Ford Deluxe, Mr. Smith's Pontiac Chief sedan or Aunt Emma's Style Master Chevy coupe. I knew my friend Susie Ryan and her grandmother were in town when I saw Rena Rickett's car because I had often been picked up in that car for school. In her late seventies, Susie's grandmother was still driving her large, black 1938 Buick Special. It featured comfortable plush gray seats that always smelled like lavender and had far more get-up-and-go than an automobile driven by a woman that age needed. Frank Meyer's car was another one I recognized. Frank always owned very large used cars. His two-toned 1940 Hudson Commodore captured my interest even as a little tyke when he pulled into our driveway to pick Dad up for township meetings. I immediately spotted it on the other side of town if it were parked in front of Al Stewart's Feed Store or George Ratz's Hardware. At my age I didn't know who owned most of the cars I saw but I was intrigued, nonetheless, by the lineup parked in front of stores when Dad drove to that side of town.

There was one car in town in those days, however, that both piqued my curiosity and made me envious. It was almost always in front of Uber's Drug Store and I recognized it because I saw it so often at Uncle Louie and Auntie Ruth's. It belonged to Chug Smith, who after the war was able to select any hard-to-come-by car he wanted at the Ford showroom on Grand River near North Street. He had sold his '41 sporty coupe back to the dealer when he enlisted in the army with the provision that he be allowed to have first choice picking out a new car once peacetime production lines had revved up. Chug had always been the town's best wheeler-dealer and the flashy Ford he drove was next to impossible to get. But the car had to be paid for and so did the big Oldsmobiles and Buicks he switched to a few years later. No wonder then that not long after returning from China in '45 his passion for bigger cars with more power required a better-paying job. That led to his thirty-year-long career as a test driver at the General Motors Proving Grounds. Pay at the "Grounds" was as good as anywhere around town, and with peacetime prosperity it quickly grew into one of the principal employers for the community.

Chug bought nice cars not just because of his passion for them but also to drive his mother around town in a "respectable" automobile. Bea Smith had worked hard and sacrificed all her life and it was her son's way of showing his thanks to her. Besides, it was an apology of sorts, since his mother had begged him not to enlist back in '43. The '49 Futuramic 98 coupe that he drove in 1949 caught my eye like none others I saw in town. It was bright yellow that sometimes appeared to be orange—the same color as the setting sun at dusk. It had white wall tires, posh seats and so much chrome that it dazzled the eyes. I wished I were one of Chug's relatives when I chanced seeing his nephew and nieces—Eddie (Bub) Case, his sister Ann, or my cousin Carolyn—riding around town in it, top up, on a hot summer day. My mind was made up! When I was old enough to own a car—or just persuade my parents to buy a different car—it too would be a flashy convertible with a bright color. Chartreuse or bright red would be fine, as long as the top came down and it was like Chug's Olds ninety-eight.

One chilly Saturday evening, when ice and snow made walking on most town sidewalks that were already riddled with cracks in the cement dangerous, Dad broke his routine and parked across the street from Paul DeLuca's. Even with the family wearing galoshes or overshoes, he felt more comfortable parking in front of Squee Squire's Electrical Shop. Mom knew, though, as she watched Dad carefully crossing the street to DeLuca's to fetch the paper that there was another reason for parking in front of Squire's. Since Aunt Emma worked at the bank and got wind of most town happenings before they were to occur, she had heard from Squee himself that he was going to stock Brighton's first ever television set by the end of the week! It could not be missed because Squire had placed the television in his show window where people outside were gathering to watch it. The door to the shop was propped open and the set turned up so loud that it was impossible not to hear the booing and cheering of the program with the best reception that evening—wrestling. Viewers, including Dad, were in awe of the maneuvers of the fighters, though many were horrified that at any time a member of the tag team would be badly injured, even knocked unconscious. "Don't take it too seriously," Mom told me, knowing full well that at that time it was more of a staged drama than an athletic event. "It's not as serious as it seems." Squee recognized us and invited us in for better viewing and to get warm, demonstrating the programs on the other two Detroit channels that evening. "I can sell you one easy as anything," he told Dad. "They're hard to come by right now but all you have to do is give me a small down payment and I will bring it to the house—I'll even kick in the aerial for free."

It was a tempting offer but Mom knew our finances. As the post-war economy grew and wages increased, farm prices stayed the same or even went down. In far better circumstances than most farmers because the farm was paid for due to the generosity of my dad's father, it still was not always easy. "No, definitely not," I heard her say emphatically to Dad on the way home. "It might be nice for the boys, but the price is just out of the question. The electric and Phil-gas bill is due next month and George Woodward tells us the furnace can't be fixed one more time." My hopes had been dashed, because next to a big, flashy Oldsmobile or Buick, I wanted that Motorola television as bad as Dad and Eddie did. But when Mom switched from addressing my father as *Dad* to *Ed*, I knew that the case was closed. After twenty years of marriage, she knew how to deal with my father. I knew deep down, too, that she may not have liked some of the programs on the television lineup she had heard about, but she wanted a television as much as anyone. "Maybe by next year, when you add a few more shorthorn cows to the herd, we will be able to afford one. For now, we can always go to the show for a twenty-five cent matinee. Wendell will get one for us when the time is right," she said in her usual calming way.

The time was not right for the Weber family to purchase a television. It *was* right for Chug Smith.

Chug, who was still a bachelor, saw to it that his family joined him often at Bea Smith's small home on the hill, just off Flint Road at the end of East Street. He and his mother also spent a good many hours at Uncle Louie and Auntie Ruth's with my cousin, Carolyn. The main activity for the Weber's and Smith's was either listening to or *making* music! And whether it was because they were so much alike—their sense of humor, outgoing personalities or just their gift of gab—Chug was especially close to Carolyn. He was always available if Uncle Louie's old Ford broke down to take Carolyn to Northville for saxophone lessons or drive her to band or *Hungry Five* practice.

The *Hungry Five*, also known as *Slim Gage and the Hungry Five*, was a remarkably talented group of young Brighton musicians—all except

Carolyn upperclassmen at Brighton High School—who regularly got gigs in and around Brighton. Their unofficial leaders were Kenny Gage (accordion player), son of local realtor Elmer Gage, and Gus Wybrew (drummer), whose father managed the American Auto Hardware Store on Grand River. Harold Bidwell, who played trumpet in the BHS band, and Shirley Ann Hills on trombone joined Carolyn as the group's other instrumentalists. They played '40s big band music—Glen Miller favorites were their specialty—complicated jazz selections, ragtime and blues, even old favorites from the '20s and '30s; no musical piece was unknown to them, none too complicated to master.

By mid-1949, nearly everyone in the area had either heard about the *Hungry Five* or heard them play. One Sunday Kenny and Gus managed to secure a gig out of Brighton at First Presbyterian Church in Howell. Because it was to be a church social occasion—the annual congregational meeting—and because Howell's Presbyterians were recognized as fun-loving and congenial, the group added comedy routines to their program. But Kenny, their emcee, kept them as "respectable" as possible out of deference to some of the members of the highly esteemed "founding" families of Howell. The evening was a great success, including the group's rehearsed routines. Among other things, they played the country songs that Chug Smith was so fond of and had taught them. They incorporated props like rag-mops, buckets of water and washing scrub boards and used the hokiest musical instruments they could come up with. They wore outrageous wigs, blackened their front teeth and dressed like hayseeds that had just left the hills. To add to the drama and comedy of the hour-long program, two or three members of the group disappeared regularly, followed by surprise re-entries. Carolyn was instructed to squeak her saxophone loudly, feigning disgust afterward. Shirley Ann yelled "Oh no, not again!" when her slide crashed to the floor. The audience could not refrain from howling with laughter from the moment the performance started. But Kenny Gage pulled off a daring vaudevillian stunt, slightly on the naughty side, that was the hit of the night. Dressed as a country bumpkin and wearing a wig, his loose fitting dungarees dropped to the floor as the combo sang Vic Damone's hit song *You're Breaking My Heart!* Kenny pretended that it was an accident, pulled his dungarees back over his long boxer shorts and bare chest and continued the production unscathed!

Word spread fast around the county seat, among the more "open" Protestant churches, at least, about the slapstick and musical talent of the Brighton combo. It was not long before representatives of no less than three churches contacted the *Hungry Five* about appearing during their congregation's fellowship hours as well. Not to be outdone by the Presbyterians, First Methodist reserved a date before any others in young Kenny's engagement book. Only two weeks after their successful performance at First Pres., the group was in Howell again driving down Grand River, past the historic courthouse, ready to perform. Not entirely sure where the Methodist Church was, they turned south at Michigan Ave, finally reaching a church on a side street just before the dim city lights came on. It was light enough to see cars parked up and down both sides of the street, though, and late arrivals were still wandering in. It would be another packed house!

"Must be the place," Kenny shouted as the group quickly unloaded their instruments. Dragging their props—two or three home-made mountain country instruments of questionable design, the essential mop and pail, the washboard—they charged through the wooden sanctuary entry doors into the church that was filled to capacity. On Kenny's signal—a loud out of tune rendition of *She'll Be Coming 'Round the Mountain*—the Hungry Five marched to the front of the church down the center aisle, and without hesitation began another song. This time, Kenny chose to move his dropped dungarees routine to the beginning of the show. And, much to the quintet's chagrin, they were not applauded, laughed at or recognized in any way afterward! In front of them was a stoic group of stone-faced Howell residents completely aghast at what they had just witnessed. Kenny had arrived at a church on a Howell side street, all right, and one with a lot of cars. Unfortunately, though, it was not First Methodist. *Hungry Five* had interrupted a prayer service at another of the town's churches that had just begun!

Performing one number by mistake at a Howell church did not sully The *Hungry Five's* reputation. If anything, they were in more demand than ever! Then came an appearance that all of Brighton was talking about. The group was invited to appear on *Starlight Staircase*, a live Saturday evening television variety show on WJBK, the CBS television affiliate in Detroit. WJBK had already billed the lineup for the evening as an exciting one, featuring a "very talented five member musical combo from our neighbors in Brighton." Auntie Ruth was on the phone almost immediately to tell my mother about the exciting news. She was understandably very proud and wanted to pass on an invitation from Chug and her mother to watch the program in the

Smith home with family and a few neighbors and friends. I remember that conversation well because Mom seemed every bit as excited as my aunt and could not wait to tell my dad at supper that night. Not only would we see Carolyn but it would be our first opportunity to watch a television program in its entirety! In typical "Chug" fashion, he had driven to Ann Arbor only hours after hearing about *Starlight Staircase* and purchased a twelve-inch RCA television for $199.95 in cash!

I was slow to shake hands with Chug that Saturday evening as he stood at the door of his house greeting guests. I had never been as close as I was to *that* car, and this was my chance to stand beside it and dream big dreams about my parents one day owning something equally as flashy. It too would have the same new car smell, white wall tires and it would have a flashy, bright color like Chug's Oldsmobile 98. Too soon, though, Chug beckoned me to join my parents, Eddie and the rest of his guests in the house.

"You married yet?" he inquired, his standard greeting for me as long as I had known him. "Better get in the house before all the good seats are taken."

Everyone was noisily catching up on Brighton news when I walked in but a few, including my mother, Bobby Richmond and Bobby's mother had already sat down to watch the television that Chug had just turned on. "It's on two, I think," he told us as he rotated the television's channel selection knob counterclockwise. The CBS national news with Douglas Edwards, its news anchor, had just started. The former radio commentator with a distinguished career and rich baritone voice had just reported that the President and members of the foreign relations committee in Congress met with Pentagon officials that day to discuss the decaying political situation in China. The look on Chug's face changed noticeably after hearing that. He was deeply interested in China's future after his service years and the news about Generalissimo Chiang Kai Shek's flight to the Island of Taiwan with Nationalist forces and the Communist takeover of mainland China was disturbing. "Should have gotten rid of the *Reds* when we chased the Japanese out," he said assertively. "Now we have both the Russians and Chinese Communists with a knife at our backs!"

Bea Smith was entertaining Bub and Ann Case in one of the nooks of the house but she immediately headed toward me when she saw me. She scooped me up in her arms and hugged me as lovingly as she would have embraced the two grandchildren near her. "You have grown like a weed, *Paulus!*" she exclaimed, calling me by the pet name many knew me by. I did not know her as well as Chug or the Cases but I remembered her charming, grandmotherly way. A member of the prominent Brighton Hyne and Hicks Families, she had beautiful snow-white hair, was as outgoing as her son, and was one of the kindest persons in our town. "I want you and Eddie to sit next to me tonight when we watch Carolyn on the new television set," she said as she pointed to the davenport and television in the living room.

Bobbie Richmond, Eddie Weber,
Eddie Case and Paul, 1948

Auntie Bess, a close Smith family friend, was working busily with Chug's sisters—Auntie Doe Case and Auntie Ruth—in the kitchen preparing refreshments for the evening. They had two large percolators of coffee brewing and were finishing their preparation of deviled eggs, ham salad sandwiches and two relish trays. No less than four pies, all of state fair championship quality, had been baked for the occasion and flanked either end of the Smith's kitchen dinette set. I knew my dad, Uncle Louie and Bub's dad, Charlie, would not be content with just one piece and the pies would be gone by the end of the evening, judging from all the picnics we had been on together.

But who was the blond woman with a long pony tail assisting in the kitchen? She was attractive, wore fashionable shoes with low heels, trendy trousers with a high waistline and a bright, long-sleeve patterned blouse. I could tell that Chug's sisters liked her and Chug certainly did, because when the kitchen work was finished she sat down very close to him on the two-seater couch in the living room. It was Chug's friend Richard Baron's sister, Janet. Even at my age, I knew that most of the adults in the living room were already speculating about Chug's prospects. Was he finally getting serious? Somehow Eileen Hecht, his army buddy's sister in Chicago whom Chug visited soon after being drummed out of service, was not cut out to be Smith, nor were the other girls—sisters of friends, friends of friends, cousins of friends—that Chug dated off and on. A wife, it appeared, was not in Chug's immediate future, just like two or three of his single buddies, Jack Teeple, Dick Baron and Jack Mullaney. He was enjoying the single life a little too much anyway, having a grand time driving fast cars, taking trips to his cousin's in the winter in Sarasota, going to country music concerts in Kentucky or Tennessee and the Indy Five Hundred.

The room was full of anticipation as the time approached for the event everyone was waiting for. Chug and Charlie Case had connected the new television just a few days before. Chug had scaled the roof to mount the antenna as Charlie, from below, got him to tweak it for the best possible reception—probably the best anywhere in Brighton, situated as the house was atop a hill. "Turn it up, darling," I heard Bea say to Chug. Then, following a brief pause for station identification, a familiar voice my mom recognized from one of the Detroit radio stations announced with more drama in his voice than any of us had ever heard on the radio:

"Coming to you live from Masonic Hall in the Cass Corridor of Downtown Detroit WJBK CHANNEL Two brings you the STARLIGHT STAIRCASE..."

And almost before anyone had time to react Auntie Ruth shouted "There's Carolyn! Yes! It's Carolyn!" Producers of *Starlight Staircase* had been so impressed by the *Hungry Five's* warm up routine—for once only popular songs with no slapstick routines—that they were to appear first in the lineup and end the program with everyone in the auditorium singing the year's hit song, *"Dear Hearts and Gentle People."* Though winter was just around the corner, *Hungry Five* played what had come to be their theme song, *September Song*, composed by Kurt Weil and Maxwell Anderson, first released in 1938 but recorded later by Bing Crosby and Frank Sinatra. Even without being introduced, the group appeared on the steps of a brilliantly lit stairway, singing and playing with so much gusto that the studio audience broke out in applause. When they were finished, everyone in the Masonic Temple studio stood up and cheered:

"Oh it's a long long while from May to September,
But the days grow short when you reach September...
And these few precious days I'll spend with you,
These precious days I'll spend with you."

There was not a dry eye in Smith's small living room when the lights dimmed on the starlit staircase on Temple Street in Detroit and *Hungry Five* finished performing.

"*September Song* always has been my favorite," Uncle Louie managed to say, breaking the silence. "I had Carolyn memorize it when she first got her sax."

A Hungry Five jam session c. 1951. **Left to right:** *Gus Wybrew, Shirley Ann Hills, Carolyn Weber, Harald Bidwell and Kenny Gage.*

Kindergartner Paul, 1950

CHAPTER THIRTEEN

Holden, Chappel, and West   **1949**

Now here's a dance you should know
Oh Baby when the lights are down low
I said grab your baby then go
Do the hucklebuck (yeah!) Do the hucklebuck!
—Andy Gibson/Roy Alfred

IF MY MOTHER COULD NOT FIND ME amusing myself outside feeding a stray kitten or building a fort in the hayloft of our barn on lazy summer days, I would invariably turn up somewhere nearby exploring the neighborhood. Down Rickett I would go, carefully crossing the road at Fred Kunz's greenhouse, then making my way east along beautiful maple tree-lined Maltby Road. Sometimes I stopped at the Green Oak Plains cemetery, half way between Rickett and U.S. 23, dodging rabbits escaping from their warrens and killdeer nesting in the high, uncut grass. I tried hard to read names on the gravestones of the township's founders and prosperous farmers—the Lees, Maltbys, Holdens, Van Amburgs and Peaches—resting peacefully beside shady trees and surrounded by cornfields and Fred Kunz's gladiolas. Often I visited my Scottish friend, Mrs. Christine Smith, in the farmhouse across the road, delighting in her lilting brogue from the Isle of Lewis in the Outer Hebrides Islands of Scotland. Normally alerted by my parents when I set off that I was bound for her house, I was treated to cookies and a drink when I arrived. After our "wee" visit, my father was sent to pick me up, but I would not leave until I played a game with him, hiding in the bedroom under Mr. and Mrs. Smith's bed with Nancy, their golden retriever.

Less than a quarter of a mile to the east of Christine Smith's home, at the end of Maltby near U.S. 23, was my first school, Holden School. It was a white, framed two-room structure, built at the end of the nineteenth century, supervised by the Livingston County Rural School System but funded and maintained primarily by Green Oak Township. Its main entrance was on Maltby but another one faced U.S. 23 to the east. The school's only driveway, playground and water pump—from which a common metal drinking cup hung—were just outside its doors. (That large cast iron pump was always an ideal target for older boys' pranks! In winter they mischievously dared unsuspecting younger kids or siblings to lick its shaft, only to laugh when they saw their tongues sticking stubbornly to its surface!) On the west side of the building there were doors which led to two small boys and girls outhouses, later replaced by a cinder block bathroom. Inside were two classrooms, each with large windows facing both east and west, and two cloakrooms for galoshes and "wraps." At the front of each was a blackboard that extended across much of the room. Above it in black and white cardboard cutouts were numbers one through twenty and the letters of the alphabet—printed and in cursive in both lower and upper cases. The schoolrooms were divided by rows, sometimes with more than one grade per row, making it necessary for teachers to include multiple grades of students in their lesson preparations. Wooden desks of varying sizes filled the rooms, at the tops of which were inkwells and grooves for pencils or fountain pens. Each desk had a drawer underneath, big enough for papers and books.

The grades taught by teachers varied. Longtime Brighton elementary school teacher Evelyn Musch, whose husband Jonathan owned a dairy farm on Winans Lake Road, was assigned the upper grades. Bernice Chappel continued to teach at Holden after Dad and Frank Meyer hired her during *the war*; she taught kindergarten through second or third grades.

Eddie began kindergarten at our country school in the fall of 1947. My brother, however, never held the same sentiments about school as I did. He much preferred recess time when he could play robust games outside with his friends Gary Griffin, Reed Spicer or the Morrow brothers, especially in the winter. Every chance they got, they insisted on venturing to the frozen pond nearby. One cold winter day, Ed was actually sent home twice, sopping wet after falling through thin ice on the pond while sliding with Arnold Morrow! Despite the grumbling I heard almost daily from my brother about his new environment, however, I was envious. I sometimes walked with him to school, dreaming of the day I too could have fun playing at recess or learning to write, as he was doing. Never keen on having his little brother tag along—in school or elsewhere—Eddie tolerated me only because of my parents' intervention. One such occasion was his birthday, Jan. 29, when my mother had made her famous million-dollar chocolate fudge for him to share with his schoolmates, a plan to which he steadfastly objected. Undaunted, my mother charged me with the task. As she waited outside, I proudly offered a piece to each student in Mrs. Chappel's room, eventually making my way through the door leading to Mrs. Musch's classes, there to do the same for her third through sixth grade students. Eddie survived the ordeal and even managed to smile when his classmates asked him if they were allowed to have more than one piece!

I looked forward to my first day as a kindergartner, despite the fact that there was still an air of sadness about the house on Rickett Road. Both of my grandmothers' deaths that spring and summer had resulted in a long period of mourning, a vacuum that was difficult to fill. To bring up our spirits, my mother invited Aunt Emma to live with us. Her upbeat and loving presence always made Eddie and me happy! She always produced Hershey or O'Henry candy bars when coming home from the bank as well as new comic books or toys. At night, she was never too tired to play with us, challenging us to games of hide-and-seek or tag in our large living room, sunroom or dining room. She also enjoyed reading stories to us—Bambi over and over—or something from the junior version of the *Jungle Books*. Because of hers and my mother's patience in reading, I was eager to learn more about everything from why ducks like Donald both quacked and talked, where tigers lived and why some people named "Sambo" were not white like me. I was also desperate to make sense of the different sounds of words made up by circular or upright letters found on every page and underneath the pictures I loved.

After the first Monday in September, the day finally arrived for me to attend school for half a day! Mom made me clean up as I usually did on Saturday nights before church and comb my toe-head locks neatly for a change. Then I put on one of the new school outfits she had bought me on a Wednesday afternoon shopping trip to Ann Arbor with Aunt Emma. It was chilly and rainy so our neighbor, Frances Griffin, had agreed to drive Eddie and me to school with her son, Gary, and her niece, my pal Susie Ryan. Outside the main entrance, Mrs. Chappel and Mrs. Musch were greeting new students for the 1949-50 school year and ushering them into their classrooms. Sixth graders Irene Spicer, Gloria Kroczak and a few of their friends remained outside where they were talking about new boys they had crushes on over the summer and dancing to the verses of the latest pop hit, *Do the Hucklebuck*:

A little bit of Twist, a little bit of this,
And if you don't know how to do it, Ask my little sis...
Wiggle like a stick, wobble like a duck,
That's what you do when you do the hucklebuck.

I knew many of the kids at school because they were neighbors— Gary Griffin, Susie Ryan and Ray Maltby, among others. Chester Sak's niece, Sally, who lived on Maltby Road, was in Eddie's class and normally met us on the corner when we walked to school on nice days. Susie Cowie, the daughter of George Fink's tenant farmer, joined us as well and so did Bonnie and Nancy Lou Bennett, who lived just north of us on Rickett. I also got to know Maltby and Lee Road neighborhood kids like Mary Caldwell, Bonnie Raub and Everett and Doris Holcomb. Gary Potter, Glen Price, Bill Spicer and Davina Hughes were a few other new faces that first day of kindergarten who were my classmates through high school.

Mrs. Chappel and Mrs. Musch took turns ringing the bell in front of school at the beginning of the day and after recess and lunch, chatting with each other while monitoring us on the playground. They were never too busy to listen to us if we interrupted their conversation nor see to it that we had the proper coats, snow suits, boots and mittens on when the weather was cold. We brought brown paper bag lunches to school and often exchanged part of our lunch fare with others. I have no idea what goodies Glen Price liked that I brought to school but I will never forget the delicacy he shared with me on several occasions— chocolate and snow ball coconut Hostess cakes and potato chips! Secular and religious holiday times like Halloween, Thanksgiving and Christmas were fun and celebrated without regard to offending anyone. Valentine's Day was made special with sweet treats and an exchange of cards with everyone in class. We looked forward to having cake or cupcakes at the end of the day on students' birthdays and there were egg and candy hunts at Easter time. We were expected to follow a few simple rules, like not being tardy, and rarely do I remember any cases of students acting out in class as they sometimes did at West Elementary School in Brighton a few years later. Mrs. Chappel and Mrs. Musch served as custodians in addition to teaching but were helped by all of their students in keeping the school rooms neat and clean. It was considered an honor to be selected to do routine chores, like wiping or washing the blackboard or making the rounds with a waste paper basket at the end of the day to pick up discarded paper.

It was common practice to ask students to read aloud in Mrs. Chappel's class. I learned to read quickly, volunteering often, and was complemented for it. I loved animals and our reading books had endless stories about Sally and Dick's pets—Spot the dog and Fluffy the cat—as well as their friendly neighbor, Zeke. But while the written word came easily to me, I recognized even at an early age that some students had great difficulties reading about a furry cat and Dick's unruly dog. Mrs. Chappel was an excellent teacher who often devoted extra time to these students. Nonetheless, they often shrank in their seats during the reading period, afraid they would be called upon. Reading well accelerated my ability to write well and excel in a number of other disciplines while my friends who read poorly lagged behind in those same reading-based subjects. Unfortunately, at a time when special programs for challenged students were not readily available, reading poorly was often not properly remediated, as were such things as dyslexia and speech impediments.

Probably my clearest memory at the Holden School in kindergarten and first grades was the final day of school. I liked school, my fellow students and Mrs. Chappel; summer vacation was not necessarily something I looked forward to like so many of my friends. Before leaving class both years, Mrs. Chappel kneeled beside every student in her three grades, handed us our report cards and whispered "You passed!" The news was happily received by all of us, for even at that young age "You failed" were two words we dreaded. I was marked in kindergarten using the standardized "A" through "F" marking system of the Livingston County Rural Schools. The following year the reporting system was the same, but one adopted by the newly formed Brighton Area School System. In kindergarten, the remarks and grading criteria likely were the same nationwide, yet today they seem unusual at best, considering the maturity of a five-year-old. In *Reading*, I "used expression," "was interested" and "read smoothly." *English Expression* found me "trying to speak correctly," "planning what I said," and "listening well to others" while in *Writing* I "used correct position." My *Science* remarks were not quite as positive. In "contributing to the exhibits," I was given a grade of C−! In *Art*, however, I "noticed the beautiful" and in *Music* "expressed rhythm in activity."

At the bottom of my kindergarten report card was a "Certificate of Promotion." "This certifies," it stated, "that *Paul Weber* has completed the work of kindergarten and is recommended for promotion to the 1st grade of the Public Schools of this State" and was signed by Bernice Chappel.

LIVINGSTON COUNTY RURAL SCHOOLS	BRIGHTON AREA SCHOOLS
Primary Report	Brighton, M.
19 *49* 19 *50*	ELEMENTARY REPORT
Paul Weber NAME OF CHILD	*Paul Weber* grade *I*
Holden SCHOOL — *B* GRADE	for the school year 19 *50* - 19 *51*
2 DISTRICT *Green Oak* TOWNSHIP	*Bernice Chappel* Teacher
Bernice Chappel TEACHER	Kindly accept this report as a personal message to you relative to the standing of your child in school. We especially urge the importance of regular attendance. A day missed now and then seems harmless to the casual observer; but to the teacher who is working with children every day, the harm is quite noticeable. We shall thoroughly appreciate any assistance you can give and trust you may find opportunity to visit the school frequently. Let us work together for the good of your child and the school.
GLADYS McCALLUM SUPERINTENDENT OF SCHOOLS	Superintendent of Schools.

In the late 1940s there were heated arguments throughout the Brighton area about a trend that was sweeping the nation—school consolidation. Small country schools were said to be ineffective and lacking the resources that town or city schools offered. There were pro and con editorials in both the *Brighton Argus* and *Livingston County Press* (the latter always called by my father, an ardent Republican, the

"Republican Press"), some even proposing compromises to keep certain township schools like Holden open as agricultural-vocational schools. With two boys in primary school, my parents favored consolidation. Convincing others who had no school-age children and were opposed to the inevitable higher taxes, though, was not easy.

By 1950 the arguments in favor had won out. At the end of the 1950-51 school year the new Brighton Area School district closed historic old

The Holden School, 1950.

country schools like Holden, Bethel, Lyons, Hollister and Ratz and opened up a new K-6 elementary school on the northwest side of town just off Seventh and State Streets. High weeds such as burdock and thistles soon surfaced at the corner of U.S. 23 and Maltby, choking out the hollyhocks, forsythias, irises and lilacs that Mrs. D. G. Van Amburg and Mrs. Joseph Holden had so lovingly cultivated on a small plot of land in section 5 of Green Oak since the end of the nineteenth

century. Like an old schoolmarm forced to retire due to advanced age, the quaint school where I began my education was locked for good and shuttered, never to open its doors again.

On summer Sunday afternoon rides with my parents following church and dinner, I had seen the sprawling, three-wing mid-century modern building rise that was to be my new school. It was as different as night and day from the two-room schoolhouse on Maltby Road where I had spent two formative years of my education. I was as apprehensive as a six-year old could be about going to town to a school that seemed enormous! But my parents, ever positive, helped me accept the transition in my life whenever I brought the subject up. "Your dad and I both went to school in town," was their standard way of convincing me that I would like the school they now referred to as "elementary."

"And don't forget that Mrs. Chappel will *still* be your teacher!"

The first memory I have of West Elementary School in town was the long school day! My friend Larry Herbst's father, Don, was charged with driving one of the first school buses in Brighton, the now old-fashioned red, white and blue no-frills student mover that sometimes spent more time broken down than on the road. His route was a long one, taking one hour or longer to complete. At the end of the day, with a full load of noisy and often misbehaving students, Mr. Herbst drove us resolutely up Third Street then south out Brighton Lake and Hamburg Roads. We crossed the Huron River Bridge at Campbell Town, eventually reaching the westernmost point on the route, Parishfield, an Episcopalian center run by my friend, Susan Ayres's, father. The circuitous route then took us east across rutty township roads, crossing Rickett and U.S. 23, finally turning north where my neighborhood friends and I were the last to leave the bus. Like U.S. Postal Service workers, Larry's dad and his fellow drivers stayed true to the motto "neither snow nor rain nor heat nor gloom of night stays these couriers from the swift completion of their appointed rounds."

Bernice Chappel was a welcome sight in my second grade classroom at West Elementary School. She stood in front of a sea of new faces—students who ten years later were to graduate with me— classmates like Larry Herbst, Randy Marx, Nancy Newman, Nancy Elliott, Suzanne Wahl, Carol Carney, Carol Hall, Keith Robertson, and Carol Ann Davis. They had come from country schools but also from schools held in one of three locations in town—the Federated Church on Grand River, St. George Lutheran and the town's oldest primary school, the Rickett School. But many of my Holden pals—Glen Price, Mary Caldwell, Davina Hughes, Bonnie Raub and Bill Spicer—were also in the brand new room, filled to capacity with 35 students. I think it was actually Bill who the first week of class broke out laughing when I boldly raised my hand to answer our teacher's question about what rhymes with the word "it," "sit," and "mitt." "TEAT," I answered enthusiastically, asserting my expertise in the vocabulary of a farmer's son. Mrs. Chappel, who was herself raised on a farm in Fowlerville, corrected me in her classical, erudite way, writing how *that* word was spelled on the chalkboard and calmly going on to the next part of our spelling lesson!

Rickett School *Federated Church*
(Brighton Homecoming-from the Pages of Time, Brighton Fire Dept., 1961)

St. George Lutheran Church

With television programming in its infancy and the use of audio-visual equipment very limited, primary school teachers had to be particularly good at both story-telling and story reading. That was indeed one of Bernice Chappel's strong suits. She read stories to us after recess and lunch that engendered a life-long love of reading in us. She also allowed us to select books to take home from her own sizable classroom library to broaden our horizons. That year I went from reading and loving *Bambi* and classic Disney children's stories to having the same passion for *Paddle to the Sea*, Holling C. Holling's novel for children, and a geography book with lives and illustrations of children around the world. I envisioned myself as the Native American boy in Canada hewing a canoe out of wood with a paddler aboard, placing it on the icy slopes near Lake Nipigon in Ontario and waiting for the melting snow to take it to the Great Lakes and big waters of the Atlantic. I joined Eskimo children Netsuk and Klaya in the frigid Arctic and the nomadic wanderers of the Kirghize Steppes of Kazakhstan in their exciting daily lives. A widely read children's book about a day in the life of a carefree grasshopper—*Happy Hopper and His Friends*—written and illustrated by Mrs. Chappel and her colleague, Doris Smith—is a testimony to their commitment to making the written word come to life for children, as it indeed did for me that year.

Time outside of class during the school day was probably the hardest for me to deal with. I often stared through the wide bank of windows on the north side of my room at the large playground area wondering who I would be playing with that day. There were, after all, close to three hundred students at West Elementary, far more than the fifty at Holden School. Eddie, of course, would be of no help since younger brothers are always in the way on playgrounds. But I soon fit in there as well as in the classroom. It was easy to get the traditional games of tag, pom-pom-pull away and "Mother, May I?" going or simply daydream or wander around from one end of the playground to the other with a new friend.

Next hardest was the stern face that always seemed to be looking over all of us. Carl Lindbom was new to Brighton that year and determined to do his best job as principal, a new position in school for most of us. And that he did, staying at the school for the rest of his career, even having the school named after him. Mr. Lindbom delegated the responsibility of monitoring the playground and bringing classes to the lunchroom to teachers but the school cafeteria was his domain. There he acted as a drill sergeant, not allowing any kind of misbehavior lest students be called out and sent to his office! Tables were strictly monitored, a lesson I learned the first week in my new surroundings since I had begun eating cooked meals rather than bringing a brown paper bag lunch to school. When I balked at eating everything on my tray that first week—including a generous helping of stewed tomatoes, which to me were worse than liver and onions— Mr. Lindbom was not pleased. He showed no favoritism. "Eat all your lunch, son," he said to me, "or you will *not* be excused to go to the playground."

When we passed Mr. Lindbom's office in the middle wing of school going to lunch or to recess, we dreaded doing something wrong and being called into that office. Spanking was a routine form of punishment in that era and we took to heart what we had heard— it was the punishment town school principals used for obstreperous students. My friend Karen Kirchbaum later told about being mortified when she was sent to the principal's office by a teacher, note in hand, until she learned that it was only a request for a jar of paste! More often than not, however, Mr. Lindbom chose to have a serious "face to face" conversation with a student who had misbehaved.

One day soon after school started two town ruffians, the McDewey brothers, decided to chase me across the expansive school playground. At West Elementary, I learned quickly that having older, not-so-nice kids, pick on you only to have kinder, older kids come to your defense was a common occurrence and part of life at recess time. But that day the "nicer older kids" were nowhere to be seen. I eluded the two miscreants chasing me for a long time because having Eddie chase me after a fight had made me fleet of foot if nothing else. When the two bully brothers eventually caught up with me and knocked me down, there were no kinder older kids to come to my rescue. Luckily this raucous event did not go unnoticed. By the time they pounced

Second Grade, West Elementary

on my back, two teacher monitors had noticed and the rowdies were marched off to the principal's office! There was a serious "face to face" conversation with Mr. Lindbom for them *that* day!

One of my new friends at West also had an altercation that year but for a completely different reason. Suzanne Campbell was the only Afro-American in our school. The Brighton Gardens resident had always liked her country school—Bethel School in Brighton Township—had done well, was close to her many friends and never experienced any of the racism she faced that day shortly after the new school year started. Nick Strait, a town boy with an attitude, blocked her at the entrance to class and taunted her in front of a group of other students just before the first day in Mrs. Smith's second grade began. "Don't want any n*****s at this school!" he shouted.

Suzanne was quick to react, hitting him and throwing him to the ground. In a fury she pinned him in a neck hold, much like the one both boys and girls used at Bethel School, but in mischievous, playful skirmishes during recess. "Don't you ever call me that name again!" she managed to spit out in tears as their teacher and Principal Lindbom arrived to break up the fight. By then Susan Ayres and a few of Suzanne's other friends had arrived to support her and watched in disbelief as Mr. Lindbom grabbed the antagonists by the collar and marched them to the dreaded office. In less than an hour, the parents of both of Mr. Lindbom's new "problem kids" were in his office to discuss what had happened.

Suzanne's mother protested. Her daughter had never heard the "n" word nor had she ever been in a fight. Defending herself from prejudicial behavior and language—not the last time in her Brighton school career as it turned out—was to be expected, not condemned.

At the end of the year Mr. Lindbom consulted with Eleanor Hornung and her third grade teacher colleague about who would be Suzanne's teacher the next year. "Which of you would like to teach the *negro* girl?" he asked.

———————

Elsa Martin Stegenga was the daughter of Adolph Martin, a German immigrant and the last remaining blacksmith in Brighton. Married to General Motors Proving Grounds photographer Dan Stegenga, she had been in the school system since the 1930s. Elsa was a gifted teacher with a bubbly personality who often cheered students up with sing-alongs during recess at West Elementary on rainy days. Loved by all of her students for her innovative "hands-on" creative art projects and excellent teaching techniques, the town blacksmith's daughter would likely have been a recipient of a teacher of the year award, had it existed in the early 1950s. Not a single student who thrived in Elsa Stegenga's class—friends and classmates of mine like Ed Case, Suzanne Campbell Conerway, Karen Herbst Stapleton, Joann Ludtke Maier, Hugh Munce, Karen Kirchbaum Geffert and Susan Ayress Weyburn—fail to laud this remarkable Brighton educator and musician. And numerous students of hers credit her amazing skills with their decision to become educators. To this day they remain puzzled why her brilliant career was never fully recognized by the citizens and school board members of the Brighton school system.

Mrs Stegenga was also Brighton High School's first band director. In her own words, one day early in 1934 Guy Pitkin, chairperson of the Brighton School Board, summoned the energetic first year elementary school teacher into his office and asked her if she might do him a favor. Despite all the community bands Brighton had supported enthusiastically since the turn of the century, there was no high school band. Pitkin inquired if Elsa, with her musical talent and recognition in the community, might be interested in starting one. That suggestion was all the third grade teacher needed to immediately organize what became B.H.S.'s first band. "The little band flourished," she later wrote. "By 1937 we were giving a concert a month for which we charged a dollar...The band kept growing and when I left in 1938 it was a nice little organization." *

Mrs. Stegenga responded without hesitation and as enthusiastically to Carl Lindbom's request at articulation time that day in 1952 as she had to Guy Pitkin's plea to begin a band in 1934. "I will take the *child*...

and gladly! Suzanne Campbell will be in *my* third grade classroom in September."

Despite falling ill twice in mid-winter with virtually every childhood sickness that existed and missing more than three weeks of school in second grade, my grades were good to very good—in social development, arithmetic, art, language, reading, spelling, music, science, and handwriting. I grew an inch that year, gained eight pounds and in June Mrs. Chappel again whispered "You passed!" in my ear.

The next year I had obviously become more accustomed to the students at my new school, for I received my first mark below a "B"— a "C " for social development and citizenship! I doubt that Bill Spicer, Larry Herbst or Randy Marx were responsible for the nose dive in my grades; I had just become a typical primary school kid who liked to talk. But even though I was apparently the class chatterbox, I did not fare poorly in third grade. Language, reading and spelling again were my best subjects and Miss Horning, a talented, veteran teacher, wrote "It has been a pleasure having Paul in my room, he has done excellent work," on my report card. And in June on the last day of class Eleanor Hornung, who 40 years later was to have a school named after her, leaned over me and whispered the same words I had by then heard for three successive years, "You passed!"

My fourth grade year was a busy one outside of the classroom at West Elementary. I was allowed to walk to St. George Church on Mondays for piano lessons in its multi-purpose basement with Mrs. Alice Essic, whom I had had as a teacher at home since second grade. After my lesson I was allowed to go to my Uncle Carl and Aunt Anna Westin's, whose house was practically in the back yard of the church at Madison and Fourth Streets, to be spoiled with a piece of Aunt Anna's freshly made cake and a glass of Vernor's ginger ale. Music remained a life-long interest of mine and in addition to going to St. George Church on Mondays after school, I followed the same routine on Wednesdays. That day of the week was set aside for Junior Choir practice for the following Sunday's service. We were directed by Rev. Paul Geiger and later by my cousin, Charles Westin. I was joined by several fourth grade classmates at West—all girls—including Joann Ludtke, Karen Herbst, Karen Kirchbaum and Vickie Benear.

The St. George Lutheran Church Junior Choir, c. 1957
Director Rev. Paul Geiger, top left

I also became a cub scout in fourth grade. Many of the scout gatherings were held at West Elementary but the weekly den meeting was at Silver Lake at my classmate Marwell Smith's home. For those meetings I rode home with Marwell on the school bus and enjoyed the weekly routine of doing crafts, learning scout rules and procedures and being treated to a snack by our den mother, Mrs. Maxwell Smith, Marwell's mother. Probably the highlight of that year—in what was to be a very short stint in scouting—was marching in the Memorial Day parade on Main Street, Mrs. Smith joining us to make sure that our ranks were neat, our marching disciplined.

Mrs. Maxwell Smith's Cub Scout den marching down Main
past the Baetcke Law Office, 1954

A lasting memory, and one for which I have always been grateful, is the *Little House* book series by Laura Ingalls Wilder that my fourth grade teacher at West introduced me to. Every day after lunch we settled down quickly and with great anticipation so our teacher, Mrs. Norma Stonex, could read a new chapter about Wilder's early life, from the woods of Wisconsin to the expansive prairies of South Dakota. Would Pa return safely to the cabin in Indian Territory while Ma protected her girls from the crises arising from their unfortunate move to the wrong territory? Would the family survive the endless Dakota winter threatening the family with starvation as they twisted hay for fuel to stoke their cook stove?

Our art and music teacher that last year at West Elementary was Wilhemina Swarthout, a floating faculty member who was also an instructor at Brighton High School. She was an enthusiastic teacher who taught us a wide range of songs, from American classics and pop tunes to the fun campfire/spinning song, *Sarasponda, Sarasponda, Sarasponda Ret Set Set* and Mel Brooks's popular rendition of the *Looney Tunes* hit *I Taut I Taw a Puddy-Tat*. An ambitious teacher, who had an engaging way with kids eager to get a break from their routine schedule of lessons, Mrs. Swarthout was by far one of the best teachers in the Brighton school system in my student career.

Mrs. Swarthout and Mrs. Essic, both Pinckney residents, put their heads together to involve me in the annual all-school Christmas program in December of that year. I was not enthusiastic about playing in front of my peers but there was little I could do to dissuade Mrs. Stonex, Mrs. Essic, Mrs Swarthout and my parents from making me a student accompanist. Though in retrospect I have always been grateful for the music fundamentals Mrs. Essic taught me, as a fourth grader I was far from what one would call "accomplished." But alas! There was no way to bail out. At the appointed time, I played a very simple arrangement of *It Came Upon the Midnight Clear* as my fellow students sang and marched to the stage where they were to perform. Despite practicing that carol with Mrs. Essic, Mrs. Swarthout and my mother, my rendition of that beloved New England Christmas carol became one of the earliest misadventures of my life. I nervously thumped out the melody, inventing accidentals the composer, Edmund Sears, never could have dreamed of, creating dissonant chords the likes of which have never been heard again in Brighton schools! When the evening was over, I sulked, even as I was consoled and told how well I had done by Mom, Dad and my teachers. A "maturing" experience some would say, but not one for which I was prepared.

In Feb 1949, the *Livingston County Press* noted in a Brighton events article that the student council of Brighton High School was planning a minstrel show at Sloan Memorial Field involving students in multiple classes, fourth grade and above. It was an event to help fund student programs that became somewhat of an annual tradition, for which Mrs. Swarthout drafted her upper elementary students. At West Elementary, she prepared ours and Mrs. Musch's fourth grade classes by teaching us some of Stephen Foster's classic antebellum songs, like *Old Black Joe* and other popular and ragtime hits. *The Dark Town Strutters' Ball*, popularized in the early 50s by Dean Martin was another:

> "*I'll be down to get you in a taxi honey, You'd better be ready bout half past eight,*
> *Ah baby don't be late, I want to be there when the band starts playing…*" (Jack Brooks)

The songs we sang at Sloan Memorial Field remain as fresh in my memory as if I had learned them only yesterday. Other than my mother blacking my face with burnt cork just before the show, however, the event itself (unlike my piano performance the preceding December!) remains very sketchy. For that I am grateful. Even as that same year in *Brown vs the Board of Education* the United States Supreme Court rejected the legal segregation of American public schools, our school had participated in yet another racist manifestation of American culture nearly a century after the Civil War and abolition of slavery.

———————

Just as the Ingalls Family survived *The Long Winter*, so too had I survived five years with many new faces and experiences at a Green Oak country school and new school in town. My life was touched by good friends, the dedication of three talented classroom teachers, an art and music teacher whose patience was monumental and a principal who realized the importance of a stable school environment. Chapter one in my educational career had drawn to a close, even as the second chapter atop a hill on Main Street in Brighton was about to begun.

———————

*Trail Tales, the Brighton Area Historical Society, July 2021

*Classmates, 1953 -55. Top: Joann Ludtke, Susan Ayres,
Suzanne Campbell; Middle: Paul Weber, Jim Davis, Karen Herbst;
Bottom: Deanna Dixon, Karen Kirchbaum*

Pres. Harry S. Truman,
1945 - 53

Pres. Dwight D. Eisenhower,
1953 - 61

CHAPTER FOURTEEN

Hope 1953

"The buck stops here." (Harry S. Truman)

*"If a political party does not have its foundation in
the determination to advance a cause that is right
and that is moral, then it is not a political
party; it is merely a conspiracy to seize
power."* (Dwight D. Eisenhower)

IN THE SUMMER OF 1950, my parents and I took a long planned trip
with Aunt Emma to Washington D.C. That trip was the first of many
that were to follow and was the beginning of my deep love of traveling
and politics. It also acquainted me with a new world very different
from Main Street or Maltby and Rickett. The geography and culture of
places outside of the Midwest were intriguing; the sights and sounds—
even the people—of cities such as Philadelphia and Washington
captivated me even as a five-year-old. I sat in the back of our green
Chevrolet entertaining Aunt Emma and vice versa while Mom, in
front, saw to it that Dad followed the right route. True to character,
Eddie chose to stay at home with Uncle Louie and Aunt Ruth and be
spoiled riding horses with Bobby Richmond and his town friends.

We stayed in a centrally located "tourist home" in Washington,
a two story brick attached house. There our car remained, as Dad
acceded to Mom's and Aunt Emma's request that we see the city and

outlying attractions by bus, on foot or with the assistance of a paid guide. After our first round of sightseeing, it became apparent that my parents had a new concern as we toured the city—a son who never stopped chattering! I was allowed—or relegated—to sit in front of the large tourist taxi beside the very knowledgeable driver and talked non-stop for those four hot Washington days! I interrupted him in the middle of sentences, parroted what he said and asked him questions before he had time to come up for air! For four long days my family and two members of our group who had booked an educational tour of the Capitol building, Arlington Cemetery and Mt. Vernon with only *one* tour guide found themselves in the company of a real life *Dennis the Menace!*

Mount Vernon, Washington D.C. Trip, 1950

Fortunately, our tour group was spared from hearing my commentary at Washington's number one tourist attraction, the White House. President Harry S. Truman was living at nearby Blair House during a long overdue renovation/rebuild of the Chief Executive's residence and there he stayed until the spring of 1952. At such a young age, I was not yet aware of the very deep division in politics centering on the President that was unfolding as we toured our nation's capital that summer. Nor did I understand the scope of the international crisis rocking the country. Truman, in his second term as President after proving all the pundits wrong in the 1948 presidential election, dealt daily with negative political criticism—some well taken, some completely unjustified. On the domestic front, measures Truman instituted in civil rights threatened to divide the Democratic Party. Internationally, the Soviet Union's ever-widening sphere of influence after World War II was testing the resolve of Western democracies to the limit, forcing the President to be defensive and firm. An *Iron Curtain* divided communist and non-communist nations of Europe and tensions in Asia were so high that a Chinese and Russian supported invasion of South Korea by the north appeared to be imminent.

Just after our D.C. visit that happened. Only five years after World War II ended, President Truman was forced to make the difficult decision to commit American troops to a U.N. police action to stop communist aggression on the Korean peninsula. The Korean War, officially called a *conflict*, raged on for three long, indecisive years, taking nearly 40,000 U.S. soldiers' lives. With no apparent end of the fighting in sight, President Truman's popularity, already waning in opinion polls for being "soft" on communism, was plummeting. In 1951, stoked by criticism for relieving W.W. II hero General Douglas MacArthur of his duties as Supreme Commander of the U.S. Forces in Korea, the President's approval rating sank to an all-time low. The stage had been set for the nation's five star general and hero of World War II, Dwight D. Eisenhower, to enter the political arena.

Soon after our Saturday evening trip to town when we viewed television for the first time, Mom gave in to Dad's wish to purchase a television. We had been filled with wonder at the exciting new medium taking the nation by storm in front of our very eyes in Wendell Squire's showroom and in Chug Smith's living room. Somehow, though, I feel that spending $299.99—a substantial amount of money in the late 1940s—was as much Mom's call as anyone's. She was always eager to experience more of the world around her and a television in our sunroom seemed to be the perfect way to do it. It could only add to the pleasure she got from reading the latest *Book of the Month Club* selection or listening to Edward R. Murrow's or Lowell Thomas's news programs and commentaries on the radio.

The Motorola television Dad purchased from Squire's had only a 14-inch screen and the reception was by no means the best. The rooftop aerial had to be re-positioned several times to tweak the signal and every few months it seemed necessary to replace a tube that had died in the middle of an exciting new episode of *Hopalong Cassidy* or Dave Garroway's dry humor on the *Today Show*. But the black and white television was our newest household "gadget" and we soon became accustomed to daily program lineups and shows we just could not go another week without watching! Mom or Dad frequently ended up refereeing when disagreements arose between Eddie and me over what programs to watch. *Howdie Doody* was my favorite afternoon program. I felt I actually was on the set with Buffalo Bob

Smith sitting in the "Peanut Gallery" watching the antics of the ever-silent Clarabelle the Clown, Phineas T. Bluster—Howdy's tight-wad nemesis—or Thunderthud, the Native American chief. Eddie usually opted for the scary adventures of *Captain Video and His Video Rangers* or *Tom Corbett's Space Cadets*. Mom and Dad arrived at a compromise on Saturday evening programming when two favorites were on at the same time. Dad was allowed to watch a boxing match and smoke his R. G. Dunn cigar one Saturday while the following week Mom viewed the television adaptation of the radio soap opera, *One Man's Family*.

Newscasts or news commentaries were boring to Eddie and me but I at least was patient enough to watch two special events in the early fifties that pre-empted regular programming. Broadcast journalism by then had rapidly advanced and through the new medium Princess Elizabeth's succession as Queen of the United Kingdom was widely covered by the BBC and major American networks. Despite the time difference, we were spellbound in 1953 watching Elizabeth II's spectacular coronation at Westminster Abbey! Dad was not particularly a fan of "things British" but even he seemed to be awed by it all. He watched every moment enthusiastically, captivated just as he was the summer before when everyone in the nation tuned in to the Democratic and Republican national conventions.

Both national parties' nominating conventions in the summer of 1952 were widely covered and among the first to be televised. As the war in Korea dragged on, General Eisenhower had at last been persuaded to enter the political arena, running for president with anti-communist crusader Sen. Richard Nixon on the Republican ticket. Unlike the other contender for the nomination—Sen. Robert Taft of Ohio—who favored a more aggressive policy against Communist China and its support of the North Koreans, Eisenhower did not favor widening the war. He also refused to put the world at risk of an atomic war by using nuclear weapons, as some hawkish critics in both parties had suggested. Yet he was a vocal critic of President Truman's wartime policy and argued that the stalemate in the fighting in Korea could not go on indefinitely. If elected, Gen. Eisenhower would journey to Korea to seek a truce in the fighting. This pledge, along with his immense personal popularity, at last secured his nomination at the party's July convention in Chicago.

Dad and Mom, though very moderate in their politics, were lifelong Republicans and hopeful that the Democrats' hold on the presidency since 1933 would at last be broken. Would the divisions in the Democratic Party and lack of political clout of its nominee,

Gov. Adlai Stevenson, seal the deal ensuring a Republican victory in November? The summer of convention watching was an exciting one and continued to kindle my interest in politics. I was intrigued by my parents' passion for their party and even followed through on their suggestion that I write a letter to a particularly ardent supporter of President Truman and Gov. Stevenson who spoke on the convention floor denouncing "our" Republican Party. I even used a word I later found useful in discussions with friends when I had become an independent in politics: *"Demagoguery,"* Mom had suggested, might be an appropriate word to use in my letter, though it was certainly not in my every day vocabulary.

Politics continued to monopolize the airwaves throughout the fall. We were drawn to television news like a magnet and every night watched the results of the latest polls. Enthusiastic crowds, tired of two wars in one decade, chanted "We like Ike!" as the nation's most honored soldier, Dwight Eisenhower, waged an active campaign in the waning months of 1952 from big cities in Delaware and California to small hamlets in Ohio and Oregon. At the same time, Gov. Adlai Stevenson, one of the most articulate and intelligent nominees for president in our nation's history, defended his party's record and eloquently solicited votes affirming the Democratic Party's platform. In the end, despite the harsh rhetoric (with not a little demagoguery!) and hard fought political battles, most of my town and family were delighted at the outcome of the election. Dwight David Eisenhower was elected President of the United States Nov. 4 in a landslide, carrying fifty-five percent of the popular vote. The future of the New Deal and other Roosevelt and Truman-era policies was questionable as Ike and Mamie Eisenhower moved into a newly renovated White House Jan 20, 1953. One thing, however, was certain. The nation's thirty-fourth President was serious about ending the needless loss of lives in Korea. And no amount of pressure or political posturing from Democrats or Republicans would deter him from this mission nor his objective of unifying the nation.

Following the outbreak of hostilities in Korea in 1950, the *Detroit Free Press* published daily lists of casualties, lists which grew longer with every passing day. By the late fall of 1950, following China's invasion of Korea, the numbers had become staggering. Like other small towns across the nation, Brighton was not exempt from telegrams sent by the adjutant general, telegrams tragically similar to the ones Mary

Margaret Carmack, the Fred Richmond's, the Thomas Family and Eric and Elva Singer received in another war only a few years before:

"...regret to inform you of your son's (husband's) death..."

One such telegram reached Esther and Clarence Seeling, who lived on E. Grand River at Hope Street, early in November. Esther's second son, Victor Atwell, a marine with the First Marine Division, was killed in action Oct. 27. Words can never express a mother's shock and anguish hearing such news nor does the hurt ever diminish. Rev. Paul Geiger of St. George tried his hardest to console his congregant. So did neighbors and the women of St. George's Women's Missionary Society. Her Victor was gone, killed defending some frozen, desolate hill in Korea, and nothing could change that. She could not even receive hugs or consolation from Danny, her youngest son. Danny, who had enlisted in the army just a year earlier, was thousands of miles away serving with the Second Division of the Eighth Army, defending yet another God-forsaken hill. But there was a *third* son. At least she could speak long distance on the telephone with Leroy. He had served in W.W. II and already done his service to the country. But would that make a difference in these perilous times? Recently that son too had been recalled to service. Now at Camp LeJeune in North Carolina, the probability that he could be deployed to that far-off Asian peninsula fought over by two world super powers served as no consolation to a grieving mother.

Cpl. Danny Atwell

Time, some well-wishers told a mother in mourning, would be the great healer. But that adage rarely is true in war time and it was by no means true for a mother who feared hearing more bad news, receiving another crushing blow. As the situation in Korea continued to deteriorate the following year, as the war of attrition dragged on, she knew that neither Danny's nor Leroy's lot could be improving.

No news coming out of Korea was promising. In fact, it was just the opposite. With General MacArthur's military leadership called into question by President Truman and his eventual firing as supreme commander, nothing was helping her sons' prospects. That spring a mother's intuition proved to be right: Corporal Danny Atwell was reported missing in action May 18. On July 21, Esther received a letter from the personnel officer of the 38th Infantry in Korea, Capt. Thomas O'Brien:

> *"Reference is made to your letter 19 June in which you request information on the status of your son, Corporal Daniel Frederick Atwell, RA 16296146, Company "B." Daniel was reported missing in action on 18 May 1951. On that date his unit was forced to withdraw from its position in the vicinity of Mug-gol, by an enemy attack. When the unit reassembled Daniel was not present."*

Time may not heal all the sadness life brings our way but it sometimes has a way of making it more *bearable*. Esther heard nothing as fighting continued fiercely in Korea throughout the summer and fall of 1951, but for Christmas she received a gift she thought was the best one she had ever gotten. Yet another dreaded telegram arrived that December and her heart sank. But this one was different—her Danny was alive! Behind enemy lines, to be sure, but Danny was alive. At last, there was hope! And the New Year brought hope, too. The President-elect traveled to Korea one month after his victory in November, fulfilling his campaign pledge to search for the best, the most practical way of achieving an end to hostilities. The stage had been set for a true peace offensive.

The President's victory and his trip to Korea were the source of lively discussions throughout the nation, none more than at the Westin Swedish Christmas Eve dinner in 1952. The venue by then had changed from Second Street—*Up Home*—to the brick house at the top of the hill on East Grand River, the home my Grandfather Weber built in 1926. Uncle Joe Westin had bought the house from my dad the year my grandmothers died and within a year it was to become home to three of my aunts and uncles. Christmases were now spent at a different place but the menu, warmth and liveliness of our family get-togethers were no different.

As the after dinner news conversation became more political and speculative than fact-based, Mom offered her opinions. Her views, as always, were based on the latest news columns she had read in the *Free Press*, radio commentaries and opinions aired on *Meet the Press*, a Sunday television news analysis program hosted by the renowned publisher and journalist Lawrence Spivak. With the election over and both North and South Korea desperately searching for a peace that had taken more than three million civilian and soldiers' lives, Eisenhower, she thought, could only have a captive audience on both sides of the 38th parallel, the line dividing the two Koreas. Echoing his words, she said

"...Small attacks on small hills would not end this war..."

As more and more Swedish *glög* was consumed, the discussions became more heated. My godparents' sons, though Democrats like their parents, were W.W. II veterans who had seen enough fighting to hope that a President they had not voted for could achieve something eluding President Truman far too long. Uncle Carl Westin, a staunch Republican and never shy about expressing his opinion, lauded Eisenhower for his action as a soon-to-be civilian leader. He and Aunt Anna Westin had spent more hours than they cared to remember worrying about their son Charles's future in time of war just after graduating from college, getting married and joining the army. They shared a degree of relief in the summer hearing he was to be stationed at an Arctic base in Thule, Greenland, instead of Korea, where most of the recruits at his basic training camp were sent. "Ike will get the job done right again," my uncle said, praising the President-elect for his bold action.

My mother, cousins and uncle were *not* disappointed in Dwight Eisenhower's skills as a general-turned-statesman, his "bold action."

The Brick House, 407 E. Grand River

Nor was Esther Seeling! Between the President-elect's December mission to Korea and his succeeding months as President he managed to break through the entangled network of political systems and national rivalries that alone could bring peace, working tirelessly with Congress, the United Nations and all parties involved in the conflict to achieve a truce, if through limited goals. An armistice was signed July 27 between North and South Korea. Lt. General Wm. Harrison Jr., speaking for the United Nations Command, announced the truce would

> *"...ensure complete cessation of hostilities and officially end all acts of armed force in Korea until a final peaceful settlement is reached."*

Shortly afterward, Esther learned that an expedited exchange of prisoners of war was announced and on August 21 received the amazing news that her son had been released! Headlining page one of the *Livingston County Press* five days later were these words:

Second P-W from County Released
Cpl. Daniel F. Atwell, Once Thought Dead, Expected Home Soon

Corporal Danny Atwell, wounded by shrapnel during an American retreat in the eleventh month of war, boarded the *Gen. John Hope* bound for San Francisco the second week of September, 1953. He had spent twenty-eight months of his young life in a North Korean prisoner of war camp. The household at Hope St. and Grand River that had for so long experienced the darkest days of America's second war within ten years could once again breathe a sigh of relief. And the jubilance and optimism of a mid-twentieth century "era of good feelings" was about to begin. * **

For a few years, at least, no mothers like Esther Seeling of Hope Street in Brighton would receive a devastating telegram that their son or daughter was killed or missing in action in some distant land fighting a super-power's war.

> *"We lay down our arms so we can reach out our arms to one another."*
> —Amanda Gorman, 2021

---

*Korean Conflict information from Wikipedia
**Articles about the Atwell Family are from Livingston County Press editions Nov 14, 1950; Aug 1, 1951; Dec 19, 1951; Sept 17 and 24, 1952 and Dec 10, 1953.

Paul and Virginia DeLuca behind their soda fountain, late 1940s
(Courtesy DelVero-DeLuca Families)

CHAPTER FIFTEEN

The Back Porch 1952

*"If you make listening and observation
your occupation, you will gain much
more than you can by talk."*
—Robert Baden-Powell

NOT LONG AFTER MY PARENTS BOUGHT MY FIRST BICYCLE for
me at Gambles when I was seven, they allowed me to ride it to town. I
plowed through the loose gravel on Rickett Road, rounded the uphill
curve just south of Uncle Louie's, crossed the railroad track not far
away and finally reached the paved streets of town. I crossed Grand
River carefully at the brick house where my godparents lived (usually
finding them relaxing on the glider of their screened-in back porch)
and headed down Piety Hill to Main Street, there to make my first
stop. At his Sweet Shop just a short distance to the west, Paul DeLuca
hand-dipped a six cent ice cream cone for me. That *Americana* image
could easily have been another Norman Rockwell subject that summer.

Surely, those kinds of scenes that are part of my tapestry of
memories are still part of life in Brighton these days. The screened-in
porch where people spent much of their leisure time in summer is one
of the easiest settings for me to recall about my town. Acquaintances
were made there, business sometimes conducted, important life-
changing decisions made and yes!—guys often got romantic with

their girlfriends there. Mothers scolded their children several times a day for slamming the screen door or leaving it open long enough for flies or mosquitoes to swarm in. Wooden tables formerly belonging to parents, grandparents or neighbors, now plastered with multiple coats of enamel paint, occupied a central place. They were positioned close enough to the kitchen to serve summer feasts of fresh sweet corn smothered with butter or strawberry short cake with mounds of ice cream on top. Easy chairs, lawn chairs and antique chairs occupying every square inch of that center of family life made getting from one end to the other difficult sometimes. But it mattered little. Anyone who dropped in would find some place to sit, even if it meant spending an evening stretching out on the floor with one of a dozen old pillows stacked in a corner for occasions like those.

Biker Paul and his Hiawatha Bicycle, 1952

Our farmhouse on Rickett Road also had a cool, breezy porch. It was on the west side of the house facing our back lawn and the hill leading to our barns. In winter, its screens and a wooden deck floor were more often than not covered by snow; in the summer dust blowing from Rickett and Maltby was deposited on them—so much so that Mom sometimes was forced to sweep and dust or wash every surface twice per day. There were no fewer than five easy chairs, a rocking chair and an antique wooden table to keep clean as well. We ate both supper and dinner on that drop leaf cherry table, conveniently located on the wall closest to the dining room door and very accessible to the kitchen.

My dad and grandfather must have been thinking about the future when they remodeled our house in the mid-1920s. The farmhouse just within the city limits on East Grand River where Con and Gustie Weber raised their sons had two spacious porches and in the summer both were transformed into the family's main living area. Rickett and Maltby would be no different. After a hot summer day working in the fields, the porch provided a refuge for Dad, his farm help or Eddie and me as we grew older. As soon as we cleaned up in the evening in the adjacent washroom or bathroom, we stretched out on an old recliner to rest before sitting down for supper. Afterward there was company to look forward to or a Detroit Tigers baseball game on WJR to listen to.

The back porch was the main entry to our house as well. In the winter it was the classic "lean-to/mudroom" where people immediately felt warmer ducking out of blowing snow or wind that made its way past the tall pine wind-break bordering our back lawn. It was a convenient place to stomp your feet on a mat before entering Mom's neat dining room and to deposit wet galoshes, skates, sleds or umbrellas. In summer, the porch was not only a place to relax and visit; it was also the best observation point for the farm buildings and fields. Any livestock that had managed to break out of fenced-in fields or the barnyard could easily be spotted there. And what better vantage point for seeing Rickett or Maltby Road neighbors racing south from town? George Fink, the "gentleman farmer" on Maltby Lake to our south, passed by often in a limousine driven by his chauffeur. Uncle Carlos Weber was easy to recognize from the porch as well, creating large dust clouds driving his Oldsmobile Custom Cruiser station wagon at a fast clip down the road. Dad's older brother often stopped for a brief visit and cup of coffee on business trips between Detroit and his office at the Highway Department in Lansing, where he was an assistant commissioner. He was always welcome to reminisce about boyhood days, catch up on family affairs or captivate us with progress on the ambitious engineering job he was engaged in, building a suspension bridge connecting the Upper and Lower Peninsulas. More than likely my uncle, an ardent Republican, would also pass on stories or complain good-naturedly about his Democratic friend, Michigan Governor G. Mennen (Soapy) Williams.

In summer, the porch was the best place for Mom and Dad to watch neighborhood boys like Alan Wunderlich, Billy Sawyer, Duke Williams, Bobby Altenburg or the Werner brothers join Eddie or me in a game of football or baseball. The grassy area between our U-shaped driveway and Rickett Road had been turned into a combination horse riding ring, baseball diamond and football field, complete with backstop and goalposts. Normally the team captains, who were older, chose me to play center or blocker in football while Eddie, who was leaner and faster, was the first choice for quarterback. In baseball, he pitched or played third base. I had to be content being an outfielder so I could chase the fly balls that always seemed to elude my glove.

In all seasons, we played basketball far from the back porch on the second floor of the barn. Eddie and Dad had built the perfect court there, installing one basket on the side of a grain scaffold and another one on a barn door. It was a popular hang-out, both for neighborhood and town boys. Often Eddie invited school friends from his basketball team to practice for their next scrimmage or game there, like Donnie Burt Appleton and my classmate, Randy Marx. Anyone who shot hoops was welcomed by a sign painted on the granary wall by our neighbor, Alan Wunderlich. "ORIGINAL BARN TROTTERS," it proclaimed!

The back porch at
Maltby and Rickett

When there was no pick-up football or baseball game to watch, the porch was also the perfect place to oversee kids who stopped by to enjoy riding horses, playing tag or chasing our dogs—Bob, Becky or Boots. Kurt and Chuck Werner's sister, Martha, was a good pal of mine and always seemed to be around. A lover of all farm animals, especially horses, she seemed to spend more time on our farm brushing horses or feeding Eddie's or my 4-H livestock projects than at home. Once in a while, Uncle Bill and Aunt Emma Lietzau's niece and nephew, Deanna and Paul Dixon, spent the afternoon with us. Deanna—my classmate and life-long friend—and her brother were city kids from Buffalo when they first started visiting. The farm, they later told us, was a place where they were naturally drawn, not just because of our families' close friendship but also because of the number of neighborhood kids that always seemed to be around.

Eddie with Deanna and Paul Dixon and Ranger, 1954.

Visits from two family members in the spring of 1953 were particularly memorable. Uncle Louie and Cousin Carolyn drove in shortly after the farm chores were done one evening in their gray Buick Special. It was unusual because Auntie Ruth and Uncle Louie always came together on visits. But this time, Auntie Ruth had chosen to stay home, tasking Carolyn and her dad with breaking some good news to us and with a very special request. By then, at only 16, Carolyn had made a name for herself at B.H.S. under the gifted band director, Russell Rowe, and in summer music programs at Interlochen, the University of Michigan and Michigan State University. Her talent was no longer just that of an amateur; she was being recruited by music schools throughout the nation, including Amherst College in Massachusetts. That day Toots (a nickname she had earned by then) had been selected by Dr. Clement Schuler of Amherst to be lead saxophonist for a twenty-four piece music ensemble called *Kids from Home. Kids* was sponsored by the Dept. of Defense and led by Schuler. That year, the group was to travel to Bermuda, Iceland, the Azores and Scotland to entertain American forces stationed there. Departure was in just two weeks!

Though *Kids* had already traveled for three summers around the globe, Auntie Ruth had legitimate concerns. The war in Korea was still raging, though prospects for a truce were increasing daily. All of the members of *Kids* were college age; Carolyn was only 16 and still in high school. And even though there would be no expenses for travel or food, she would be expected to purchase her own formal wear and have spending money for eight weeks, the length of time the group would be on tour. But despite her hesitation, Auntie Ruth realized what a wonderful opportunity her daughter had been given. She would allow Toots to join the group under one condition—her godparents must approve.

In Lutheran tradition, being godparents was a sacred duty in every sense of the word. Should anything happen to either of a child's parents, godparents were expected to help with a child's upbringing. My dad, Carolyn's godfather, took this duty seriously. And so did her godmother, Auntie Ruth's sister, Doris Case—Auntie "Doe." Along with her grandmother and a favorite aunt, they were always very close and always included in most important decisions in Carolyn's life.

Carolyn was not worried. She, not her dad, had been told to ask for my dad's permission. She knew her uncle would likely not veto the trip but her mature approach to my dad's sense of family values framed how she worded her request:

"We just came from Case's," she told Dad. "Auntie Doe said 'Yes! Certainly! You will always regret it if you turn down an opportunity at your age to see the world. But you know how much your mother and your grandmother worry. You have my permission to go, but only if you make responsible adult decisions, stay safe and give them no cause for concern.'"

She paused before asking Dad the important question…"What does my godfather say?"

My dad knew only too well how much Auntie Ruth worried. And he could not argue with anything Carolyn's aunt said. He also knew how important this trip would be.

"Toots," he said without hesitation, "of course you should go." But he could not help but offer a caveat, one god-fatherly piece of advice. "Just try to go to church whenever you can."

Carolyn toured with *Kids from Home* for seven years and those trips were remarkable experiences. They took her around the globe—to France, Germany, Belgium, North Africa and Japan as well as Scotland, the Azores, Iceland and Bermuda—wherever there were American army or air force bases on foreign soil. Less than a year after the July 1953 truce in Korea, *Kids* played where once fierce fighting occurred at the 21st Transportation Port in Inchon, Korea. Greeted by foreign leaders, celebrities, and generals over the years, the group received personal commendations from the Department of Defense and high-ranking military officials, including Maj Herbert Jones, Adjutant General of the Army. The trips were memorable and always resulted in standing room only audiences. They provided amazing boosts in morale to American soldiers during the Cold War and jump-started the careers of amateur *Kids* musicians from throughout the nation.

There were romances, heartbreaks and life-long friendships made on tour. There were also tense moments. In Iceland, the USO transport bus *Kids* was riding was in an accident. And there was more than one close call on aging transport planes that crisscrossed oceans flying from one continent to the other. But, above all, there were joyous moments. In Korea, just miles away from the three-mile wide demilitarized zone separating North and South, Carolyn and the other female members of the show worried about how they would cross a wide stretch of an army base to get to the stage where *Kids* was to perform. It was raining and they would be mired in mud in their formals and high heels. GIs to the rescue! The girl from small town Brighton was dumbfounded when someone in the sea of soldiers in combat boots and olive green and khaki fatigues shouted "Toots?" It was Jim Siford, one of the best looking recent graduates of BHS, she had dated for a year! He swooped her up beside his friends and carried her to the stage without even asking. The show's emcee did not fail to announce that incredible coincidence moments later, either, just before the group serenaded whistling and deeply grateful soldiers from Maine to Mississippi with Doris Day's pop hit *"If I Give my My Heart to You."*

Kids from Home on tour, 1956.

Carolyn Weber, second row-middle, and a few of her buddies, Kids from Home, 1956.

News reaching our back porch retreat was not always good, like Carolyn's invitation to join *Kids from Home*. Frank Meyer was usually the person neighbors counted on to keep everyone informed about Rickett and Maltby happenings, to be the bearer of both good and bad news. A jovial, white-haired Wisconsin transplant with a kind expression and tanned, wizened face, Frank always appeared wearing his trademark denim dungarees and engineer's cap. He had a certain way about him that all of us respected and loved, never changing his demeanor nor attempting to put on airs, a man of stellar character. If Frank drove up in his Hudson car, no matter what time of day or the season, we knew he had something very important to tell or ask. An excellent organizer and problem solver, he was the go-to person for Green Oak Township issues—bad roads, tax questions, town hall meetings—because he was so well respected at the Livingston County Courthouse. And anyone requiring assistance—like the blood transfusions George Fink's farm manager, James Cowie, desperately needed after surgery—could count on Frank to provide help or needed insight.

We knew by the look on Frank's face in mid-April 1952 that something was amiss. First, there was the small talk. Yes, Dad would certainly volunteer to join him at the Green Oak Town Hall in the fall presidential election as a Republican election observer. Yes, his sister—Aunt Hattie to us—was doing just fine. And, yes, so were his daughters—Grace and newly married Charlene in Howell. Then, the real reason for his call. Judy King, the girl with the smiling, welcoming face I remembered from my earliest days at the Holden School and from riding the school bus, was dead at only seventeen. She had sustained a fractured skull from being thrown from her boyfriend's motorcycle in Ann Arbor April 26. Her parents and brother, David, as well as the families near her home at Lee Rd. and U.S. 23, were devastated. Mom offered to send a casserole along with Aunt Hattie's dessert to the King Family and she and Dad would join Frank, Hattie and the Griffins at the funeral at the Methodist Church May 3. One of the saddest that congregants had ever attended, it was also one of Rev. John McLukas's most difficult services. Judy King was memorialized and buried just a month before she was to have graduated from Brighton High School.

Frank was back in early July, the same troubled look on his face. Page one of the Aug. 6 edition of *The Livingston County Press* reported that there had been an outbreak of polio in the county. Noting that adults were not immune from polio, the local infantile paralysis chapter in Howell listed symptoms of the dreaded disease reported by doctors and precautions parents should take. Symptoms included a low fever, upset stomach, intestinal disturbances, headaches, backaches, stiff neck or back, tenderness or weakness of muscle groups, extreme tiredness or nervousness and a sore throat. Among others, precautions recommended by the Michigan Department of Health were to insist on rest periods during the day for children, prohibit activities resulting in exhaustion and not allowing children to become chilled, particularly during and after swimming.

The newspaper also reported the alarming number of county cases of polio in 1952. Thirteen children had come down with the disease before the summer but by July eleven more cases had been reported, one as young as two years old! No area in Livingston County was spared from the ravages of the disease, it seemed. Howell, with the largest population, had been the hardest hit with six cases. *One victim was from Brighton.*

Our neighbor Alan Wunderlich's older brother, Kenny, was stricken July 8. When my brother and I learned about Kenny, we had difficulties both accepting and coming to terms with the misfortune life had dealt him. We had learned about infantile paralysis from Mom and Dad's warnings and in school during the annual March of Dimes charity appeal. We also knew what its symptoms and treatment were. We had learned about its most prominent victim, President Franklin Roosevelt, and were well aware that our Uncle Carl and teacher Bernice Chappel had had polio as children. Yet there were questions no one could seem to answer: Would we too get polio? What about our friends and family? This was just too personal, too close to home.

I can never forget visiting Kenny with Alan, Eddie and my parents at University Hospital in Ann Arbor the fall after he was stricken, where he had been in an iron lung for many weeks. There he lay with many others in a polio ward, only his head and neck protruding from the surrealistic machine that seemed to be regularly convulsing yet was keeping him alive. Kenny's expression was his usual one—the trademark smile no one could miss—and his speech totally unchanged as he greeted us enthusiastically. I recognized the worried yet reassuring look on his parents' faces as they welcomed us, encouraging us to huddle around their older son, even as a tear appeared on my mom's face. Eddie and Alan talked about how the Lions were faring that season, how they may well be able to beat the Packers Thanksgiving Day for a change with their heroes, Les Bingaman and Doak Walker, driving the team.

"Wouldn't count on it," Kenny quipped, winking at my dad. "I've seen Eddie throw more complete passes to Alan on Rickett Road turf with no cleats than Bobby Lane sometimes does at Briggs Stadium!"

Billy Sawyer, Eddie and
Alan Wunderlich, 1954 at Billy's
house on Rickett Road

Kenny's recovery was nothing short of a miracle. He was a fighter who had great support in his many friends and parents—Don and Dotty Wunderlich—as well as Alan. His positive attitude, inspired all of us. Though he was paralyzed from his waist down, no obstacle was too great to overcome. He learned to walk as well as anyone with crutches and even how to drive a specially equipped car again! Graduating from Brighton High school less than two years later with honors in art, he went on to attend and receive a degree from Olivet College.

We did not need to hear about weather events—thunderstorms, blizzards, wind storms or tornadoes—from Frank. *We witnessed them.*

Southeast Michigan's summer weather was usually ideal. People took advantage of sunny days on its many lakes to enjoy boating, water skiing, swimming—or simply to relax under sprawling, shady trees. Humidity levels could sometimes climb to extremes but temperatures were usually moderate. Yet there were times when the weather at Maltby and Rickett turned on us and was merciless. Heavy rain and winds were not uncommon, something to be wary of that posed major threats, especially to farmers. Each year, hundreds of thousands of dollars in insurance claims for lightning strikes or wind damage in our corner of southeastern Michigan alone were filed. It was not unusual for ancient burr oak trees in fields or shady maple and elm trees lining Maltby or Rickett to be struck and uprooted, sometimes blocking access to homes and farms for days. Grain crops or even hay fields that were an integral part of farm income could be totally wiped out.

In those devastating storms, barns, houses and outbuildings were often destroyed. One such storm, a cyclone, in the early part of the century completely downed our large barn. In my own time, our nearest farm neighbors, the Glen Griffin's, lost virtually everything in a freak Fourth of July tornado. The seventy-five year old brick farmhouse where Frances Rickett and her siblings were raised *and* the large barn built by her father were completely destroyed within an hour on one ugly afternoon in July. A big part of Glen and Frances Griffin's livelihood had been taken from them. With two sons to raise, the future of their farm—even with insurance—was in jeopardy.

Living off the land was based on good fortune as much as anything and there were occasions when good fortune simply did not come farmers' way. Virtually no farmer was exempt from bad luck—be it wind or thunderstorm damage, flooding, drought or a collapse in the market values of livestock or crops. As visitors stopped by to visit on the back porch in the summer just to chat about ordinary happenings, those misfortunes too often were the subject of conversation. That is how we heard about another weather-related farm incident, one that was as hard to fathom as the tornado destruction Glen and Frances Griffin experienced.

Dad raised Milking Shorthorn cows, known for having a far higher milk fat content than other cattle. Uncle Louie, on the other hand, prided himself in his herd of Holsteins, a breed known especially for its high milk production. Like his father's, they were registered with the Holstein-Friesian Association and mostly "true types"—cattle that were especially prized for their marking, a wide white vertical stripe running from the top of the head to the nose. By the mid-50s, Uncle Louie's outstanding herd of true types—and pride—had grown, enough so that he had built a new milk house to accommodate more milk production and expanded and improved his dairy barn. Things were looking promising for Dad's younger brother.

Only a year after Carolyn shared the news about *Kids from Home*, Uncle Louie came to sit on the back porch late one afternoon with somber and devastating news. He came to be consoled, if that were even possible; his herd of outstanding Holstein-Friesian cows had just been radically reduced in size. The hard rainstorm earlier that day had forced his cows to seek refuge beneath a stand of white oak trees in the pasture nearest the farm's pond. In one fell swoop, five cattle were struck and killed by lightning. When milking time came that day, Uncle Louie discovered them with his neighbor Bobby Richmond, who sometimes helped with chores. Those magnificently marked registered cows—the best milk producers in the herd—lay piled up like dominos, already bloating, in an oak glade. My uncle, a grown man of forty-eight, knelt on the ground and tried to hold back tears.

"What am I going to do?" he tasked my parents. "If Ruthie were not working in town at Refrigeration Research we could not survive. A quarter of our farm income is lost. And insurance will never cover the cost of replacing those championship cattle."

Dad and Mom listened to Uncle Louie talk for over an hour that day, commiserating with him. Listening well and empathizing is one of the things they always did best. They offered no optimistic assessment for the future, for though they were compassionate, they were realists. Dad had also lost good milk producing cows to bad weather or sickness as well as numerous sheep. It was an unfortunate lot of farmers to be at the mercy of the weather; he could not very well tell his brother that everything was going to be all right.

Uncle Louie's question could not and would not be answered. Sometimes questions even in the secure environment of a back porch refuge are not answerable.

"Can I offer you a cup of coffee?" my mom finally said, breaking the long silence that followed his breaking the awful news.

"Yes, thanks," my uncle replied. And then a request. "I wonder if maybe you can stop in tomorrow when the insurance people come if there are questions you think I need to ask?"

"And can you come too, Ed? The soap truck comes tomorrow to load the cows. You can probably help Bobby and me take down my gates to the lane going back to where they are piled up so they can make it through."

Brighton High School, 1940s

CHAPTER SIXTEEN

School Hill 1954

> *"Education is the most powerful weapon*
> *we can use to change the world."*
> —Nelson Mandela

STUDENTS AND TEACHERS WHO MADE THEIR WAY to class the first day of school in September 1928 later remarked that they could not determine whose smile was broader that day, Superintendent P. L. Bell's or that of an honored guest, real estate developer Tom Leith. As promised, Brighton High School's new building was completed in the last days of August, a dream-come-true for the two men. With the support of the community and a dedicated school board, they had seen the project they worked on tirelessly for almost two years become a reality.

The new school was a two-story red, face-brick building. Designed by Detroit architects Wilhelm and Moiby, it was located on Church Street just south of Main in Brighton Heights and commanded an outstanding view of the town to the west. A row of old, stately Spencer Road residences stood to the south and rolling green hills, the highest in Brighton, framed the building to the north and east. To complete the campus, Leith had donated a sizeable amount of vacant land adjoining the new building for an athletic field, a panoramic vista dotted by picturesque brick Tudor ranch houses within a decade.

The three hundred forty-one K through 12 students who began school that day discovered an educational plant as different as night and day from the overcrowded sixty-one year old Union School on Rickett Road. They must have thought they were in a large city school as they gawked at the long hallways, stairs to the second floor on either side of the building and so many classrooms they wondered if there were enough students to fill them. There was ample overhead lighting and expansive windows in each room, each one large and well furnished. For school assemblies and music and theater functions, there was a large gathering facility. Not far away was a study hall that could accommodate ninety students. Commercial, manual training, domestic science and chemistry rooms had been included in the plans to facilitate every student's educational needs. Like the newest schools in the nation, there was also a clinic, faculty room, exercise and shower room and individual student lockers.

With time, the 1928 rectangular brick building that I remembered as a child became outdated and over-crowded. Even before school consolidation in 1951, serious long term planning by local educational leaders for enlarging the high school and constructing a new "West Elementary School" had begun. Nation-wide, baby boomers were already making it necessary for school districts to expand old facilities or build entirely new ones. Pedagogical theories had also changed dramatically by mid-century. Allowing children in primary and junior high grades to be educated in the same building as high school students, even in different areas, was no longer acceptable.

At the same time West Elementary was constructed, Superintendent James Pepper oversaw the building of both a vocational shop annex to the north of the high school and a gymnasium and administrative offices to the south. "It is now possible," he wrote in the 1952 school yearbook, "for you and students of coming generations to enjoy buildings and equipment comparable to the best schools in Michigan..." Two years later, H. Gordon Hawkins, Pepper's long-time and much respected successor, addressed the already overcrowded conditions at West Elementary. In the summer of 1954 a sizeable upper elementary wing, including a band and chorus room, additional office space, a clinic and five classrooms, was added to the southeast side of the high school building just west of Sloan Memorial Field. Only two years after that, prompted by an ever increasing enrollment, a four classroom junior high school addition with a multi-purpose facility was built to the southwest.

Superintendent of Schools 1952-1965,
H. Gordon Hawkins

"Paul Weber, I never knew you had two left feet!"

Robert Scranton was standing beside me in the P.E. area just outside our classroom when he shouted at me half-joking as I did the *Do Si Do* and headed back to my square dance partner for the day. Square dancing, which Scranton loved, was a new part of his gym class curriculum that year. He had even been able to get the school system's permission to showcase it in an evening program for parents and teachers featuring a talent show, special music and social hour in the school gymnasium.

Bob Scranton's sixth grade P.E. classes in Brighton demonstrated dance steps for parents and other students in the winter of 1956 in the school gymnasium. Pictured above are Lorraine Mason and her partner (left), Paul Weber, Nancy Elliott, Marwell Smith, Diana Cain and Carl Mitchell (middle), and Dale Cooper (right).

By then, the junior high principal knew me well. I liked him and he liked me. One of H. Gordon Hawkins's hires—a University of Michigan master's candidate who had been a prisoner of war in Germany during World War II—Scranton was to make a big impact in the Brighton school system, remain in it for the rest of his professional career, and eventually have a school named after him. Dancing was one of his great loves and he made sure that his students would be exposed—or at least permitted—to learn as many forms of it that they could, as long as he made it a part of his curriculum. That could not have suited me more, for participating in team sports in his or Robert Wolcott's physical education classes was a disagreeable part of the school day I could have done without. Normally I was low-keyed at school and took everything in my stride. But changing into and out of gym clothes in the dingy, smelly locker room next to the old high school furnace room and enduring the day's athletic activity (inevitably chosen last for a basketball or baseball game) made me uncharacteristically irritable.

Bob Scranton knew that Superintendent Hawkins would secure permission for our square dance exhibition for parents. It was the most popular indoor winter social activity for many people in Brighton in those days, second only to playing cards. Evenings featuring this unique American form of dance occurred so regularly that families or clubs would vie months in advance to host one, provided they had ample room for musicians and the crowd they expected. Our family was no exception and I dreamed of a day when I could join the adults, especially Auntie Ruth and Uncle Louie, who were always the center of attention on dance floors around town. At one such dance, held at Dad's cousin, Carl Musch's, old home near Chilson, Carl and his wife, Irene, had invited Chug Smith to provide the music. Chug was accomplished on practically every musical instrument, from piano (black keys only!) to the laundry board, and the friends in his country music band were as well.

To make room for the crowd they anticipated and to prepare for the event, Musch's emptied the furniture out of the house and removed the threadbare rugs covering its hardwood floors. Except for a few corner niches, where bags of grain from the summer harvest were still stored, not a single space downstairs in the large old farmhouse was unoccupied. The party continued into the wee hours of the morning, until all of Irene's homemade doughnuts, cookies and cakes as well as Carl's home-brewed hard cider and wine were gone. Exhausted at last, no couples responded to the caller's plea for one more selection from his play list and Chug and his country band could make music no more.

Square dancing during gym class brought back nostalgic memories of that lively winter evening in the old Musch farmhouse. But the B.H.S. gymnasium where our program took place—the scent of its varnished basketball floor, the dance music and loud banter of teachers, students and parents—brings back memories equally as memorable. That mid-fifties winter event allowed Bob Scranton to share his biggest passion with his students—next to relishing food and being a friend to all.

Robert Scranton

I was comfortable dancing with my partner, Nancy Elliott, who had been in all of my classes since second grade. When we paired up for class earlier in the week, we seemed to be a logical match, just as Fred Nettles, who was African-American, seemed to be the logical match for my friend Suzanne Campbell. Fred was an outgoing, popular boy who showed outstanding potential as an athlete and was mentored by Dr. Herdis Lewis, the long-time Brighton dentist whose practice was on the second floor of a building on East Grand River. Suzanne made it clear to me in later years that neither she nor her mother were in favor of the dance decision. It had little to do with Freddie, who had seen a great many hard knocks in his life; it had everything to do with color being the sole determining factor in the choice of partners.

To avoid controversy, pairing a black boy with a black girl was just the way decisions were often made in those days. So too were decisions about academic matters. For no justifiable reason, Suzanne had been shuffled from one sixth grade teacher to the other that year. To make matters worse, she had been diagnosed as "retarded," even though she had always gotten good grades. The reason was never fully explained to her or her parents.

That sixth grade year was a hurtful one. While Randy Marx, Larry Herbst, Susie Uber or I were routinely called on when we raised our hands to answer questions, Suzanne, Freddie and students in the last row of class, both black and white, were ignored. Her year sitting at a desk in the "slow learner" section of class was not a pleasant one. She admitted later in life that if it had not been for some of her close friends that year, especially Susan Ayres, a fellow youth group member of St. Paul's Church she had known since pre-school days, she does not know what she would have done. Not until she came into her own in junior high school and later as a percussion player under the mentoring of long-time B.H.S. band director Carl Klopshinske was she able to put that year into perspective.

While Suzanne struggled in sixth grade, I fared well that year. Looking back, all four years in the two new, mid-century annexes were good ones. The old familiar faces—secretaries, custodians, bus drivers and cafeteria workers—from West Elementary were no longer there but I quickly felt at home with the new school personnel. Among others I remember fondly were Mrs. Kramm, Mrs. Borst and Mrs. Morrow in the cafeteria; two classmates' custodian grandfathers, Mr. Brown and Mr. Carney; Dad's friend Earl Crawford, transportation director; St. George member Pat Lueker, Mr. Scranton's secretary; Helen Mae Michaels, Gordon Hawkins secretary and Mrs. Harry Seger, the school nurse.

Most of the teachers were different from West Elementary, yet they were also veterans of our small district where school personnel remained unchanged for decades, as did teaching methods. The local connection for teachers was not to change on School Hill either. Three women who taught fifth grade—Georgia Fitzpatrick, Zelma Beers and her sister, Georgia Apps—had gone to school with my parents and Mrs. Beers was in their graduating class. Ina Shannon, one of the sixth grade teachers, was in my aunt's 1917 Brighton High School graduation class. Her colleague, Blanche Rickett, was close to being a Brighton native and so was their fifth/sixth grade colleague, Mrs. Joe Ryan.

I never felt that it was surprising, nor much of an accident, that in September of 1954 Mrs. Beers, an excellent educator, became my fifth grade teacher. Through the years, she had kept in touch with my parents and they were delighted that I was in her class. Fifth grade was to be my best year in school thus far, my grades exceptionally good. In June, as a reward for good citizenship, we made our first school field trip. It was to the Detroit Zoo and a highlight of the year for all of us—*if not* for Earl Crawford's crew of bus drivers who were forced to experience our soon-to-be-sixth-graders raucous behavior and listen to loud, repeated refrains of *Ninety-nine Bottles of Beer on the Wall…!* The May 25, 1955 permission slip for the outing, which each student wrote in his best cursive in penmanship class, had to be signed by a parent, dated and returned within five days. "Our room is planning to go to the zoo on June 1," it stated. "May I bring 8 cents to Mrs. Beers for the Jo Mendi Show and train ride? It has been decided that each fifth grader should not take more than 50 cents for spending money." All of us were in awe of Jo Mendi that day in 1955! We could not believe our eyes when the chimpanzee who succeeded the star attraction of the famous 1925 Scopes Monkey Trial not only drove a car but changed its wheel as well!

A new music program made a big impression on almost everyone in my fifth grade class that same year. David Jones, an accomplished jazz musician who played gigs in Detroit nearly every weekend, was hired to replace veteran band director Russell Rowe in high school and was joined by his accomplished wife, Marilyn, in the choral music department. My cousin Carolyn, a senior, encouraged me to play clarinet in Mr. Jones's beginning band and I have always been grateful for giving something other than a piano a try. A good friend of both the Joneses, Carolyn often strolled into the band room to see how I was doing with the used clarinet she had found for me at the music store where she worked in Ann Arbor. She was also fond of annoying me by tickling my neck in the middle of some musical piece I was trying to master as David Jones simply shook his head while directing his new charges.

We found band fun and stimulating, a nice change of pace from being in the classroom. Most in the group were already close friends and remained so through graduation. Karen Herbst, Joann Ludtke, Deanna Dixon, Vickie Benear and Susan Ayres joined me in the woodwind section and we challenged each other in a friendly way for the next five years for first and second chairs. Town friends Suzanne Wahl, Barb Love, and Dale Cooper were also part of the woodwind section while Jimmy Davis, Brian Musgrave and Larry Herbst tooted away on the coronet, trombone and bass across the aisle. Suzanne Campbell began a long professional career playing percussion standing in back of all of us. David Jones had the patience of a saint and never seemed to complain as he listened to his new recruits attempt to make music despite the honking and squeaking he was forced to endure.

Fifth Grader Paul Weber

Scranton did not need a "curriculum" excuse such as gym class to encourage dancing during school hours in junior high school as he had for his sixth graders. He made sure that the school sponsored social events after athletic games—the ever popular "sock hop," "turnabout" and other theme dances. *And* the event girls loved and boys hated—the Sadie Hawkins dance! When a small multi-purpose room was included in the junior high addition to the high school, Mr. Scranton made it clear that he intended to use it as a place for students to gather during their lunch hour—to listen to music *and* to dance if anyone so chose! When the weather was bad or our schedules allowed it, my friends and I spent more time congregating there than any other place on campus. We danced the *chicken* or improvised movements listening to rock and roll hits—the newest musical genre sweeping the nation in the 1950s. We also stuck to "slow dances" when a classmate brought in the latest Elvis Presley release like *"Love Me Tender."* We swooned when someone chose to play a stack of 33 r.p.m. "oldies but goodies" that had been added to the music queue. And we could bet that Scranton would be in the corner enjoying the music as much as we did whenever he was not busy with his official duties as principal or simply spending time in his office with students who were naturally drawn to him to chat or be informally counseled.

Robert Scranton was just one among many faculty members in junior high that almost every student respected in what always seemed to me to be the most innocent and enjoyable of our school years. Often we had outstanding teachers working on their master's degrees at the University of Michigan, such as Susan Murphy, the first teacher I ever had a crush on! Mrs Murphy, whose husband was an Olympic swimmer and on the diving team at Michigan, was our civics teacher. Years after graduating, her students still remembered a segment of her curriculum very different from any we had ever had. It was on vocation and personal responsibility. We spent long hours thinking about our life goals and what we would do when we finished school. We interviewed people in diverse occupations, learned about a myriad of jobs we never knew existed and ultimately wrote a paper on what best suited our needs and skills.

One assignment was both provocative and innovative, making all of us, as young as we were, think about our vocational aspirations and how realistic they were. We were required to take the Kuder Occupational Interest Survey, already a standard in school guidance and counseling departments. My friends Karen, Joann and Susan wanted to be teachers; Deanna Dixon and a few other girls hoped to be executive secretaries or work at newspapers; Suzanne Campbell had been singing at her father's nightclub in Detroit since she was a little girl and loved playing in the band—she would hear of nothing else than a career in music; Randy Marx wanted to be a professional athlete; my buddy Hugh Munce was determined to be a journalist like his grandfather who worked for the *Detroit News*. Since church was so important to me, and an integral part of our family life, I had decided at a very early age to go into the Lutheran ministry. My parents always told me that one Sunday, as my mother was helping other women after church in the chancel, I announced with great certainty that I would be "preaching" like Rev. Geiger from the very pulpit where he had just been standing! No wonder then that I was troubled when the survey results were analyzed. Numerous questions had to do with interest in marketing, being a salesperson and, in particular, convincing others. Being a salesperson or convincing people of the value of a product were of little interest to me and I had responded in the negative to any survey question reflecting the subject. Imagine my disappointment when, in red, Mrs. Murphy wrote on the paper (for which I received an A+) *"Paul, a minister must be very **persuasive**, don't you think?"*

My life-long love of history began in my U.S. History class that year, another of Mrs. Murphy's teaching assignments. Mrs. Murphy made history come alive and her encouragement of students who were not as gifted academically as well as her insistence that they participate in class discussions and projects set an excellent example for the entire school. My parents had always loved American history and explained to me at an early age that the house we lived in was an "Old Colonial" house and over one hundred years old. I was quick to inform Mrs.

Murphy about this when she started a unit on Colonial America. She blushed slightly explaining how the New England courting process involved couples sleeping in the same bed before marriage, but in "bundling" beds to honor their strict Puritan beliefs. "Thanks for sharing that," she said, "but it's doubtful that you have a bundling bed in your *Old Colonial* house!"

Not long after that the class was encouraged to assist with an exhibit in the trophy case at the entrance to the high school, which I enthusiastically helped create and gave the name "Mementos of Colonial Life in America." Our efforts were duly reported in an article entitled *"Articles over 100 Years Old"* in the Nov 1, 1957 edition of the *Bulldog Banner*, the Brigton High School newspaper:

> *"...Take a peek at the display in the showcase which you will likely never see again. The exhibit was prepared by the Eighth Grade, Section B. An 1818 German Bible and 1776 prayer book and saddle bag were brought in by Paul Weber...On exhibit also are models of stocks, a whipping cart and dunking bench used in Colonial New England for punishment...Vickie Benear brought in a collection of old coins, Suzanne Wahl her great-grandmother's blouse, Tommy Stone a pewter pitcher and Karen Herbst a flat iron which is over 125 years old..."*

Our class was chagrined one day in the winter when someone we did not know in the school system appeared to teach our U.S. history and civics classes. Mrs. Murphy's husband had been in a diving accident and was in an Ann Arbor hospital in serious condition. Our favorite teacher had asked to take a leave of absence to help take care of him and Christine Christensen had been hired as a long term substitute. After explaining the circumstances leading to Mrs. Murphy's absence, Mrs. Christensen wasted no time stepping beautifully into her shoes. By the next week we were convinced that she was the perfect replacement. Like Mrs. Murphy, she did not tolerate misbehavior and demanded strict adherence to her very simple and reasonable expectations. Her assignments were interesting, her classes well planned and—most important—her professionalism admirable. What is more, I now had my second crush on a witty, very attractive blond teacher!

Chris Christensen, who was to remain in the Brighton school system longer than any teacher we had ever had, taught in much the same fashion as Susan Murphy. Class participation—essential! Lessons made relevant to the present day—essential! Coaching *every* student to strive for excellence—essential! Putting students down unnecessarily—never an option! She also did not hesitate to take on very good students whose work she believed was not up to a standard she expected. My grades in Mrs. Christensen's class were even better than in Mrs. Murphy's and one day I expected an A (A+ would have been better) on an essay I wrote for a test on the presidency of Theodore Roosevelt. The question had to do with being altruistic as a nation: "Was the United States morally right in encouraging and funding rebels seeking independence from Colombia so President Roosevelt could have Congress make a treaty with the new nation of Panama, thus facilitating the construction of a canal?" Theodore Roosevelt was a Republican. He was a hero in the Weber and Westin households and that colored everything I wrote. Of course he was right! I was disappointed when my favorite teacher returned my paper virtually illegible because she had written an essay (in red!) herself over my justification of the imperial actions of a U.S. President. *"Have you really thought through this, Paul?"* she wrote. Some of her comments were in especially bold ink: *"American foreign policy and diplomacy ought always be tempered by conscience and morality, not by partisan politics."* I had aced most of the objective questions on the test but been taken to the woodhouse and challenged by my highly principled teacher. That sense of fair play and objectivity, shared by my parents, church and community and instilled in me from a young age, had just been reinforced by a teacher I highly respected.

My school days in two additions that morphed out of a 1928 building on *School Hill* came to an end too soon in June 1958. But life as an underclassman in that Collegiate Gothic style high school, the educational setting dotting scores of cityscapes throughout America, was about to begin.

> *High upon a hill in Brighton, 'neath the sky above,*
> *Stands our noble alma mater, school we'll always love.*
> *As the sons go marching onward, sing her praises high,*
> *Hail oh Hail our alma mater, Brighton we are proud!*
> B.H.S. *Alma Mater* (C. Weber, Russell Row, 1952)

Carl Klopshinske posed with the B.H.S. senior
band his first year of teaching in the fall of 1959.
Sophomore classmates pictured included Suzanne Campbell, Suzanne Wahl,
Joann Ludtke, Vickie Benear, Deana Dixon, Karen Herbst, Billy Zellman,
Dale Cooper, Larry Herbst, Jim Davis, Barb Love and Brian Musgrave.
(I am seated fourth from left in the second row.)

CHAPTER SEVENTEEN

Bulldog '62 Scrapbook   **Jan 1959**

> *"Fight the team across the field, for B.H.S. is here,*
> *set the earth reverberating with a mighty cheer: 'Rah Rah Rah!'*
> *Hit them hard and see how they fall, never let that team get the ball!*
> *Hail, Hail, the gang's all here, so let's beat every team this year!"*
> (B.H.S. Fight Song)

LONG AFTER I HAD DISCOVERED my mom's daybook from 1943—before I even knew how to read—I picked it up again out of sheer curiosity. Its ink by then was starting to fade, the corners of its graying pages dog-eared, some already torn out. I was, as usual, procrastinating—not studying animal *phyla* that my ninth grade biology teacher, Ed Smith, had assigned for the test the following day. I liked Mr. Smith's class, but found that part of the biology curriculum far less interesting than what I was studying in Mrs. Hoag's English or Mrs. Wilson's Latin I classes.

I was so intrigued as a young adult reading that daybook for the first time that I read it from cover to cover. I found my mom's narrative to be a compelling story about how the *greatest generation* sacrificed so much for the good of the nation rather than striving for individual gain. I was amazed at how she coped with shortages daily, how she made it through the day as a young mother making due with what was available and how inventive she was. Decades later, I thought a lot about what Mom told me when I interrupted her from her usual daily household tasks after reading it.

"Why don't you start your own diary?" she asked. "You like to write and you like history! Besides, years from now you may be happy you have it."

Ironically, soon after that discussion I received a pocket diary as a Christmas present from my Uncle Carlos and Aunt Frances Weber. It was a faux leather, two-and-a-half by five-and-a-half inch pocket notebook—a freebie my uncle had gotten from the American Bridge Division of the United States Steel Corporation. Properly speaking, it was more of an appointment book and almanac, with very little room to write much of anything on each page. But that probably served as an incentive for me to write something each day in it—through the month of October, at least. Many years later, and quite by accident, I discovered that I still had that 1959 American Bridge pocket diary! It was buried in a mildewed box beside a scrapbook Mom started for me shortly after I was born. Like her wartime diary, it too was dog-eared, its pages worn, the ink fading. Yet everything I had quickly jotted down as a freshman and sophomore in high school more than sixty years before was still legible, the events and places still very fresh in my memory. And, like that day I read my mother's daybook from cover to cover without stopping, I read it without putting it down. I was no longer living far from Michigan in a 21st century world. I was *in touch* once again…with those *remarkable* Brighton days.

My mom was right. *"Some day you will be happy to have it,"* she had said.

I could not help but recall my first week at B.H.S. as a freshman before I even started recording things in that diary. The laughs we shared during the then-obligatory freshmen initiation the second week of school were so infectious that years later my classmates and I still talk about that week. It felt wonderful to be totally subjected to the whims of upperclassmen, dressed like simpletons as we washed the wooden floors of the first floor hallway with toothbrushes. We felt like we all *belonged* to the B.H.S. student body, that we had been officially accepted as underclassmen.

*Looking a bit overdressed and
far too sober, I posed for my freshman
class picture in October 1958.*

I wrote descriptively, if briefly, about the end of my freshmen and beginning of my sophomore years, mostly entering upbeat kinds of things that, in retrospect, I am grateful to have. Among the more memorable classes in our first two years at B.H.S. was algebra, which I referred to without being hyperbolic as *"bedlam,"* in my diary. Mr. C. was short, elderly and kind but he had little or no control of his class. How any of us managed to be placed in geometry the following year or advanced algebra two years later is still a mystery. The large windows in our classroom facing east at the north end of the first floor hallway seemed to be open intentionally every day of the year, even in winter. It was usual for two or three classmates, led by my fun-loving friends Dale Cooper, Dennis Pearsall and Randy Marx, to bolt class through those windows and face little or no disciplinary action. All the daily entertainment, however, came to a screeching halt in the middle of the second semester when Mr. C was fired and replaced by a genuine educator who put up with no such behavior. Much to Superintendent Gordon Hawkins's and Principal Orville Snellenberger's delight, he was not fond of any of our attempts at humor and resolved—like it or not—to teach us about balancing equations rather than acrobatics and comedy.

I liked my teachers and most of my classmates. With a student body of less than 400, Brighton High was still small enough at the end of the 1950s that there were few students you didn't know—older brothers and sisters of classmates, neighborhood friends and relatives—and few that you could not kid or choose to stop and talk to between classes. Eddie was a junior, though we rarely saw each other during the school day. But I knew many of his friends when I passed them in the hall or on the stairs. Duke Williams, Billy Sawyer, Jerry Schoeppey and Bob Loveland often came to the farm just to hang out or play on our basketball court.

Many of the faculty members—Coach Fosdick, Stewart, Wolcott, Prieskorn and Kucher—and teachers, were more like friends at times. All of us knew, for example, that Alice Wilson, our Latin and government teacher, was always on our side and that there were days when talking about serious concerns as students was more important than conjugating verbs or memorizing the Preamble of the Constitution of the United States. When she enthusiastically agreed to participate in "Be Kind to Teachers Day" in our first year Latin class, the class chose me to be the student teacher. Mrs. Wilson complimented me privately immediately after class. One month later she asked me to teach class once again when she had to leave school briefly for a doctor's appointment. *"They* (the students) *weren't as good as before,"* I wrote in my diary May 13, *"but they were pretty good."* Alice Hawkins, the superintendent of schools wife and one of two home economics teachers, was another educator much like Alice Wilson. She was outgoing, extremely intelligent, her smile contagious and we knew we could always rely on her to give us sage advice.

Ed Smith was also a much loved ninth grade teacher. He never had an objection to groups of students meeting in his room after school just to chat or check on grades in his biology class. He was a deeply empathetic man and chose to include subjects in his curriculum about sicknesses that had struck friends or family of virtually everyone in his class. We marveled in March at home watching a cataract operation broadcast live on television that Mr. Smith had assigned as an optional activity and talked about it the next day for almost an entire period. Another part of his class that touched us all was making us aware of the myths plaguing people afflicted with Hansen's disease (leprosy) and advances in the treatment and understanding of that sickness. There were no dry eyes in Ed Smith's class that day! In recent times, when there has been grossly unreasonable criticism of the discipline of science by skeptics seeking a political platform, learning to respect the legitimacy of the scientific process Ed Smith instilled in us has always been something for which we have been grateful.

During the Cold War in the 1950s and 60s, civil defense drills were held frequently in schools across the nation. We looked forward to these and hoped they would go on for the usual twenty minutes or longer as we scampered under desks, our protection should a nuclear war break out! Normally the drills were during our excellent English teacher Anna Marie Hoag's class. She was always chagrined when hearing the loud, shrill signal that forced us to break ranks and fall on the floor, as we were conditioned to do. It was hard enough making it through our literature anthology textbooks with selections like *David Copperfield* or short stories and poems by American humorists H.L. Mencken and Ogden Nash without those annoying interruptions the state felt necessary to mandate in school.

| *Ed Smith* | *Alice Hawkins* | *Alice Wilson* |

The year 1959 was one of the most memorable years of my life while at the same time the year I miraculously lived to tell about it. Apart from the occasional cold, bouts with poison ivy or typical childhood illnesses like mumps and chicken pox, I had missed few days of school since second grade. During my second semester as a freshman, that pattern changed. Many of my diary entries mention having headaches, nose bleeds, colds or the flu; by June I had missed thirteen days of school. Three weeks into my sophomore year, on Thursday, Sept 24 I wrote *"I am feeling weak for some reason."* The following day *"felt good in school all day..."* yet after doing my farm chores, I felt a pain in my stomach. I was only able to lie on one side when I went to bed that night, it had gotten so bad..."*a terrible night,*" I wrote.

My pain had not lessened by Sunday and that night my parents gave up their bed so I could sleep downstairs. Alarmed because of my condition, my mother phoned Dr. Archibald McGregor the next morning. Dr. McGregor agreed to make a house call immediately, diagnosing my condition as a burst appendix, and ordered a hospital room at the newly built McPherson Community Hospital in Howell.

Never known for mincing words, McGregor told my frantic parents that I was in critical condition and immediate surgery was necessary to save my life! Within minutes my Uncle Louie, who worked with Dad at the time, was speeding down Rickett Road and Grand River with me in the back seat of his 1955 Buick Special, on our way to Howell.

I remember little from the time I stumbled into my room at McPherson until I found myself late that night in a daze, somewhere between the unconscious and otherworldly, an ethereal world where I imagined the walls around me enclosing a prison cell, the lights outside my room emanating from some distant inhabited world in the universe. Slowly regaining my senses, I felt a needle stabbing my arm and a tube uncomfortably inserted into my nose. I heard sounds that seemed vague but were actually coming from my parents standing at my bedside next to a private nurse Dr. McGregor had secured to monitor me.

"You can go now, Mr. and Mrs. Weber," she said in comforting words I will never forget. "Your son is going to be all right. Dr. McGregor has promised to be on call and I can assure you that if Paul has any medical needs during the night, he will be taken care of."

My parents were already more grateful to Dr. McGregor than anyone might imagine. In 1936, he treated them for an extremely dangerous farm incident. On a hot summer day a rabid horse in our barn bit Dad and Dr. McGregor, whom he summoned immediately, insisted that both he and my mother receive a long course of painful injections that in all likelihood saved their lives. My mother's brush with death when I was born in 1944 and her treatment by McGregor for nearly a year afterward was yet another reason to be thankful for the family physician's expert and timely treatment.

The next morning at 10 o'clock, Dr. McGregor walked into my room and greeted both my mom and me warmly. He was in his surgical scrubs and, without taking time for small talk, removed the tube that had been in my nose for the past 24 hours. Our family doctor was only in his late forties but his graying hair and stubby mustache, the premature wrinkles in his face, his vintage wire-rim glasses and his general manner had always given me the impression that he was far older than he actually was. A native of Detroit, our family physician looked more as if he stepped out of an Ivy League lecture hall in the Northeast than the head doctor at our small town hospital. Graduating in 1931 from Wayne State University, Dr. McGregor interned at Detroit Receiving Hospital and began practicing in Perry, Michigan. He moved to Brighton in 1936, replacing Dr. Duncan Cameron at Mellus

Hospital when Cameron established his private obstetrics practice on Main Street. After long-time Brighton physician Dr. Horace Mellus died suddenly in 1939, McGregor took over full operation of Brighton's stately Georgian red brick hospital.

My mother was normally the most even-keeled person anyone could think of. But that day her face was pale, the area surrounding her eyes dark, and signs that this normally stoic woman had been privately shedding a great many tears were very evident. She had stood to greet Dr. McGregor moments before and I saw tears forming in her eyes, obviously enormously relieved that I had made it through surgery and that the man who had saved yet another Weber life was now standing beside her.

The doctor spoke then in the calm voice of a friend rather than a medical professional. "You know, Anna, we very nearly lost Paul," he said in his trademark professional yet deeply personal way. "Peritonitis had already set in and had you not had the presence of mind to call me first thing Monday morning, he would not be with us as we speak. Luckily, his good physical condition and your quick action were contributing factors in saving the day. He is going to be fine. He should be here for a week; I expect to release him next Monday."

Dr. Archibald McGregor

True to his word, Dr. McGregor released me exactly one week after I had had surgery. With each day at McPherson, there was a lessening of my pain and I quickly regained my strength. The week passed quickly, with visits from my parents, Eddie, aunts, uncles, and cousins. On Friday, I noted in my diary that I was "lonely" but the same day got a welcome visit from Suzanne Campbell, my pal going back to West Elementary days. Suzanne brought letters from every student in my Latin II class that Alice Wilson had instructed her to deliver. Always aware of the latest romances and feuding among students in my sophomore class, she spent more than an hour catching me up on the most recent news about my classmates.

"Didn't you tell me that you had problems in geometry before you switched to another class a few weeks ago?" she quizzed me. "Hughie (my close friend Hugh Munce) and Miss B are feuding in that second period geometry class...she gave him a bad citizenship mark in study hall for a mid-term grade, making him ineligible to stay on student council. He spoke to her about it but she told him he deserved the grade and would not change it!" Suzanne stopped talking for a while to take time for a deep breathe then continued reporting on the latest comings and goings at B.H.S. "You can probably guess who everybody voted for as our sophomore homecoming attendant," she said with a chuckle when she had finished and started walking toward her mother in the hallway. "She's been your friend since you learned to walk!"

"Don't have to guess very hard," I said with a grin. "Joann, of course!"

My recuperation was quick, though catching up in Latin II, typing, geometry—even in band—was challenging. My G.P.A. plummeted to the lowest it had ever been, though through some miracle I still managed to be on the honor roll at the end of the quarter. Yet in spite of the mountain of work I had to make up, in spite of summoning all the strength I could to make it to the end of the school day that fall, there was a bright light shining at the end of my recovery tunnel in the form of one Carl William Klopshinske.

Carl Klopshinske

"Mr. K," as he was known to his students, began his long and distinguished career at B.H.S. the beginning of our sophomore year, a position he held until his retirement thirty-three years later. Klopshinske earned his bachelor's and master's degrees from Michigan State and Wayne State, later serving a four-year stint in the U.S. Army Reserves, where he played trombone in the Army Band. Not yet having found a teaching position in the late summer of 1959, he was working at his second home for much of his youth, the Charles Howell Boy Scout Camp at Brighton Lake, when he got a call from Superintendent of Schools Gordon Hawkins. Hawkins had still not found a replacement for the band director at B.H.S. who resigned at the end of the last school year and he was anxious. He had heard that Klopshinske was not only looking for work; he was also highly qualified.

Determined not to let another good prospect slip by, Hawkins was insistent that the young Wayne, Michigan native come to his office for an interview. "Like for you to come to my office today," Hawkins told him.

But Klopshinske, still in his scout uniform, was sweaty and tired from an afternoon of counseling duties and digging a new latrine. "Can't do it now, Mr. Hawkins," Klopshinske answered politely, disappointment very apparent in his response. "I'm wearing shorts and a t-shirt, I'm sweaty and the only thing I have in my tent to wear is another pair of shorts and a t-shirt!"

Hawkins never regretted his decision to hire Mr. K that very day—-he wearing his customary stylish suit and white shirt, the twenty-six year old Boy Scout counselor donning drab green shorts and the cleanest t-shirt he could find. Klopshinske started his career in Brighton with so much enthusiasm that it was hard at times for Hawkins or Principal Orville Snellenberger to keep him reined in!

"This is a new day for the B.H.S. band," he told his thirty-seven students the first day of class in September 1959, imitating the style of his army drill sergeant. "From now on you will be in your seats with your instruments and music out when the bell rings, you will vow to practice at least one hour every night and you will show your fellow students and me the respect they merit."

Following a long pause, during which his charges looked aghast and not a little intimidated, Mr. K ended his introductory speech. "And if any of you do not choose to abide by my rules…if your heart is not into playing those instruments with enthusiasm and representing our school proudly, I would advise you to change your class schedule by the end of the day!"

The list of achievements for the B.H.S. band under Mr. K's leadership defies imagination. By the time of his retirement, the band had grown to over 200 members. It played at Detroit Lions games every fall at Briggs Stadium. It participated annually in Band Day at the U. of M. Stadium in Ann Arbor. The band marched in a myriad of town parades and J. L Hudson's Thanksgiving Day Parade. Band members took part in all-conference bands regularly—always with a large contingent of Brighton students. The two crowning achievements in Klopshinske's long career in Brighton for which he was proudest, however, occurred in our nation's bicentennial year and just two years before he retired.

In 1976, the Brighton High School Band was invited to play at the Tomb of the Unknown Soldier in Washington D.C., the only non-military band ever to do so at that time. In 1990, it took first place at one of the nation's most competitive contests, the prestigious Smoky Mountain Music Festival in Gatlinburg, Tennessee.

Klopshinske was also the recipient of numerous individual awards, distinguishing himself twice by his election as president of districts four and eight of the Michigan Band Directors Association and later being inducted into membership in the American Academy of Band Directors.

Probably Mr. K's greatest legacy though, like that of Alice Wilson, Alice Hawkins, Ed Smith and Anna Marie Hoag, was his dedication to and love of the students he taught. Sometime in the middle of my freshman year, for reasons which elude me to this day, I decided to switch from playing clarinet to oboe. Too much—and better—competition in the clarinet section? Some innate need to stand out from the crowd? With the help of my cousin, Carolyn Weber, who worked for Paul's Music Store in Ann Arbor, I purchased an oboe at a discounted rate of $300.00, using money I was making from my budding sheep raising business on our farm. If the truth be told and to set the record straight, I never tried hard enough nor practiced long enough to play anything but shrieking, mournful notes on that unique and difficult woodwind instrument. *"Played my oboe before band—if you could call it that—and attracted quite a crowd,"* I noted the January before Carl Klopshinske was hired.

Eight months later, however, an enthusiastic new band director was not content to have a student in his band who possessed an instrument but *did not play it!* He patiently encouraged me to take private lessons at Paul's Ann Arbor store and one day even worked with me after school on the fine art of oboe fingering. When he learned I did not have a way home in the busiest part of my dad's day he offered to drive me home himself. *"Mr. K drove me home after school today,"* I wrote in my diary September 22. *"Really nice of him; had a few laughs since he already had volunteered to drive two friends home and we were packed into his Volkswagen beetle like sardines!"* Almost all of Klopshinske's former students have similar stories—supervised tutoring after school, delivering students without rides home or to extracurricular regional band events, having heart-to-heart conversations with struggling students and frequently paying for band expenses out of his own pocket. Though neither mastering the oboe or remaining in the band for another two years was to be in the cards for me, I can never forget Mr. K's kindness.

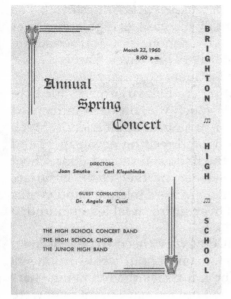

Carl Klopshiske's first B.H.S. spring concert featured Dr. Angelo Gucci, Director of Wayne State University's bands, as guest conductor in a well-received program that included widely diverse selections. Among them were "Waltzing Cat" by American composer Leroy Anderson and "Sakrava," a tune written by Prince Norodom of Cambodia.

I took part in some of the extra-curricular activities offered during and after school my freshman year, still managing to make time to study, work on 4-H projects and remain active in church organizations at St. George. I was president of our Luther League and even tried my hand one summer at teaching Bible School with a friend, Chris Klages. Joann Ludtke and two students new to Brighton schools our freshman year—Ruthie Worrall and Kathy Wright—joined Brian Musgrave and me in the local Youth for Christ Club at school and soon were recruited to be on a quiz team that competed with Howell High and other nearby schools. English class was my favorite that year and because my teacher, Anna Marie Hoag, knew of my interest in entering the Lutheran ministry—and most likely would need to polish my skills in speech—I was persuaded to enter our school's forensic contest, writing an original oration on the American Revolutionary War.

The following year I pursued my training in a speech-related class and was the only sophomore on the debate team, coached by Mrs. Bergman. *"Mrs. Bergman is a nice teacher,"* I scribbled in my diary after my classes had been changed the second week of school to include debate, *"but I don't think my team partner likes debate!"* "Resolved: The Federal Government should substantially increase its regulations over labor unions," was the topic that year, as the national political pendulum began swinging to the right. Fellow debaters Jim Bayes, Carolyn Love, Kenny Haller, Donna Murray, Chuck Madden, Rosemary Forsythe, Jay Herbst and I struggled at times writing credible arguments for both pro and con sides, depending on how much we had been influenced by opinions filtered down to us by our parents or adult friends. Much of our class time was spent researching and reading newspapers and periodicals like *Time* or *Newsweek* in the hallowed second floor school library. That room was zealously overseen by the school librarian, Mrs. H.C. Snyder, where not even whispers were tolerated and creaks from floors the only noises one could hear sitting at tables surrounded by book stacks.

That year, we could always count on experienced upperclassman Jim Bayes and Jay Herbst to make up for some of our weak arguments at Wayne-Oakland League meets. The hot issues the following years after Bayes graduated and Jay remained our primary point man were "Resolved: The United Nations should be significantly strengthened," and "Resolved: Should the Federal Government equalize educational opportunities by means of grants to the states' public elementary and secondary schools?" Underclassmen Diana Durbin, Chris Klages, John Park, Jacque Carney, George Bufford and Joyce Gibson—who was often my partner—proved to be formidable teammates for the next two word-sparring seasons when English and speech teachers Pat Taylor and Rosemary Twomey replaced Mrs. Bergman.

Pep rallies in the gym, with competition between classes for the most enthusiasm, were regular Friday events. Indeed, our first year in high school we had much to celebrate as our Class "C" basketball team won the Wayne-Oakland League championship Feb 27 and the district championship March 7. Often there were assemblies for musical events as well. The best performances were by renowned violinist David Rubinoff April 2 and, just one day later, by the Michigan State University Glee Club. There were even addresses by inspiring speakers like veteran Hollywood film star Thomas Mitchell and an assembly that appealed particularly to the more adventuresome in our student body on deep sea diving. Class meetings in the gym to plan for freshmen or sophomore dances and other events like class banquets or electing officers were also held regularly. At one of them, we made plans for a freshmen-sponsored Friday night dance a week before Valentine's Day. *"Bought new black shoes at Roberts for the Cupid*

Caper dance tonight," I entered in my diary Feb. 7. *"Danced with Joann* (Ludtke) *and Deanna* (Dixon) *all night; wonderful!"*

Showing livestock at the Fowlerville Fair in July with the Green Oak Livestock 4-H Club was an annual event for Eddie, my friends Martha Werner, Bob Altenburg and myself from 1956 – 1960. I won several ribbons, including Grand Champion in the yearling ewe class with PWW 3, one of my registered Corriedale sheep.

My freshmen and sophomore years were for the most part good ones—I even wrote *"Bored...wish I were back in school!"* the second week of vacation. Not all of the entries in that tiny pocket diary with my microscopic cursive writing were about school, however. Every day there was news about my "Farmer Boy" life on Rickett and Maltby. In January, our new neighbors, Reed and Rita Altenburg, purchased fourteen acres from Dad and Mom that adjoined their farm to the southeast on Maltby Road. Land values were ever increasing around Brighton once again in the 1950s and the $10,000 Dad and Mom received from that purchase was a welcome addition to a farm income that seemed to be ever diminishing.

I kept busy caring for my fast growing flock of sheep, which I bred to exhibit with the Green Oak Livestock Club at the Fowlerville Fair each July. My pride and joy were my registered Corriedales, which Dad helped me get through advertisements and special sales. Often I stayed up all night during early lambing season if the need arose or cared for weak or sick lambs near the furnace in our basement. With the expertise and help of my dad and uncle, I even learned the fine art of bobbing all of the lambs' tales!

My labors—supplemented by the greatest possible encouragement and tons of free feed from my dad—eventually paid off; my flock grew to more than forty and eventually helped pay for my college education. I noted in the diary in the winter and spring that I began to derive a profit from my labors—*"received a check for $90.00 for the 145 lbs. of wool Phil Gage* (our 4-H club leader) *sheared,"* I wrote in one entry, and *"made enough money from the sale of lambs to pay for my oboe"* in another. In August of 1959, I made a valuable addition to the flock, purchasing a ram in Upper Sandusky, Ohio for what seemed at the time like an outlandish price of $250.00. But my dad's eye and my own for quality livestock paid off. That ram was to produce some of the finest medium wool lambs the area—and Livingston County—had ever seen. I was amazed one month later when the breeder I had purchased the ram from, E. E Wolfe, personally delivered the pride of his flock to our farm when I was still in school. Late that Wednesday night in early September, I did not fail to record Wolfe's words to my dad that day: *"Smart purchase your son made here, Mr. Weber...showed the ram at the Michigan State Fair where he took Grand Champion!"*

The back porch at Maltby and Rickett continued to be a summer meeting place for family and friends. When no one dropped in for the evening, our entertainment after chores was usually listening to Detroit Tigers baseball games. I still associate the sound of cattle lowing in the fields around the barn and the sight of June and lightning bugs on porch screens with broadcasts of those games. I can never forget the excitement when Al Kaline came to the plate, the clip Massachusetts accent of the Tigers' Hall of Fame announcer, Mel Ott, and the malapropisms and folksy humor of former Tigers pitcher-turned-announcer, Paul "Dizzy" Trout. Another vivid summer memory is seeing my friend and neighbor, Martha Werner, outside the porch mounted on "Beauty." Beauty was my cousin Carolyn's spirited pinto gelding that she had given Eddie and me after her parents sold their Rickett Road farm in 1955. Many of my friends enjoyed riding Beauty but there was something unique about Martha's and Beauty's bond, a bond that lasted for many years. Martha had no second thoughts about caring for Beauty at all hours of the day or night when he came down with laminitis in the summer of 1959. Nor did she hesitate to show her prize steed in Fowlerville the last year the Green Oak Livestock Club participated in the Fowlerville Fair, even though Beauty was all of 10 years old.

Eddie on Beauty, 1961

*A/FC Edwin Weber Jr.
Home on leave from the
Air Force*

In mid-June 1959, Dad and Mom became the new owners of a two-toned aspen green Chevrolet Bel Air sedan. We were all proud of that two-door car, whose rear fins made one think more of a monster fish than anything else! Eddie was by then driving and probably put more miles on the car dating his latest heartthrob than Dad ever did. Having a new car and not taking a short motor trip somewhere in Michigan on Dad and Mom's wedding anniversary June 12 was simply incomprehensible! Off we drove a few days after getting the car, bound for the Upper Peninsula, Eddie at the wheel the whole way. We had not yet seen or crossed the two-year-old Mackinac Bridge that Uncle Carlos had spent so much of his time in the Highway Department designing. As we drove through Mackinaw City, our first glimpse of it towering over the azure blue waters of the straits connecting Lake Huron and Lake Michigan literally took our breath away! We could not have been prouder of Dad's older brother as we cruised across that beautiful span, still the longest suspension bridge between anchorages in the Western Hemisphere. We spent the night in Sault Ste. Marie, where we had spent the afternoon watching ships by-pass the St. Mary's River navigating on locks from one Great Lake to the other. Setting off for home the next day, we first made the short trek by ferry to Mackinac Island, paying what seemed like far too much for the round trip ticket of $1.65 from Mackinaw City. Dad, Mom and I took in the amazing views of Lake Huron and Fort Mackinac while Eddie wandered off on his own, less interested as always in sightseeing than jumping into the driver's seat of the new "Chevy" for the trip back to Maltby and Rickett.

Uncle Carlos Weber

That was the last trip Eddie was to take with us. In June 1960, he graduated and began working for a member of our church at a farm implement repair shop in South Lyon. The broken leg he suffered working there and uncertainty about his career path in life led him late that summer into joining the U.S. Air Force with his friend, Bob Loveland. There was a large void in our house that summer after Eddie left for the military but probably my Mom felt it the most. I was still home—and in fact never strayed very far away from home!—but there was something heart-rending about Mom's first-born leaving Maltby and Rickett, like a fledgling leaving the safety of its nest. Off my brother went with his best friend to Detroit where he had enlisted, seeking his fortune as a Tactical Air Command mechanic in the Far East, just as the perilous times for soldiers now known in history books as the Viet Nam War Era began.

Dad was less sentimental than Mom when he said good-bye to his older son. His words as he hugged him, nonetheless, were halting as he turned to Eddie saying, "I'll be waiting for you to come back to the farm. I always relied on you to fix things around here like your Grandfather Con used to." Then, like the time on the back porch seven years before when his niece asked his permission to join *Kids from Home*, his parting words to his son were *"Don't forget to go to church!"*

CHAPTER EIGHTEEN

Pomp and Circumstances 1960-62

> *"Wisdom is the principal thing; therefore get wisdom:*
> *And with all thy getting get understanding."*
> —Proverbs 4: 7 (Cover of B.H.S.
> Baccalaureate Program, June 3, 1962)

"FLEETING" BEST DESCRIBES how members of the B.H.S. Class of 1962 remember our final high school years. As September 1960 approached, most of us could not comprehend that in less than two years we would be following separate paths, some near, some far away from the halls of the building atop School Hill in Brighton where we became so close. Yet one sultry evening in June 1962, we began that exodus.

Our high school years were coming to an end. And they had indeed been fleeting.

———————————

There was hardly time to get caught up with the latest news from friends the first week of school of our junior year. I soon found that everyone was far more interested in talking about the classes they were taking, which teachers they liked or didn't like and B.H.S.'s prospects for repeating the 1959 Wayne-Oakland basketball championship that winter. Listening to a typical "How I spent my summer" story was not high on our priorities the first day of school that year.

Besides, an exciting presidential election was probably the most important subject on everyone's mind that fall. I spent many hours researching party platforms and both Sen. John F. Kennedy's and V.P. Richard Nixon's candidacies for an assignment our English teacher, Pat Taylor, gave us the first day of class. I tried to be as objective as possible, not easy considering that both the Weber and Westin Families were staunch Republicans. It was one of the most interesting assignments in my high school career, probably because in later years I broke with family tradition and independent thinking in politics became foremost in my mind. I received an A+ on the assignment and I was chosen—if a bit reluctantly—to present the *Democratic* platform and John F. Kennedy's views in a debate with Dennis Pearsall, my Republican opponent.

Pat Taylor wore many hats that year at B.H.S. She was a ninth and eleventh grade English teacher as well as cheerleading and debate coach. In addition, she directed both the junior and senior plays. I tried out for the junior play, expecting to be a shoo-in for a part in *"Heaven Can Wait,"* that year's drama selection. I was a good student, involved in forensics and debate and thus far had a 4.0 average in English class. I stood in disbelief the next day when my friends and I checked the cast that was posted in the first floor hallway trophy case. All of my friends were part of the drama but my name did not appear on the list! That same day in English class, Paul Sheng, a good friend of mine who was the son of the new Chinese-American doctors in town, raised his hand to answer a question Mrs. Taylor had just posed about Stephen Crane's *Red Badge of Courage*.

"Why didn't you choose Paul Weber for the play?" he asked.

Paul's off-task question silenced the room of 30 students and Mrs. Taylor was at a loss for words.

I had no reason to feel that I had been slighted by Pat Taylor. She was one of my favorite teachers and had even selected me for a scholarship that summer at MSU's continuing education program in forensics. I had gotten a taste of college life for a week there, stayed on campus in a dorm and got to know students from all over Michigan. Competing in speech contests every day was both challenging and fun, an inkling of what I would be in for in just two short years in college. "Can you stay after class to talk about it, Paul Sheng?" she answered. "Your question is a good one and I would be happy to discuss it with you."

Paul and I were both satisfied with Mrs. Taylor's reasoning. I was indeed disappointed to see many of my classmates in the cast but as I sat on the sidelines serving as an off-stage prompter, my bigheaded wounds were assuaged and I actually enjoyed the production. My debut as a B.H.S. Thespian would have to wait.

Before anyone could believe it, it was spring and time to prepare for our first school prom. Beautifully decorated by a junior class committee and sophomores, the "J-Hop"—held in the high school gym after "Pine Lodge" at Woodland Lake burned down in 1957— was always the highlight of the year for upperclassmen. I invited my long-time friend from St. George Church, Karen Herbst, to the formal dance at the beginning of May in both our junior and senior years. It was my first official "date" and I looked forward to the occasion, reserving a tuxedo at Robert's Men's Clothing Store and ordering a cymbidium orchid for Karen from Winkelhouse Florist in Whitmore Lake. As juniors, Karen and I "quadruple" dated with Chuck Uber and his date, Joann Ludtke, and Hugh Munce and George Standlick and their dates. That memorable evening was made even more special by a midnight dinner at Topinka's Restaurant in Detroit and a picnic feast at Kent Lake the next day hosted by Barb Love.

Both the junior and senior proms took place at Hawkins Elementary School—only a quarter of a mile from Maltby and Rickett! The school had just been built and, much to our delight, there almost seemed to have been a metamorphosis of the large cement block multi-purpose room/gym when Karen and I literally waltzed in! A B.H.S. Review story a few days afterward featured headlines in bold type and an article about the dance at the top of the page:

**"Moments to Remember, The Senior Prom
Featuring the Herb Law Quartet."**

The nondescript multi-purpose room had been transformed into an enchanted spot for a gala spring affair, literally an orchard in bloom! There were flowers, arbors and trellises everywhere, even an entrancing swing and wishing well made up of spring flowers! Soft colored streamers were playfully suspended above the magic spot, with refreshment tables in every corner and centerpieces made up of punch bowls crafted in ice!

A little over three months after the junior prom, Karen and I were on a train headed down the Eastern Seaboard toward Miami

Beach, Florida. We had been elected to serve as delegates from the youth group of St. George to attend the first triennial Luther League convention of the newly constituted American Lutheran Church. I had been to Florida once before but it was Karen's first trip to the South. The scenery along the way, especially the broad, glistening expanse of Chesapeake Bay, captivated us and we were excited to be staying directly on the Atlantic near the center of activities at the Hotel Delano in Miami Beach.

The highlight by far, however, was the convention speaker, Dr. Martin Luther King Jr., who left us with a life-long, treasured memory. The amazing oratorical style and prophetic message of the civil rights leader inspired the fourteen thousand delegates, clergy and guests present beyond belief, filling everyone with a zeal for mission during the exciting yet turbulent days of the movement for racial justice. Dr. King's central message was the necessity for Christians to heed, not just read about, Christ's commands, to fight against injustice and for the dignity of all God's creation. "The world in which we live is a neighborhood as a result of scientific advancement," he said. "Now we face the moral responsibility to make it a brotherhood...We must learn to live together as brothers or die together as fools." *

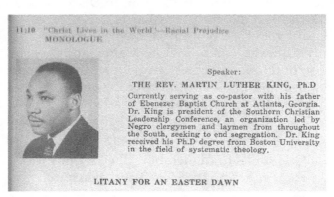

Convention organizers chose part of the early Church's Easter dawn litany as a liturgical selection after Dr. Martin Luther King's speech at the first triennial convention of the Luther League of the American Lutheran Church August 18, 1961.

Sandra Carson's yearbook staff and journalism class our senior year met in her southeast second floor classroom next to the stairway. Even today, when I see Gilbert Stuart's classic portrait of George Washington, I think about that classroom. Stuart's painting hung prominently on a wall next to the teacher's desk and was drenched with sunlight during our morning class. The "Father of our Country" seemed to be watching over our every move! Or was it simply affirmation of the class Mrs. Carson was teaching and her method of teaching? She was blond and short in stature but let none of her students—even the tallest and burliest boys—get away with anything. The Chicago native and U. of M. graduate student had made it clear on day one of class that she expected us to work hard, complete all of our assignments and not waste her time if we chose to socialize rather than to work. In a teacher profile I had written about her for B.H.S.'s monthly feature *Brighton Argus* page, she had said "the free press is indicative of a well-informed public and objectivity—bringing the news to the public without an interpretation of it—is the most important aspect of journalism." Taking on thirty upperclassmen and engendering in them one of the most important principles of American democracy—freedom of the press—was even more important to Sandra Carson than being assured she would receive a paycheck at the end of the month!

The goal of the 1962 *Brightonian* under Mrs. Carson, whose staff met after school on Wednesdays, was to produce a yearbook with a distinctly different style and to incorporate the most recent advances in photojournalism. She carefully selected staff members who were disciplined, hard workers and representative of the student body. I greatly respected her, yet with pressing assignments to complete in journalism class for our *Brighton Argus* column *and* deadlines to meet for the yearbook production, our afternoon yearbook staff meetings were occasionally a bit trying. But the more we commiserated with each other or mentioned how much we had to do outside of class, Mrs. Carson's response would always be the same. "*You* chose your class schedule and to work on the yearbook staff. *You* knew you would be working hard when you made your choice. Most of you are seniors and college bound. Now don't you think you need to act more like young adults and spend more time being positive? Try not to complain as much and put more effort into making your writing better. And while we're on the topic, journalists have deadlines to deal with constantly. How about trying harder to get your assignments done in a more timely manner?"

*The staff of the 1962 "Brightonian." **Top, from Left:** Peggy Rimes, Sharon Goodrich, Janet Albert, Dale Cooper, Jacque Carney and Diana Durbin **(editor). Middle, from Left:** Sandy Holmes, Joyce Gross, John Park, Dianne Pearsall and Karen Bigger. **Bottom, Standing, from Left:** Larry Schaffier, Joyce Gross, Bobbie Shekell, Nancy Krause, Paul Weber and Pat Dougherty. **Seated:** Roger Orndorf **(photographer)** and Suzanne Campbell.*

Truthfully, all of us knew that Mrs. Carson was right and we respected her for it. She had gone out of her way to make us better writers, better reporters and better journalists. It seemed as if every week there would be a face we did not recognize in class, a guest speaker Mrs. Carson had invited to address us on careers in journalism or writing. We were in awe of the amount of work and expertise involved in running a weekly newspaper after listening to Walter Ruch, editor of the *Brighton Argus*, one of many who agreed to a B.H.S.

speaking engagement. He had been invited to talk to us just a few days before our monthly column, *The Brighton High School Review*, went to press. But Mrs. Carson was not content with speakers coming *to us*. November saw some of the class at the studios of television station *WWJ* in Detroit to hear a presentation by the popular "lovelorn" syndicated columnist Abby Van Buren, sponsored by the *Detroit News*. The vivacious *"Dear Abby"* received us warmly for an autograph signing session in the station's large auditorium after her presentation. "I never smoke or drink...don't plan to begin," she asserted. And then came something that was hugely unpopular with a number of B.H.S. students—even a majority of her readers. "I do not approve of going steady either!"

Somehow I knew that Mrs. Carson's admonishments about "putting more effort into completing assignments on time" had been discretely directed at me. She could not be too direct because I had worked hard in her journalism class and seemed to get more key assignments than anyone else. My solid 4.0 average spoke for itself. Rather, it was about my performance on the yearbook staff. My pal Suzanne Campbell's heated complaint at one of our staff meetings undoubtedly reflected Mrs. Carson's sentiments. Suzanne, however, was anything but discrete. I was neglecting to do a difficult assignment that no senior on the staff volunteered for, and for good reason. Suzanne knew that as well as I did; nonetheless I had taken it on. My neglect was *not* an acceptable option.

Five members of our journalism class attended a presentation by
"Dear Abbey" columnist Abigail Van Buren in Nov. 1961. **Standing,**
Left to Right: *Karen Bosquette, Roger Orndorf, Paul Weber.*
Seated, Left to Right: *Dianne Pearsall, Hugh Munce, Abigail Van Buren.*

Many adjectives and qualities come to mind when describing my life-long friend Suzanne. She is jolly, reassuring, honest, true to friends, upbeat and positive. I had never seen her upset nor experienced anything resembling negativity from her. Not surprising then that I did a double take when I saw her changed demeanor and upsetting facial expression as she interrupted a heated discussion John Park, Dale Cooper and I—three of Suzanne's close friends—were having rather than concentrating on our yearbook assignments. President Kennedy was dealing with deteriorating relations with the Soviet Union and attempting to get U-2 spy pilot Francis Gary Powers released from a Russian prison and the three of us were praising his efforts. "Kennedy and the Soviet Union can wait," Suzanne blurted out. We need to talk!"

Frustrated beyond words, Suzanne told me that the dedication to one of our classmates that I had been assigned several weeks earlier was long overdue and a rough layout of the yearbook page it was supposed to be on was to be sent to the publisher in just a few days. "You said two weeks ago and again last week that it would be ready today. *Paul*, Mrs. Carson is fit to be tied! I told her you were one of my best friends, that I had known you since second grade at West Elementary and never known you to be unreliable. I promised her I would see that your tribute was done by today. *Well, it is not done!* What am I supposed to do?"

I barely spoke to Dad when he picked me up after our staff meeting that day.

"Want to drive home?" he asked, as he got out of our green Chevy Bel Air and walked to the passenger side. "The roads are icy today but you have to learn sometime how to deal with slippery Rickett Road."

"Not today, Dad," I answered evasively.

That evening, even before doing chores, I spread my schoolbooks out on my desk in a new downstairs bedroom and slumped in my chair. Even though it was not yet early spring, there were already a few ewes that were lambing that needed immediate attention. Dad's response was an uncharacteristic impatient one when I told him I would be dealing with them later. It was far below zero that night, there was no moonlight, it was pitch dark out and the lights in the front lambing stable just barely shed enough light to find the latch opening the gates.

"If you have more pressing things to do for school, then do them. But I expect to see you in less than an hour in the barn with a flashlight if you expect to see your favorite sheep birth healthy lambs!"

Gifted in writing and always on top of current affairs, Mom enjoyed occasionally reading my homework assignments, sometimes even giving me suggestions about what I had left out or added unnecessarily. That night I needed her help, but it was not about a government, English, journalism or debate assignment. It was about the yearbook. I stopped what I was doing after Dad left and walked into the sunroom where she was watching the evening news.

"I was waiting to talk to you," she said excitedly. "Got a letter from Eddie today from Japan. You know how anxious we were to hear if everything went well after his furlough last month. Let me read it too you..."

I could tell that Mom was taken aback when I interrupted her in the middle of a sentence. "Maybe later," I said. "But right now I need your input. I need to work something out."

I doubt that I will ever forget the reassurance I got from her that evening.

"I will be happy to help you with a word or two of that yearbook assignment and I will gladly proofread what you write. But first I want you to try drafting something yourself. Most important, write it from your heart. With your ability, you can write a tribute to Billy better than anyone, and that includes me. By the way, Mrs. Carson was *right*. Suzanne was only trying to help you."

What followed was a dedication that, though short, was indeed from the heart, words that expressed what everyone in our senior class felt. Billy Zellman was a friend, a fellow member of St. George Church and one of the most popular students in our class. We shared a table in study hall one semester of our junior year and despite the policing eyes of the teacher assigned to monitor us, we delighted in sneaking in conversations about cars, music, girls, politics, teachers—just about every topic two teenagers talked about outside of class. He was one of the best members of the brass section of the band—an excellent trumpet and cornet player—a scout, and actively sought after to play *Taps* at Memorial Day and veteran ceremonies. That year he looked forward to the occasion more than ever.

Billy never made his Memorial Day engagement. On May 27, just a few days before summer vacation, he was killed driving his parent's car around a curve on Rickett Road.

My dedication was on Mrs. Carson's desk the next day:

"For our friend and classmate who was taken from our midst at the end of our junior year. Though a year has passed since we bade him farewell, time has not erased the keen sorrow we felt at the death of this fine young man, our friend Bill Zellman..."

Billy Zellman

After not getting a role in the class play my junior year, my fortunes changed as a senior. There was no surprise when I was type cast in the role of a priest in the drama club's Christmas presentation of *Why the Chimes Rang*, a one-act play set in medieval times and directed by our debate coach, Rosemary Twomey. I had resolved not even to try out for the senior presentation of *Curtain Going Up* in November but both Mrs. Taylor, who again was directing the play, and my friends convinced me to swallow my pride and read for a part. Mrs. Taylor had told me I would be good in one of the lead roles and, for some reason, I got the part! I was again type cast, this time as a nerdy English teacher pursuing a far-from-nerdy teacher, played by Joann Ludtke. In the last scene, I romantically swept Joann off her feet, upstaging even the popular star athlete (onstage and off!), Randy Marx. A lengthy round of applause followed but Mrs. Taylor was swift in adding a postscript to her praise of how I had taken the role to heart. "If Mac Pearsall could kiss Joann at homecoming ceremonies on the football field in front of hundreds of people, you had the same chance tonight! You missed your opportunity, Paul Weber," she joked with me afterward. I was kidded for weeks about the missed opportunity and my friend Dennis Pearsall found it so amusing that he wrote on the back of his senior picture "Hope you finally get to kiss a girl!"

Curtain Going Up and *Why the Chimes Rang* were to be my last roles on stage. Stage of the theater, at least!

The cast of "Curtain Going Up" **Seated:** *Beth Osborne, Diana Cain, Nancy Krause, Deanna Dixon, Vicki Benear, Carol Hall.* **Second Row:** *Judy Latimer, Jamie Harmon, Carol Davis, Ron McClements, Bob Darga, Hugh Munce, Joann Ludtke, Pat Pendergrass, Barb Love, Susie Uber, Pat Taylor* **(Director).** **Third Row:** *Don Amenson, Rich Krasuski, Randy Marx, Jim Davis, Paul Weber*

Pat Taylor's reference to Mac Pearsall smooching Joann Ludtke on the cheek took place Oct 20 at a chilly, rainy Friday night football game against Northville, just a month before our senior play. It was no surprise to anyone that Joann had been elected homecoming queen that year; all of us were happy for her and knew that she would represent the school well. As vice-president of the senior class, I was given the honor of accompanying her as she made the rounds of Sloan Memorial Field in an open convertible on homecoming night before stopping in mid-field while the band serenaded her. During Joann's crowning, Suzanne Campbell had suggested to Carl Klopshinske that the band play a hit from the Broadway play and movie *Carousel*, *"You'll Never Walk Alone."* Her musical selection could not have been more perfect nor evoked more touching memories as I presented Joann to Principal Leo Fitzgerald, 1960 homecoming queen Shari Baetcke, Student Council President Mac Pearsall and varsity football captain, Randy Marx to be crowned. Though Mac got lucky that special evening with a kiss, I did not consider myself a loser. My friend since the age of three at St. George, Joann granted me the first royal dance of the evening afterward in the school gym!

I was privileged to accompany Joann on her convertible ride around Sloan Memorial Field for homecoming ceremonies.

Karen Herbst and I found ourselves on a train trip together once again, three weeks before we graduated, this time comfortably seated beside our pals aboard New York Central's *Wolverine* bound for New York City. Our route to the nation's largest city took us through Canada, arriving at Penn Station at 9:15 in the morning May 21. I wrote a story June 6 in the *BHS Review* about that three-day odyssey, one of the last times most of us were to be together as a group. Quite intentionally, I left out many of our daring—though harmless—teenage antics on that trip in the story. I had decided to be a part-time, non-inhaling pipe smoker and was applauded for my uncharacteristic, somewhat irreverent (for a potential minister?) behavior by my peers; nor was there any objection beforehand from my parents or the adults who accompanied us, Superintendent of Schools Gordon Hawkins, his wife, Alice, and biology teacher Ed Smith, the latter two our class advisors. Little was said, either, about the unsuccessful escapade exploring the city at night by a few of the more adventuresome boys in the class who set off from our hotel, *The New Yorker*, to visit the famed Peppermint Lounge. They planned to try their hand at doing the *twist*, the dance popularized by singer Chubby Checker that year, but did not get past the bouncers at the lounge's doors on W. 45th Street! Hugh Munce, Karen Herbst and I jaunted on foot to behold the wonders of Harlem that same night. It was another attempt at showing our independence, somewhat naughtily instigated by our buddy and leader, Suzanne Campbell.

One of the first destinations after our arrival May 21st was Ellis Island, where a ferry had taken us to the Statue of Liberty. We ascended the narrow, claustrophobic steps of one of our most important national icons to her crown, out of breath but awed at the panoramic view we beheld. Back at Manhattan's Battery we boarded sightseeing buses bound for the United Nations Building, the Cathedral of St. John the Divine, the Cunard Ocean liner *Queen Elizabeth*, the New York Stock Exchange, Chinatown, and the Bowery. The next day saw us gawking at the Empire State Building from the corner of Fifth Ave and 34th Sts., our eyes fixated on the clouds high overhead all but passing through the landmark skyscraper. We craned our necks until they ached before taking the long elevator ride to the roof overlooking the Midtown skyline. Sightseeing was again on our itinerary the last day of our trip, exploring Rockefeller Center and attending the television program "Who Do You Trust," starring Johnny Carson, at the St. James's Little Theater. At Radio City Music Hall that evening, we viewed the world famous *Rockettes* doing their precisely choreographed routines. "I loved being so close to the Rockettes," Karen Herbst told me years later. "We could actually see the runs in their nylon stockings!"

———————

"Mi nombre es Pablo. Tengo diez-y-seis años y vivo en Brighton, Michigan... Tengo un hermano en la fuerza aérea de Los Estados Unidos..."

I had just started writing a composition about myself and was practicing reading it to Peggy Leith in Mrs. Kennedy's sixth hour Spanish class when Leo Fitzgerald walked into the room. Fitzgerald had become principal that year, replacing Orville Snellenberger. He was well liked, extremely competent, and had already made a number of administrative changes and hired new teachers who reflected changing educational styles. High on his list of priorities had been to stem the flow of dropouts by offering alternative curriculum choices and more classes for low performing and failing students. He was an activist and made the community aware of Brighton's educational challenges by cooperating with Superintendent Hawkins in establishing new programs, even getting the P.T.A. to devote much of their time to his agenda.

Equally as important for Mr. Fitzgerald was getting his students to aspire to do their very best in both the classes they took and planning for their future. Over thirty percent of the senior class had committed to some form of higher education, had visited campuses in Southeast Michigan and many had received college acceptance letters. Such was my case.

Already by the middle of our junior year, my friends and I were thinking seriously about career plans and college. On March 6, forty-three of us took the three-hour-long National Merit Scholarship qualifying test and later the Pre-Scholastic Achievement Test at the U. of M. in Ann Arbor. Fully supported by my church and St. George minister Robert F. Spieler, I never wavered in my intention to enter the Lutheran ministry. Buoyed up by an unexpected monetary gift from my Uncle Joe Westin at Christmas, working for a summer on Livingston County farms as a surveyor for the U.S. Dept. of Agriculture and profits from raising sheep had allowed me to consider any number of colleges. But I was particularly interested in Lutheran schools in the Upper Midwest that offered prep courses for pastors. At the same time, however, I was drawn to larger universities closer to home, especially after attending M.S.U.'s continuing education seminar in forensics after my sophomore year. The following summer I was bound for

M.S.U. again, this time to attend Wolverine Boy's State, for which my sophomore friend Ed Case and I had been nominated by faculty.

Even though many members of my family had attended the East Lansing school, I was not convinced that M.S.U. was right for me. Whether my final choice to attend the University of Michigan was colored by my less than enjoyable experience at Boy's State at MSU that summer or by the bias my mother always had for the Ann Arbor university will probably never be clear in my mind. What mattered in the end was my late winter acceptance at Michigan's oldest university, where in September I would be enrolled in the College of Literature, Science and the Arts and majoring in European History.

Fitzgerald asked me to come with him to his office for an interview for the prestigious University of Michigan Regents Alumni scholarship, for which I had applied some weeks before. As we walked down the flight of stairs to the first floor, we met Suzanne Campbell who, like me, had been called out of class and was headed to the scholarship interview. With Fitzgerald's and Band Director Carl Klopshinske's help and inspiration—mixed with a huge helping of self-determination—she had also been accepted at Michigan, but in the School of Music.

Standing in the hallway in front of Fitzgerald's office, we met two men, one we knew very well, one a complete stranger. The stranger was a Howell resident and member of the University of Michigan Alumni Club. He was part of the scholarship selection committee headed by Joe Brady of Brighton and greeted us warmly as Fitzgerald went about his normal business. We were invited to sit down in a small conference room near Olah Bidwell's—Fitzgerald's secretary's—desk and I headed in there without hesitation. I was a bit tense because of the interview and sat down, but why was Suzanne not following me? I had seen the second man—an all-school advisor and member of the faculty—motion to Suzanne to remain in the hallway as I left her yet paid it no mind.

My interview went very well. Time passed and the second week in April I received a certificate and letter in the mail informing me that I was among six hundred forty-nine seniors in Michigan who had won the Regents Alumni Scholarship. I was elated and my parents beamed when I told them. I wondered, though, if Suzanne had also received a letter from the scholarship committee—and still did not know why she had not joined me in Mr. Fitzgerald's office. With graduation planning and final exams, I assumed that she was just too busy to say anything. At the time, however—in characteristic Suzanne Campbell fashion—not a word was said about her experience. She told her parents but none of her friends.

It was not until many years later that I learned the reason. Suzanne was simply told summarily *not* to stay, she explained. Our advisor did not deem her capable of winning it, even invoking my name as being the probable and appropriate winner of the Regents scholarship.

Despite having been highly recommended for admission to the School of Music at U. of M., it was just another roadblock she had to endure that started at the end of second grade when two teachers were asked who would take the *Negro* child because she had fought back after a racist slur. Or four years later being branded as *retarded* and put in a separate row for *slow* learners in sixth grade because a teacher was looking for a pretext not to teach her.

Suzanne Marie Campbell

I was angry when Suzanne related this story to me with not the least bit of avarice, more than five decades later. That small town girl, denied an opportunity to apply for a University of Michigan scholarship as I did, went on to become the university's first female percussionist. She attained a Bachelor of Music and a Master's degree in educational counseling and returned to B.H.S. as the first African-American educator, teaching choral music. She was employed later by two Ivy League universities and, after moving to Texas, recognized by that state for her breakthrough work in the Upward Bound program at Texas Christian University. She became Director of Counseling for Tarrant County College, later returning to Michigan and retiring from Warren Consolidated Schools after a 40-year career in education.

The seventy-sixth annual commencement ceremony of B.H.S. was set for June 7 in the high school gym—just one day after the eighteenth

*Setting a pace very seriously, Carol Davis and I
marched together at commencement.*

anniversary of D-Day, one of the most valiant days in history and occurring in the year most of my classmates and I were born. By then senior pictures had been taken, mounted in a collage that would later be displayed beside the trophy case on the first floor of the high school, invitations had been sent out and the graduation ceremony planned. The school choir, of which I was a part, was to sing a time-honored choral version of Emma Lazarus's Statue of Liberty poem, *Give Me Your Tired, Your Poor*, and Superintendent Hawkins had invited Dr. Ralph L, Steffek, a lecturer in Education at the U. of M., to give the commencement address. Rev. Alvin A. C. Barker of the Wesleyan Methodist Church was to preside at the baccalaureate service June 3 and deliver both the invocation and benediction. By then both the valedictorian and salutatorian of the Class of 1962 had been named.

My mom was second in her 1924 B.H.S. graduating class. Though I aspired to follow in her footsteps, I could not have been happier for my prom date who was the salutatorian of our class. Karen Herbst's salutatory was eloquent and delivered from the heart, not flowery but, befitting her personality, in the sincerest manner possible. It captured the thoughts of so many of us sitting before her:

> *"Parents, teachers, relatives and friends...it is to you that we owe so much. You have been kind, understanding, patient and forgiving. It is to you that we give credit for the achievements and goals each one of us has attained..."*

Her speech was met with both approbation and loud applause. As I looked around me at classmates and parents during her speech, few had dry eyes, few could not help but think about the formative years of or lives starting in 1949 when we began our educational journey.

The valedictorian of the Class of '62 was Joann Ludtke. Gifted with intelligence and a great sense of loyalty to family and friends, Joann was outgoing and had a bubbly personality that rubbed off on everyone she met. Perhaps because her mother and both my aunt and Mom had always been close friends or maybe just because with my more introverted personality I always enjoyed being in her company, Joann had always been a good friend.

Joann, too, delivered a speech that night that drew an immediate, highly sensitive reaction from everyone in the B.H.S. gym. Like Karen she thanked parents, teachers and relatives for their patience and understanding. Like Karen, the scope of her speech was altruistic:

> *"We must also take time to dream, for dreaming, as has often been said, 'hitches the soul to the stars'...and this dream of ours can only become a reality when we are measured by what we are—not by our race, creed, color or nationality."*

And, like Karen's, Joann's speech was simply elegant.

The audience broke out in uproarious applause after Joann's speech just as they had after Karen spoke. But because the presentation of the class by Principal Fitzgerald was scheduled immediately following Joann's address *and* because Joann was the 1961 homecoming queen, not only was there lengthy applause but a not-entirely-unexpected round of whistles and cheers from classmates as well that only abated when Superintendent Hawkins stepped to the podium requesting silence.

I was fretting about the side of the mortarboard cap my tassel was on and whether I would trip over the scarlet red gown I was wearing when Leo Fitzgerald rose, advanced to the dais, stood before the microphone and, in his booming baritone voice, presented our graduation class to the audience.

"Class of 1962, please rise," Fitzgerald said.

Glancing at the audience for a split second, I was struck by the sea of women dressed in their finest, some donning corsages for the occasion, most of them in the latest fashions, many imitating the elegant style of First Lady Jacqueline Kennedy. Their husbands wore dark suit coats with narrow lapels and crisp, white shirts with tight snap-tab collars. Co-ed friends of graduates with ponytails and bobby socks were standing there too, some next to boyfriends who had just been to Bill Bentley's or Harry Seger's barber shop for stylish "butch" or Elvis Presley-esque Pompadour haircuts.

A myriad of thoughts raced through my mind. What would life at Michigan be like, leaving a high school with less than four hundred students and entering a freshman class with seven or eight thousand students? Could Dad take over my responsibilities with the sheep? How would I cope with leaving home and living in a dorm? And what would my upcoming sail on the *S.S. Maasdam* across the Atlantic to England be like that I was embarking on in less than two weeks, with sojourns by ferry and train to Scotland, Sweden and Germany?

Mostly, though, there were images from the past coupled with those thoughts. Most prominent among them were the faces of the graduates of the Class of 1962. I saw new students at West Elementary— Suzanne Wahl, Nancy Newman, Nancy Elliott, Carol Hall, Carol Ann Davis, Carol Carney, Linda White, Susie Uber, Bob Hartman, Jamie Harmon, Lorraine Mason, Bobby Halpin, Marwell Smith, Darrell Heller, Keith Robertson, Margie Warr, Deanna Kluck, Tom Fear, and Larry Herbst— playing tag and pom-pom-pullaway on the playground under the watchful eye of Mrs. Chappel. Holden School classmates Gary Potter, Davina Hughes, Mary Caldwell, Glen Price, Bill Spicer and Bonnie Raub joined them. I saw Mrs. Smith's second graders— Ronnie McClements (always with a smile on his face), Chuck Uber, Fred Brown, Barbara Love, Dale Cooper, Diana Cain, Linda Skeman, Diane Langley, Brian Musgrave, Dennis Pearsall, Jim Davis, Suzanne Campbell, Susan Ayres, Karen Herbst, Joann Ludtke, Karen Krichbaum, Vicki Benear, Richard Verellen and Eddie Martin—headed for good positions on the monkey bars and swings at recess. I saw Deanna Dixon bashfully mixing with them the next year when she moved from New York. Then there were Chuck Werner, George Standlick, Rick Visel, Sandy Shekell, Carl Mitchell and Mark Waite joining us in fifth and sixth grades. I remembered Randy Marx proudly displaying his mother's oil painting of *Custer's Last Stand* in Mrs. Rickett's classroom for "show and tell." I would never forget the expression on Hugh Munce's face, standing aghast at the side of the tennis courts fronting East Main as I explained the biological principle of the birds and the bees to him one day during our lunch break!

There was also the plethora of new students in ninth grade and succeeding years. I saw my cafeteria tablemate Kenny Michaels and a long list of transfers from other B.H.S. classes and St. Patrick's and other schools: Dave Denkhaus, Rich Krasuski, Mike Dunk, Nancy Krause, Ruthie Worrall, George Taylor, Ron Peterson, Kathy Wright, Louise Craig, Jim Armstrong, Bob Darga, Delores Klein, Judy Beard, Danny Backus, Judy Latimer, Carolyn McCrae, Barbara Newton, George Taylor, Pat Pendergrass, Marsha Gladys, Vickie Gosselin, twins Dan and Dale Cole, Richard McElyea, the affable Don Amenson, Englishman Alan Parker, Mike Helms, Bill Dean, Chuck Brown, Barbara Hannenberg, Roger Warner, Sharon Eggert, David Hill, Geraldine Hoskings, Dan Hines, Katherine Pierce, Pat Grob, George Kordell, Lloyce Martin, Chuck Mance Beth Osborne and sweet Fern Williams—all adding spirit and pizazz to our Bulldog '62 lineup. And how could one forget the student taken too early from us, Billy Zellman, even before we graduated?

...Paul Westin Weber. Hearing H Gordon Hawkins call my name as I daydreamed, recollecting names and faces from the past while lined up between Margie Warr and Chuck Werner just off-stage in the B.H.S. gym seemed almost surreal. Then, as Chuck nudged me when Margie began her descent from the stage to the row of seats in front of it, I suddenly awakened from my reverie. I advanced toward Gordon Hawkins, accepted the diploma he handed me and with great care switched my red and white tassel from the right side of my loose-fitting mortar board cap to the left. I managed a smile for my mother who stood up in an aisle with her Argus C-3 camera to snap a picture and returned to my seat to bow my head for Rev Barker's benediction.

"It's over!" Hugh Munce shouted at me as chaos broke out when he heard Barker say "Amen."

"Now, for God's sake, let's shed these scarlet "choir" robes and get out of here!"

Gordon Mallot, B.H.S. Choir Director

B.H.S Choir, 1961-62: **Top, Row One:** *Darlene Wegrzyn, Nancy Prieskorn, Carol Davis, Jamie Harmon, Peggy Leith, Gretchen Matthews, Deanna Kluck.* **Row Two:** *Ruth Hurst, Susie Uber, Lorraine Denkhaus, Brenda Hicks, Anne Kutnic, Kathy Cameron, Barbara Crane, Linda Skeman.* **Row Three:** *Jim Bidwell, Keith Drayton, Ricky Albaugh, Bill Dean, Ron Peterson.* **Row Four:** *Jim Armstrong, Bob Darga, Dick Elliott, Jim Arnold, Bob Warr, Bill Haughton.*

Botttom, Row One: *Lucy Kroczak, Davina Hughes, Linda White, Louise Craig, Diana Daugherty, Susie Paddock, Julie Smith, Karen Bosquette, Diana Cain, Pat Grob, Linda Saunby, Carol Hall.* **Row Two:** *Kathy Wegrzyn, Sandy Orndorf, Judy Warner, Carol Warner, Dorothy Fick, Vickie Benear, Peggy Rines, Christie Ploehn, Carol Willia, Ruth Worrall.* **Row Three:** *Lee Niles, Harry Seger, Bob Halpin, Phil Stine, Dick Demorest, Dave Parmenter, Chuck Ritter, Bob Hartman, Paul Weber.*

*The Westin siblings, two spouses and their families gathered at Mom and Dad's house on Somerset Drive in October 1966 to meet Ed's wife, Joyce, shortly after their marriage. **Front, from Left:** Anna (Mrs. Carl) Westin, Uncle Carl Westin, Emma Westin. **Back, from Left:** Aunt Jennie Carlson, Dad, Mom. Missing is Mom's older brother Joe Westom.*

EPILOGUE

Two Funerals Brighton, April 1968

> *"...I've been to the mountaintop...And I've seen the Promised Land. I may not get there with you. But I want you to know tonight, that we, as a people, will get to the Promised Land."*
> —Last Speech, Martin Luther King Jr., April 3, 1968

THE PROCESSION WOUND ITS WAY AROUND the curves of Flint Road, slowly approaching the entrance to Fairview cemetery. Across the road, flags already dotted the brightly carpeted green landscape of Brighton Hills Memorial Gardens where scores of veterans were resting in peace. The symphony of red, white and blue colors waving in the breezy eastern horizon would have brought smiles to people in cars passing by on any other spring day. But this was *not* any normal spring day.

Both cemeteries were an idyllic setting where the departed could keep watch over Brighton from the gently rolling hills northeast of town beyond the Millpond. Only a few short years before I enjoyed going there on history expeditions, unusual for a teenager who ought to be spending time hanging around with his pals making out with their girlfriends at the A & W Root Beer stand on Grand River. Better yet, frequenting the skating rink at Island Lake—enjoying a few drags on a Pall Mall, the cigarette of choice for the younger set in those days.

Randy Marx and David Denkhaus were among my '62 B.H.S. classmates who served in Viet Nam.

Those were better times—certainly less traumatic for my family. Better times, too, for families now fearing news reports broadcast every evening about the *war* in distant Southeast Asia. It seemed inconceivable that Gary Potter, my Kindergarten and first grade friend at the Holden School, was there—and would serve several tours of duty. Or that Randy Marx, named to the Wayne-Oakland All Conference Football team only a few years before, would be commanding an artillery unit in the same war. Also bound for that far-off peninsula was Jim Armstrong, Randy's basketball teammate, who enjoyed playing masterfully conceived pranks on unsuspecting members of the class of '62! Jim had signed up for the Air Force under the buddy system with Glen Price and Jerry Clark as a senior, following in the path of their friend, Dick Verellen. Based at Bien Hoa, Jim's unit was to be one of the last in Saigon before it fell to the Viet Cong. David Denkhaus, another classmate, joined Jim and Randy in Viet Nam about the same time. Ironically, both Dave and Randy graduated from O.C.S. within a few months of each other, Dave in the army, Randy a marine, both men becoming first lieutenants and earning honors for bravery. Randy's bronze star citation that same year for maneuvering his platoon to an advantageous position while under surprise enemy fire northwest of Khe Sanh stated

"Lieutenant Marx's courage, bold initiative, and unfaltering devotion to duty in the face of great personal danger were in keeping with the highest traditions of the Marine Corps and of the United States Naval Service (and)...is authorized to wear the Combat "V." *

David earned his bronze star the following year for service as a senior advisor in a mobile advisory team and advisor on a rural development cadre to the South Vietnamese in Kien Hoa Province,

"...Distinguishing himself by meritorious service against a hostile force...demonstrating unusual professional zeal, determination and enthusiasm in a demanding duty assignment...exhibiting sound judgment... * *

Left: *In clerical vestments standing with Dad and parishioners in front of Good Shepherd Lutheran Church, Robbins, Illinois, where I served as pastor from 1968 – 1969.* **Right:** *My graduation picture from Luther Theological Seminary, 1970.*

The call came about three in the afternoon, Como Avenue time.

I was in my second year at Luther Theological Seminary in St Paul, Minnesota, the largest Lutheran seminary in the country. It was a different world, one filled with classes on systematic theology and pastoral counseling, nights out at favorite neighborhood bars where cheap beer could be had, and devoutly spiritual moments attending chapel in the frigid Minnesota winter. Just two weeks before I had made one of my all-night trips back to Brighton in my '62 Chevy Impala and within sight of O'Hare International made an important decision. About nine p.m., bulletins interrupted all programming with the news of the assassination of Dr. Martin Luther King, Jr. The man I had so respected, one of the greatest ministers and leaders of our generation, was dead. I felt somehow in the moments following that tragedy that I could honor his memory by serving an African-American inner city church the next year on my internship. I explained this to my parents as they met me at the door on Somerset Drive in Brighton later that evening. Aunt Emma Westin, who lived in the brick house my grandfather built in 1927, was as supportive as they had been when I saw her the next day. As always, I knew that I could count on her encouraging words as she chanted the familiar refrain of the Civil Rights marches, "We shall overcome...we shall overcome some day..." when I broke the news to her...

"You have a long distance call that you must take immediately!" Gladys, the seminary switchboard operator who reminded me a bit of *Laugh In's* Ernestine, seemed just a little agitated by the calls she was taking from seminarians' girlfriends that afternoon as she rang me in my room in Luther's Bøckman Hall. I was back on campus, staring at the splendid neo-Gothic limestone building next to the late nineteenth century dormitory I was living in. Carved over the entryway were three words in Latin, one of the themes of my favorite Gospel writer, John—*Christus Lux Mundi*, Christ, Light of the World. Nearly every day I watched small groups of men in their twenties with distinct Scandinavian features mingling with a few foreign students from the heart of Africa exiting from that classroom building. They were leaving the pedagogical world of Gullixon Hall, hurrying to the *Diet*, the campus canteen, for coffee and heated debates about Søren Kirkegaard's theology and Eugene McCarthy's latest political posturing. My good friend and cubicle neighbor, Rollie Severson, was among them, dressed in his signature Ivy League sweater and shirt, penny loafers and light colored chino pants.

"Dad?" I said after the operator had connected us. He rarely called me; Weber men just didn't have much occasion to telephone anyone unless babies were born or St. George Church needed someone to usher or count the offering at Sunday services the next day.

"What's wrong?" I said after a long pause. Though Dad was composed, something was not right. After a few seconds he was able to talk, returning to his normal conversational cadence and voice pitch that since my childhood always reassured me that things were ok. But things were *not* ok.

"Mom was in an accident in Fowlerville today...She was with Emma and Jennie...Emma was driving. They were hit head-on. Emma and Jennie are both dead. Mom is in McPherson Hospital in Howell in critical condition..."

It seemed like an eternity before I was able to say anything; no tears, just complete shock. Only a month before my mother was enjoying Dad's long overdue retirement on the white sandy beaches of Sarasota. *"...In critical condition."* Her younger sister, the gentle, refined woman who was a fixture at the Brighton State Bank for 43 years: *"...Dead."* The older sister—my good-hearted, fun-loving godmother who was speaking Swedish with me at age three— *"...Both dead."*

Three family photos taken on Somerset Drive, 1963 – 66. Left: Mom, Ed, Aunt Emma Westin, Me. Middle: Me, Emma, Mom, Dad, Uncle Joe Westin. Right: Ed married Joyce Belcher of Kalamazoo in 1966.

"I will be there today," I told Dad. "Take care of yourself...Mom will be all right."

I knew telling Dad to take care of himself was not necessary. I was mulling that over as Rollie Severson made his white '60 Ford Galaxy groan shamelessly driving down Como Ave. on the way to MSP International Airport. Darwin Polesky, another seminary friend who knew how and when to give good council to friends, was also in the car, and fussed at Rollie for missing a turn-off in Richfield. As we coasted into MSP's departures parking lot, a disc jockey on station KDWB played *"Sittin' on the Dock of the Bay,"* the number one song on both the R & B and pop charts, a mournful ballad whose music and lyrics somewhat matched my emotional state that afternoon. It was recorded the preceding November by the artist, one month before his untimely death in Madison, Wisconsin:

*"Sittin' in the morning sun, I'll be sittin' when the evenin' comes,
Watchin' the ships roll in, then I watch 'em roll away again,
yeah...
It look like nothin's gonna come my way...sittin' on the dock of
the bay..."*

The three-hour flight to Detroit Metro seemed endless. I broke down when I saw my father standing in the arrivals hall waiting with Chuck Smith. To see Chug standing by Dad's side that evening to greet me was almost a godsend! Fifty-four years ago, family was probably the value that Brighton valued the most. On only an hour's notice, Chug and his wife, Margaret, acted with dispatch and saw to it that Dad would be at Metro to meet me that evening. Chug! A man I had known all my life, a man whose *jôie de vivre* and humor were infectious.

Dad fell asleep almost immediately as Chug negotiated his way out of Metro's crowded parking lot. He kept pace with the traffic on I-94 as I listened incredulously to him talk, telling what he knew about the senseless tragedy. By the time we passed Ypsi, he had recounted most of the facts:

Chug was the last person to see my aunts alive. The accident happened close to Fowlerville on Grand River and Hogback Road. Irony of ironies, I thought. Twenty years before, the name Westin was a household word there; now it was again. You knew you could always get the best and fairest deal at the grocery store established by my grandfather and uncles in 1922. Everybody in town knew Joe and Carl Westin, not to mention Carl's wife, Anna—one of Con Weber's many nieces—and their son Chuck. Just two blocks away on Grand River from Westin Brothers Grocery was their 1930s two-story Tudor brick home, a jewel in the neighborhood with its ivy-covered chimney, rock garden and immaculately manicured lawn...

"Didn't know Anna was back from Florida...haven't seen Emma Westin since she retired from the bank," Chug told his friend Jack Teeple as he passed Mom and her sisters just east of town. They had just paid their respects to Erv Bandkau and his family, members of St. George Church and friends for many years. Erv's wife, Molly, had died only two days before and the family was pleased to see so many Brighton folks at the *visitation*.

A half hour later, the din of voices that filled the parlor where Chug and Teep were standing was replaced by silence as one visibly shaken funeral director, looking slightly disheveled and dressed in black, gestured to another who was standing close to Molly's coffin. The two joined each other near the front vestibule where Chug and Teep were standing. Chug's face turned ashen gray as he overheard the conversation:

"There was a head-on collision just east of town on Grand River," the shorter of the two undertakers whispered to the other. He had not recovered from what he had seen even though he had dealt with countless victims of car accidents before. This was supposed to be part of the business he was in but the carnage there he would not soon forget.

"Three women from Brighton were in the car. The driver was killed instantly. The front seat passenger is unconscious and not expected to live. The lady in the back is in critical condition. We believe they had just been here at the *visitation*. You need to come with me *now*."

Enough said. Chug grabbed Jack Teeple's arm as the two men left Dillingham's without offering an explanation to the Bandkau Family.

"Let's go, Teep!" Chug finally managed to say to his friend. "We've got to get in touch with Ed Weber!"

Erv Bandkau Jr., stunned like all the mourners in the room, stopped them before they got to the parking lot.

"I'm going with you," the older of the two Bandkau sons told Chug. "Anna or Ed might need my help."

And so it happened that I found myself at home again in a familiar world where little changed when I was growing up except, perhaps, the occasional window display at Rolison's or Gamble's Hardware. George Ratz knew he could count on the same clientele from year to year, decade to decade, without bothering to worry much about windows. Miss Sadie Hicks at Strick's Store across Main and Grace Rickett next to Paul DeLuca's kept tidy visual displays in the front as they got older, though their inventory was smaller and beginning to look more out of date. George at Woodward's Plumbing and Squee Squire never bothered fussing with windows. Actually, that was not quite true. Wendell was now showing RCA color console televisions in his display window whose screens were more than double the size of the black and white twelve-inch Motorola set Dad purchased from him in 1949.

North Side of West Main, mid-1960s. (Coutesy B.F.D. "From the Pages of Time)

There were a few signs that things were changing ever so slowly in the Brighton of the '60s. Doc Shafer did a fine job of developing Horizon Hills out on U.S. 23. There was a beauty of a new post office on North Street atop the hill from where the abandoned mill used to stand that made Charlie Case, the assistant postmaster, beam with pride. Across the street, overlooking Main, was the newly built Brighton State Bank building that Whit Kimble and Aunt Emma helped dedicate in 1963. Not far away, Bob Leland, Harald Jarvis, Mary Matthias and Donna Nelson were doing just fine in their attractive new stores built over Ore Creek at Main and West Streets.

Miss Amelia Conrad's tiny house close to Grand River and Main had been bulldozed at the beginning of the decade to make way for an A&P and Chuck Uber's Drugstore. I tried working at the new A & P for a while because of the Westin grocery business tradition. Uncle Joe had told me to be punctual, always busy, and decline tips when they were offered. My friends Hugh Munce and Larry Herbst worked there too and before long seemed to spend every waking moment after school at the place. I followed my uncle's advice at the new store but management never forgave me for what happened the day the store had its grand opening. Quite by accident—and, in retrospect, to my good fortune—I tripped over dozens of cases of bottled soft drinks stored in a back room, breaking most and causing fizzing pop to cascade through double swinging doors as far as customers milling around the dairy case! I was almost relieved to get a pink slip not long afterward so I could spend more time conjugating verbs in Mrs. Kennedy's Spanish class up the hill at B.H.S.!

Uncle Carl Westin, who lived on Madison Street a few paces away from St. George Church, was doing what he could to console his brother Joe when Chug, Dad and I arrived from the airport. Uncle Joe would now be alone in an empty house where he had lived with his sisters for the past 18 years. Joe had been feeling better the day Emma, Mom and Aunt Jennie left for Fowlerville. It was spring and he would soon be getting some relief from the illnesses that had debilitated him. He could sit for a short time on the screened-in back porch on a glider Aunt Jennie had brought with her from Roseville and curse the droning choruses the blackbirds in the woods just outside the house were making instead of his arthritis and emphysema.

The older of the two Westin brothers, whose generosity had made going to the U of M more financially feasible for me, had never married. He barely made it home from France back in 1919 after World War I; gas attacks compromised his lungs and bullet wounds from Belleau Wood and Château-Thierry left him with a pronounced limp and infections that not even the best of Mr. Wilson's army doctors could heal. At last, he gave up on them at Ft. Sherman and took the fastest train home to Michigan that he could get. Alfred Bidwell's five-acre fruit farm on N. Second Street that Grandfather Westin had bought in 1920 witnessed a miracle that summer. Fresh milk, clean country air and doting family members brought a new outlook to life for Private Joseph Westin...

As the brothers sat together talking late that night, something even worse than the bullets and gas of the trenches of France were now taking Joe Westin down.

"I don't think I've been in this house since long before Ed's dad died. I used to deliver groceries here to Gustie and Con when I worked at Scranton's."

Chug tried his hardest to make conversation with Uncle Joe and Uncle Carl after Dad and I walked in the door at 407 E. Grand River with him. There were no lights on anywhere in the empty house except in the front sunroom where my uncles were sitting. Joe and Carl clearly needed to talk about other things. About the accident, about the facts they had learned that afternoon, about how Mom was doing.

"The state police tell me they were hit by a drunk driver. He may have come from a bar in Howell...Damn." That was about the only expletive that ever came out of Carl Westin's mouth and he used it with regularity in that conversation. "And to think, this happened in *Fowlerville* of all places…Damn!"

Following a long, awkward pause, Chug excused himself for not staying longer and left the room. He winced as he walked by the cupboards in the kitchen on his way out. On top of one of them, Emma Westin's bloodied black purse that had been salvaged from the wreck of her '64 yellow Chevy Impala had been placed. Next to it was the unopened thank you letter I had sent her a few days earlier from St. Paul. We thanked Chug for being so kind as he went down the steps of the back porch to his car.

"Don't forget to call me if you or Joe need anything at all," he shouted as he backed up to leave. "I would be happy to pick Eddie and Joyce up tomorrow…Margaret invited them to stay with us."

Ed and his wife Joyce flew in from Sarasota the next day. Then twenty-six, Ed's resemblance to Con Weber seemed to become more pronounced every year. Slightly shorter than I was, he was strong, had dimpled cheeks, and wide shoulders. My brother often withdrew to himself and did not speak unless there was something important to be said. Mom once remarked that he "took things too hard" and that characteristic did not diminish with age. We were brothers who were close but could not have been more different. I had brown eyes, avoided doing mechanical things and was not particularly athletic; Ed had blue eyes, there was nothing mechanical that he could not do and he always excelled in sports. There were, however, two physical characteristics that we shared with our father and grandfather—the Weber stance and gait. We were slightly flat-footed and our stride was more like a deliberate shuffle, particularly if we were in a hurry. Our stance could best be described as positioning oneself for something that could take a long time—one leg ahead of the other, one foot out at a sharp angle, the other dug in firmly.

My immediate family—the second of Con Weber's son's family—gathered in the crowded environment of an intensive care room at McPherson Community Health Center shortly after Ed and Joyce's arrival the next day. We Weber men stood with sober faces around Mom's bed as Joyce, a nurse, spoke with the attending physicians and nurses in the hallway. I could see a slight smile on Mom's face when she saw Joyce. Joyce was the daughter Mom had always wanted and her acceptance in the family had been warm and immediate.

"Joy…!" Mom blurted out weakly, not finishing her sentence as her daughter-in-law embraced her.

Though still in critical condition, we learned that Mom would make it; as for the quality of her life, that was another question. Her morphine fix was making it difficult for her to speak and she slurred her words. There were tubes everywhere and her leg was pinned; a smashed femur, among other things, we were told. Always prone to getting black and blue marks, her pale face was the only part of her body free of them, all of her limbs dotted by traces of the trauma she had been through. As a diversion, I glanced out the window. In tidy, small fields, Holstein cattle were grazing on the green grass of late spring. The bucolic sight was welcome to me that day, remembering the same calming scene the day I recovered from surgery when I was in high school, the time Doc MacGregor saved my life. I could not help but remember the words of the Psalmist, always relevant, especially that day:

> *"The Lord is my shepherd, I shall not want…he maketh me to lie down in green pastures, my cup runneth over…yea though I walk through the valley of the shadow…"*

My meditation ended abruptly. A pall descended on the room as my mother started to speak. There were lapses of memory, bewildered stares and—finally—a slurred account of the accident:

Mom remembered pointing out the Westin house to her sisters as they passed it on their way to Molly Bandkau's visitation at Dillingham's Funeral Home. "Grandma and Grandpa Weber, Uncle Adam, Aunt Maria, Aunt Lydia, Pa and Ma all had their pictures taken right there in the rock garden," she had said to them. "And do you remember when Eddie was a toddler and cousin Lila Larson came to visit just after joining the W.A.C.s during the *war*? Carl and Anna had us all for dinner. I still have a kodacolor picture of us, Ma so proud and surrounded by her four grandchildren…"

"We left Fowlerville early because Emma and Jennie did not want to leave Joe too long. I remember passing Chug Smith with another man just outside of Fowlerville on our way home. We talked the whole time driving down Grand River about our memories of Molly Bandkau and how she had always been such a good friend…then…the last thing I remember is Emma and Jennie gasping. I never saw the car that caused them to scream, and when I came to I remember Jennie's labored breaths and moans. I saw Erv Bandkau Jr. and later…"

Tears welled up in my eyes when I saw Dad gently stroke Mom's forehead as she suddenly drifted away. As Dad held Mom's hand tightly, I noticed that her wedding ring was missing—the first time I had seen her without it since Tay Rickett reset it in white gold ten years earlier. Thirty-nine years of marriage had not diminished their love and affection for one another—still his Anna, the blond "bob-haired" classmate he fell in love with in high school. Ed, still the same reliable, hard worker who had courted her in Detroit when she went to the Detroit Business Institute and lived with Aunt Jennie and Uncle Gust.

Mom was now battling something in her troubled sleep and beads of sweat trickled down her forehead. "Time for you folks to leave now," one of the nurses who had just come on duty said politely but assertively.

"Mrs. Weber will need to get as much rest as she can before she is transferred to St. Joe's in Ann Arbor tomorrow. We will see to it that she remains comfortable."

Keehn's Funeral Home on West Main, yet another of those brick Tudors from the twenties and thirties like my grandfather's, was a place that never changed much; then again, that was the way things were supposed to be in small towns. Emil Keehn, the funeral director, had not changed either in the more than two decades I had known him. Always the impeccably dressed businessperson, organized and articulate, he was someone people could count on in times such as these. As he opened the door for the scores of people who came to the funeral home for my aunts' *viewing* the next two days, Emil remained calm and personable, small comfort for the bereaved, but consoling nonetheless.

He had been observing how people mourn ever since he came to Brighton to take over Guy Pitkin's furniture and funeral business on Main in the 20s. It was, of course, commonplace for Emil to deal with people who were in mourning yet he never fully accustomed himself to it. There were times when he found it downright difficult to deal with or understand. The last couple of days had been like that. He had handled funeral arrangements for friends, strangers, even family over the years but this *viewing* was different, not just part of his job. He thought about the numerous times he had spoken to Emma since coming to Brighton—at church, on social occasions, in the bank on business or at stockholders meetings. The accident on Grand River had robbed Brighton of a woman he much admired—a woman with more business acumen than anyone he knew. Emma would be sorely missed.

Whitney Kimble, the bank cashier, said little when Emil greeted him at the door. He had at last gained enough composure to come to the *viewing* of someone who had been a mainstay at the bank since he moved to Brighton fifteen years before. He shook his head in disbelief as he walked up to the two caskets then joined his wife, June, on a sofa in another room. Alice Newcomb and Henrietta Pearsall, daughters of long-time cashier Roy Newcomb who worked alongside Emma at the bank, were with him too, friends of hers since the 1930s.

"We gave Emma quite the send-off from the bank, you know," Whitney told members of the Carlson family, childhood friends of my mom and Emma who had arrived earlier from Cleveland. "I slipped a *lei* around her neck at the *Canopy* the evening the bank's board of directors honored her at her retirement dinner. We surprised…"

Whit could not finish his sentence to tell about the retirement present Emma had received that evening, a trip for two to Hawaii. It took him a few moments to regain his composure:

"And to think, that was only a few weeks ago…"

Martin Lavan, the ginger-haired Irish immigrant who now was the most senior of the town's lawyers, cut his conversation short with Emil upon entering the crowded flower-filled parlor where Emma and Aunt Jennie lay. Without speaking to anyone, he advanced resolutely to both coffins, genuflected, and took out a starched white handkerchief to wipe away the tears in his eyes.

"My little girl was just riding her bike across the street when she got hit," he told Dad after a minute or two. "You really never recover." He recalled sitting down at Roy Newcomb's desk at the old bank then standing in front of the teller's window visiting with Emma for a long time just after it happened. "Funny how these things work. Roy and Emma—the staunchest Republicans in Brighton, me one of the few FDR Democrats—I loved the both of them. I never knew a lovelier woman than Emma Westin."

Emil left his position in the vestibule as the crowds started thinning out and checked out the cramped flower arrangements yet another time before the *viewing* ended. He thought about the *arrangements* for services the next day that Carl Westin and he had finalized not long before. There would be two funerals in one, right there in the chapel—a tough squeeze but Emil would make it happen. He was glad Carl was in charge. Carl was another person like Emma you could always count on. Never once in debt at St. George with the two of us on the council together after Carl retired in Brighton, he thought; out after an hour and a half meeting with a good joke or two afterward—just like when George Shoup was here in the 30s.

Uncle Carl Westin and Emil *did* make it happen. Esther Leibfarth, St. George's organist, comforted mourners by playing short works on the piano by Bach that were Emma's favorites and sentimental religious pieces that were much loved by Aunt Jennie. Rev. Bob Olson, the progressive pastor at St. George who was primarily responsible for my attending Luther Seminary, preached an inspiring funeral sermon based on the comforting words of the eleventh and fourteenth chapters of the Gospel of St. John. I admired Bob because he preached so well and chanted the Lutheran liturgy in the old Scandinavian State Church tradition. Bob was also a social activist who had upset a few long-time St. George members by his belief that the Word not only had to be preached but *lived* as well.

Immediately following the service, Esther played a somber recessional as scores of bereaved friends and relatives solemnly left Keehn's chapel. Preceding them, twelve pallbearers marched in perfect unison to two shiny black Cadillac hearses parked on Main Street that had been part of Emil's fleet for five years. They led a long procession that parked at Fairview on an upward slope on the west side of one of Fairview's gravel drives, only a few paces away from a red granite monument. Chiseled on it in large letters was the name *Westin*. It stood out because of its hue and size from others surrounding it and lay on a green knoll far enough away from Flint Road to be a quiet resting place. Next to it were two small cedar trees that Emma had planted in memory of her parents and beside them two grave markers with the inscription

Charles A., 1864 – 1935 and Amanda S., 1866 – 1949.

At Emil's signal, six of the twelve pallbearers removed Emma's coffin from the front hearse, already caked in dust from the gravel drive, and bore it the short distance to her newly dug grave. With little fanfare, it was lowered into the clay earth. There was a surprising serenity that moment on Fairview Hill when Emma joined her mother and father. Bob Olson then made his way to the grave intoning the words "Ashes to ashes…," with all the conviction he could muster then repeating words from St. John the Evangelist that he had used as a text earlier…"I *am* the resurrection and the life." Dad and I embraced each other during the quick interment service as we sat under the nearby tent canopy on two uncomfortable folding chairs that tipped to one side as you leaned. There were masses of flowers everywhere and the blackbirds flying overhead made us both grin. Uncle Joe Westin was too grief-stricken and weak to be there, but somehow, sitting at the brick house on Grand River, he had managed to rid his woods temporarily of the noise pestilence that drew his ire every other day!

As the second hearse made its way back down Fairview Hill afterward, two cemetery groundskeepers who had been having a quick smoke yawned lazily and approached the Westin cemetery plot, shovels in hand...

"Dust to dust...In my Father's house are many mansions..." The second commitment was concluding. Rev. Olson himself was becoming emotional as he pronounced the benediction and made the sign of the cross over Jennie Carlson's grave. Bob's wife, Mary Ann, was already sitting in their car when he walked over to it to join her. Brighton folks were pulling away by then but the Dearborn, Detroit and Cleveland Carlson cousins remained at Aunt Jennie's grave reminiscing about the Westin Family's Pennsylvania, Detroit, and Second Street days.

"...Two gray granite stones, four graves close to each other so they can visit...a bit like Con planned it that way." I heard Dad talking to Ed as I watched the two of them walk over to my second set of grandparents' grave markers next to the Carlson plot, below the massive larch tree Dad planted that shaded his mother and father's final resting places. On it were the names *Conrad Weber 1869-1942* and *Clara Augusta Weber 1874-1949*. The fragrant air from the flowering bushes lining the Hyne mausoleum next to Henry and Lydia Weber's grave a short ways away wafted downwind as he began to talk. As his father often did, Dad was gesturing at the same time as he spoke, his large hands pointing below the Weber names.

"This summer, when the sun filters through to the gravestones, the bright red geraniums from Kunz's Greenhouse will make Ma and Pa both smile. We'll put them between their names, like we always do."

Bronze Medal citation 1970 from H. W. Buse Jr., Lieutenant General U.S. Marine Corps, Commanding General Fleet Marine Force Pacific for the President of the United States
Bronze Medal citation July 16, 1970 from Headquarters, U. S. Military Asst. Command Vietnam by Direction from the President of the United States

When the purple morning breaks,
When the bird wakens and the shadows flee,
Fairer than morning, lovelier than daylight,
Dawns the sweet consciousness,
"I am with thee!"

When sinks the soul, subdued by toil to slumber
In closing eyes look up to Thee in prayer.
Sweet the repose beneath Thy wings o'er shading,
Yet sweeter still to wake and find Thee there.

So shall it be at last in that bright morning,
When the soul wakens, and life's shadows flee.
O in that moment, fairer than daylight dawning,
Shall rise the glorious thought
I am with thee."

Harriet Beecher Stowe

AFTER WORD

JUNE 2022 MARKED THE SEVENTY-EIGHTH ANNIVERSARY of the Allied invasion of Normandy. One of the most significant events in world history always had a special meaning to me, occurring just a few months before I was born, a necessary military operation leading to the end of a conflict testing the resolve of Western Civilization. This year that milestone was more meaningful than ever, coming as it did only a few months after completing a book whose first chapters deal with the part Brighton's sons and daughters played in winning that monumental conflict. Chug Smith, Ray Carmack, Don Juipe, Roy Thomas, Bill Richmond, Fred Singer, and Harry Herbst were just a few of the hundreds of residents of *my town* who made victory in that *war* possible, who gave so freely of themselves to secure freedom for their own and future generations.

June 2022 also marked the 60th anniversary of my graduation from Brighton High School. To say that I am incredulous is an understatement! Who would have guessed that after the din of parents, friends, and relatives congratulating us had died down, after all the photos had been snapped and the old B.H.S. gym started to empty we would assemble six decades later in *our town* to commemorate one of the most important events in our lives?

In a sense, we never shed our scarlet and white robes that hot, humid day in 1962 just as the Brighton veterans of World War II never fully returned to the civilian life they once knew in a small town in southeastern Michigan. Over the years, many members of the class of 1962 have stayed in touch, often getting together on social occasions or simply phoning, emailing and zooming one another to say "hi." We have laughed and rejoiced with one another, we have toasted each other after life's triumphs and we have commiserated with one another after passing through the low valleys of life. And, as we consoled, encouraged—sometimes even got angry with one another—all of us shared the special bond that was created in that two story brick building atop School Hill in Brighton in the fall of 1958.

Members of the B.H.S. class of 1962 celebrated a special weekend in July 2012, the fiftieth anniversary of our graduation. We caught up with each other—what we had accomplished in life, where we had lived, where we had worked—and shared stories about spouses, children and grandchildren. Many made a special effort to attend, coming from all corners of the country—from Washington to Florida, North Carolina to Wisconsin, Texas to New York. We were elated that even five of our teachers managed to show up! We spent much time looking at memorabilia the night of our banquet at St. Paul's Church and the touching display of framed portraits of classmates who were no longer with us. Too many of our peers had left us far too soon, too many we were so close to had not had a chance to enjoy life to its fullest!

As we made our way from table to table that night getting re-acquainted and sharing stories about our life as *Bulldogs*, all of us agreed that we could not have grown up in a better time, in a better place. It was that sentiment that prompted me three years later to begin a book about Brighton and to title it *"Remarkably Brighton—Still in touch.*

Even now, we continue to be beckoned back to that special place in the palm of the mitten—that place we still call home. We continue to write new chapters in our lives, blessed and enriched with small town memories. It is my hope that readers enjoy **Remarkably Brighton – Still in Touch**—as much as I did writing it. It is Brighton's story, it is my friends' story, it is my classmates' story. But most of all, it is my story.

Front Row: Linda (Skeman) Wintermute, Dr. Marilyn Jones (elementary school music), Nancy (Krause) Hollis, Suzanne (Campbell) Conerway, Suzanne (Wahl) Phillips), Pat (Pendergrass) Mack. **Second Row:** Gary Potter, Judy (Latimore) Farmer, Katherine (Pierce) Arnot, Diane Langley, Mary (Caldwell) Gruda, Barbara (Love) Kaste, Carol (Davis) Purdy, Carol (Carney) Haviland, Deanna (Dixon) Stagner, Pat Taylor Burkett (H.S. English). **Third Row:** Deanna (Kluck) Heikkinin, Karen (Krichbaum) Geffert, Karl Ehnis (H.S. U.S. History), Karen (Herbst) Stapleton, Susan (Ayres) Weyburn, Ron Peterson, Carol (Hall) Peterson, Jamie (Harmon) Devine. **Fourth Row:** Dick Verellen, Dennis Pearsall, Carl Klopshinske (H.S. Band), Ruth (Worrall) Danner, Dale Cooper, Dave Denkhaus, Bill Dean. **Fifth Row:** Eddie Martin, Brian Musgrave, Bob Darga , Hugh Munce, Jim Davis, Keith Robertson, Paul Weber, Mike Dunk, Jim Armstrong, Larry Herbst, Rich Krasuski, Mark Waite.

Remarkably Brighton is my second attempt at writing the "Great American Novel" and was begun in the fall of 2013—a single page, that is.

In the middle of a sultry mid-summer Sarasota day, I sat at my desk in the *Landings*, my faithful Australian shepherd *Jip* at my feet, grateful that I was at last finished with a project I had been planning and working on since the untimely death of my wife, Brigitte, in 2007. Before her death, and without my being privy to the conversation, Brigitte had asked our close friend, Bruce Halliday, to make certain that I followed up on a lifetime dream to write a book about my hometown.

Jip

Bruce took his charge seriously. Before long, I had written what I intended to be the prologue to a novel I titled *"Con Weber's Brighton: Portrait of Family, Church and Nation, 1832-1942."* I showed it to Bruce and to my cousin, Carolyn Weber, who had long tried to persuade me to write a book about our grandfather and the town where we grew up. I was proud of what I had written and so were Bruce and Carolyn. I persevered. Though that prologue did not appear in my 2014 novel, I am still proud of it. Renamed *"Epilogue,"* it has undergone a metamorphosis of sorts and in its edited form appears as the last chapter of **Remarkably Brighton**.

In the first paragraph of my preface to **Con Weber's Brighton**, I wrote

> *"For the past few years, I have had the undeniable good fortune of combining two passions—writing and history telling...In my formative years, history had a profound*

impact on me. I absorbed Michigan history much as young people today immerse themselves in video games and texting..."

Not satisfied with my life when writing no longer consumed all of my waking hours, I resolutely began my second book, also in the form of a historical novel. I titled it *Small Town* and intended it to be a sequel to my first book. It was slow going. Writer's cramps? No Bruce Halliday or Carolyn Weber to "agitate" me to write—both of whom passed away within five years of the completion of my first book?

Two developments came into play in 2015 and 2020 to reawaken my interest in writing the book I rebranded as *Remarkably Brighton: Still in Touch.*

The first was the emergence (or re-emergence?) of three diaries and one black and white photo album. The album belonged to a lifelong friend, Charles "Chug" Smith, the brother of my Aunt Ruth Weber, who passed away just as I was beginning this book. I characterize Chug in several chapters as being "fun-loving," "musically gifted," a "good joke teller" and, most important, a *"raconteur"* of the first magnitude. Growing up in Brighton, he captivated friends and family by his stories—his early life in the Brighton of the 1930s, adventures in World War II, his life as a test driver at General Motors Proving Grounds and his naming his daughter after the city in China where he was stationed in the *war*! The album was a record of Chug's service in China in 1944 – 45. It was in remarkably good condition and there were captions under every picture. I could not put the album down after I started thumbing through it, along with the 1945 "Victory Edition" of the *Brighton Argus* he had so carefully preserved with it. Chapters one, two and seven were written using much of the information gleaned from these two sources. Coupled with my interest in the *war* and the research I did teaching world history at Sarasota High School, all that remained was to write a compelling story.

The three diaries were those of my mother, her sister and Ray Carmack, a Brighton soldier who fought in the *war*. Mom began her diary just after Christmas 1942 and it covers only the first seven months of the year. She was intelligent, interested in world affairs, a passionate reader and an excellent writer who knew how to be economical with words. Raising a year old toddler while still attentive to her duties as a farmer's wife in wartime likely contributed to the abrupt ending to Mom's daybook entries. I could not have been more delighted finding another invaluable resource about the *war*! She wrote about life as an active member of St. George Lutheran Church, the antics of my brother Eddie, financial hardships, my dad's back breaking work in the fields planting and harvesting, marriages and deaths. Often she quoted excerpts from the best-seller Book of the Month Club selection she had just received or news stories from the *Detroit Free Press*, which she read religiously. Most of her entries, as one would expect, were about war developments or local events relating to the *war*. In January and February, for example, when temperatures plummeted as low as nine-below-zero and blizzards prevented milk from being sent to the creamery in town, she wrote that my dad and a friend visited neighboring farmers with county agricultural quotas for 1943. In a July entry, I learned that a church friend, Molly Bandkau, had just gotten a new job at the Advance Stamping Company which produced war materiel.

My mother's sister, Emma Westin, kept a diary all of her life. I was fortunate enough after her death to inherit her entire collection. Like my mom, she too was an intelligent woman who read extensively and immersed herself in war news. Her concise, informative writing style was much the same as that of my mother. I chose to use her diary from the date my mom stopped keeping one in July 1943 through the following July, an eventful year when the tide of World War II was swiftly turning in favor of the Allies. Emma lived in town with her mother and worked at the Brighton State Bank. Thus, the events she focused on were somewhat different from those of my mother, though war news still took center stage. Her first entry for 1943 mentions working as a Women's Auxiliary member at the blood bank, where there were 247 donors; in her last entry in July 1944 she noted that she had taken my brother, Eddie, downtown to feed the ducks on the Millpond!

Thanks to the efforts of an unknown resident of Riverside, CA, a third diary I used as a resource for three chapters of *Remarkably Brighton* surfaced in Brighton nearly three decades after it was begun. Ray Carmack was the second son of Walter Carmack, the well-known owner of Brighton's *Grand* Theater. Ray enlisted in the Army Air Corps in 1942, trained as a radio gunner on B-24 bombers and attained the rank of sergeant while stationed in Riverside in late 1943. Shortly thereafter, he became part of a crew whose orders took them to a former RAF base in Old Buckenham, England. From this Allied air base, some of the fiercest bombing missions over Germany and France were initiated, an ominous prelude to the D-Day invasion of 1944. Only weeks before Ray's crew left for Old Buckenham he had married

Mary Hitdlebaugh, his B.H.S. sweetheart, in Riverside. Fortunately for later generations, Ray documented the story of their wedding, whirlwind honeymoon and his subsequent posting in England. The small, standard-issue G.I. diary, *My Life in the Service*, that fit snugly in the envelope Mary received when she lived on Walnut Street, was issued to Ray when he enlisted and is a heart rending account of four months in the life of a member of America's "Greatest Generation."

I will always be grateful in the initial stages of writing chapters three through five for speaking often with Mary on the phone before her death in Brighton at age ninety-four. Her sweetness and amazing ability to recount facts about Ray's courtship of her were indeed touching. I am grateful as well for conversations with Mary's younger daughter, Debbie Pelkey Serwach, who very kindly gave me permission to use information and pictures from Ray's diary while providing me with much background information. Debbie's husband, Joe Serwach, was also extremely helpful. Joe had researched Ray's life extensively and volunteered to photocopy his diary for my use. Mary's older daughter, Donna Juipe Chasteen, and her husband, Joe, provided me with still more information about Ray and Mary as well as the distinguished military career of Donna's father, Mary's second husband, Don Juipe.

Though very short, my own diary is the last of the primary resources I used for the book and turned up not long before my last chapter was written in 2021. Begun when I was a freshman, it covers a little over nine months of my life in 1959. It is set in the old B.H.S. building and on the farm where I grew up, two miles south of town on Rickett Road. Like my mother's, my diary accounts are very abbreviated ones, almost illegible in places due to space limitations and replete with events of every day farm life. Family and friends, like Mom's entries, were the main focus of my writing.

Routine events in my life after 2015 led to a long hiatus from writing, drawing me away from my word processor far too long. From time to time, I picked up the first copy of *Con Weber's Brighton* I received from Peppertree Publishing in Sarasota and read a sentence or two. It occupied a prominent place on a coffee table in my living room and was a topic of conversation when dinner guests perused it while enjoying *hors d'oeuvres* and a cocktail or two.

"How are you doing with your second book?" they would inevitably ask.

"Taking some time off," was my insincere rejoinder.

And then...

I had not touched on the Spanish influenza pandemic of 1918-20 that my parents lived through in *Con Weber's Brighton* but they had talked about it often. Schools were closed and the grim reaper visited countless homes in the Brighton area. Wishaw, Pennsylvania, my mother's girlhood home, was devastated by the flu and took the lives of many of her friends. *Never* in my wildest imagination did I think that I would experience a pandemic in my lifetime! Like a thief in the night, Americans witnessed the outbreak and spread of COVID-19 in early 2020 along with the loss of hundreds of thousands of lives. Lives were changed unalterably. Masking and unmasking, vaccinations and boosters, massive hospitalizations, economic hardships and lives disrupted soon became the "new normal."

Yet as people everywhere learned to cope—or at least function with some degree of "normalcy"—I returned to my study and began to write again on my neglected computer, my faithful Australian shepherd again ever nearby. I reread what I had written, edited it far too many times, and mapped out my strategy for finishing *Remarkably Brighton*. Chapters one through seven—the *war*—were primarily non-fiction and biographical and the remaining chapters, like *Con Weber's Brighton*, would be the same. They would be autobiographical, a story about growing up in the mid-century Brighton I knew until the time I graduated from high school in 1962. They too would be written in the form of a novel.*

Most of *Remarkably Brighton* was thus written between March 2020 and the fall of last year. Again, I found much pleasure in writing, in expressing my thoughts, in fighting grammar and context battles that often took days to win. I wrote at least three chapters before realizing that if the rest of the book contained *any* similarity to an autobiography, it would be good to start with where I began life—a dairy farm south of Brighton! That account, chapter eight, was not begun until several months after I started writing again. Like the preface for *Con Weber's Brighton*** I wrote 12 years before, I was proud of it. If only my brother, Ed, or my parents were alive, I thought, to read the story of a little boy's idyllic life playing in hay fields in summer and petting stanchioned cows in the barn on a cold winter's night!

Like anything else in life, taking one's first steps is always the hardest, always requires the most determination and will power. Resolving to complete *Remarkably Brighton* was like learning to ride a bicycle on a dusty farm driveway gently sloping upward beside an alfalfa field leading to Rickett Road when I was six years old. With my dad's help, I succeeded at that laborious, sweaty undertaking. And with help from family, friends and B.H.S. classmates, I succeeded at an equally challenging task—finishing my story.

PWW
March 2022

My accounts of World War II and growing up in Brighton are primarily non-fiction. The reader should know, however, that because both Con Weber's Brighton *and* Remarkably Brighton *are historical novels, some names and the sequencing of events have been changed out of respect for individuals' privacy and to achieve better readability.*
**Con Weber's Brighton *is available at Amazon.com, Barnes&Noble.com and PeppertreePublishing.com.*

Ray Carmack's service diary made its way to Brighton and his widow, Mary Hitdlebaugh Pelkey, from Riverside, CA nearly three decades after he wrote his first entry in November 1943. Debbie Serwach, Mary's daughter, found it under her mother's bed on one of her periodic visits to Brighton.

ACKNOWLEDGEMENTS

Many people in the past seven years have helped me realize my dream of bringing Remarkably Brighton to press. It would be impossible on these pages to thank all of them but several are listed in the following paragraphs.

Margaret Smith, Chug Smith's widow, allowed me to gain much insight into what her husband's life in Asia during the war must have been like. She lent me Chug's photo albums, old copies of The Brighton Argus and shared stories about his deployment in China that were essential in writing chapters one, two and seven. Margaret also helped me fill in the blanks about Chug's post-World War II life in mid-century Brighton that were fascinating! Chug attracted friends easily, was a cornerstone of his family and remains one of the most colorful personalities I have ever met!

Chapters three through five would not have been possible without Debbie and Joe Serwach sharing Ray Carmack's wartime diary, My Life in the Service, and their insight into Ray's life and military service. Debbie also made it possible to speak with her mother, Mary Pelkey, about her recollections of Ray. I felt an immediate bond with Mary and am grateful that I was allowed the opportunity to get to know her. Through her, Ray Carmack came to life and I was inspired to tell his history. Debbie was also able to provide me with contacts for a number of friends and relatives who helped me finish telling Ray's and her mother's story. Even as I was writing the last paragraph of my book in 2021, I learned that the story of Ray and Mary's romance as told in chapter three was not complete. Gordon Collins, Ray's sister's first husband, added more details about Ray and Mary's marriage in Riverside, California. Nor was the story of Mary's second husband, Don Juipe, complete. Debbie's sister and brother-in-law, Donna and Joe Chasteen, helped me piece together the puzzle of his distinguished World War II service and marriage to Mary Carmack.

There were numerous "dead ends" doing research for this book. But one very special person helped me proceed in the right direction when I became discouraged. Norma Jean Leitz Pless and her husband, Chuck, were long-time Brighton residents and Norma Jean was a family friend of the Carmack's. Her ability to both research and recall events in Brighton's past are amazing, her contributions to the Brighton Area Historical Society simply indispensable! Whenever I had questions that could not be answered, the Howell resident and "walking encyclopedia" about mid-century Brighton history came to my rescue. Without my asking, she actually drove to Brighton from Howell one day to retrace the route state troopers would have taken to the Carmack and Hitdlebaugh homes near the Grand Theater on East Street to notify Mary Carmack about her husband's death!

I am indebted to both Jim Vichich and Jerry Damon of the Brighton Area Historical Society for putting me in touch with Norma Jean but also for answering numerous questions about Brighton's past. Thanks to both Jerry and Jim as well for helping with pre-publication publicity for Remarkably Brighton and for taking photographs of Brighton scenes. B.A.H.S. member Charlene Kull also took Brighton photographs for me and aided me with research and publication issues **(Jim's, Jerry's and Charlene's excellent photos were used on the cover of** *Remarkably Brighton*). Other B.A.H.S members helped me greatly with the final draft of this book. Bob Richmond, a childhood friend of both my brother and myself, was quick to respond to my emails whenever details about events were sketchy. Bob has lived in Brighton all his life, has been active in numerous town civic organizations and was always willing to oblige me with his input. It was especially valuable in the chapter ten narrative about the deaths of "Peanut" Cline," Larry Jackson and Trooper Bud Souder as well as information I used for chapters twelve and fourteen. Marieanna Bair, who passed away in 2021, assisted me with both Con Weber's Brighton and the sequel I have just completed. Carol McMacken, who also passed away last year, was an invaluable resource in writing both books. I spoke with Carol numerous times and she graciously gave me permission to use her book, *From Settlement to City: Brighton Michigan, 1832 -1945* (Brighton Area Historical Society, 2004), as a reference in Remarkably Brighton. Both Marieanna and Carol were founding members of the Brighton Area Historical Society and will be sorely missed.

Many B.H.S. classmates have also assisted me with both research and encouragement in writing the book. Suzanne Campbell, a special friend, always urged me to plod on—often in late night chats on the phone—and refreshed my memory more times than I can count about our days together in high school. From many years serving as president of the Brighton High School Alumni Association, Suzanne was able to provide me with numerous email addresses and other contact information for school friends. My boyhood friend Ed Case was especially helpful in suggesting research sites and discovering Brighton facts that I was not able to uncover. Karen Kirchbaum Geffert added to the narrative of the "Peanut Cline" story. Doreen Klopshinske, widow of B.H.S. band director Carl Klopshinske, provided me with extensive information about her husband. Other classmates who assisted me include Alan Wunderlich, Jim Davis, Peggy Leith Altenburg, Karen Herbst Stapleton, Deanna Dixon Stagner, Kathy Zellman-Alrubaiy, Josephine DeLuca Delvero, Larry Herbst, Randy Marx, Diane (Shekell) Denkhaus, David Denkhaus, Jim Armstrong and Joann Ludtke Maier. I will ever be grateful for getting reacquainted with Susan Ayers Weyburn who helped me edit chapters 13, 15 and 16 before her untimely death in 2021.

Several B.H.S. yearbooks (The Brightonian) from the 1950s through 1962 were used in writing the book and enabled me to verify the names of numerous faculty and students in that period. Equally as important were archived articles and information from both the Detroit Free Press and the Brighton Argus and Livingston County Press (now the Livingston County Daily Press and Argus), 1949–54.

Finally, special thanks to Julie Ann Bakker, founder and publisher of Peppertree Press in Sarasota and her office manager and editorial director, Teri Franco. The patience and amazing professionalism they have exhibited in publishing my two books have been appreciated more than they will ever know.

ABOUT THE AUTHOR

Paul Weber published his first novel, "Con Weber's Brighton: Portrait of Church, Family and Nation, 1832–1942," in 2014. A 1962 graduate of Brighton High School, he lives with his dog, Lady Juno, in Sarasota, Florida. Paul retired from the Sarasota County School System in 2006, teaching German, world history and social studies for 34 years. His wife, Brigitte, passed away in 2007. His daughter, Niki, and family live in Cheshire, England. He is an enthusiastic fan of the Tampa Bay Rays and Bucs; a choir member and Christian education teacher at Pine Shores Presbyterian Church, Sarasota; a longtime volunteer for Meals on Wheels and is a board member and officer of the Sarasota Choral Society.

CPSIA information can be obtained
at www.ICGtesting.com
Printed in the USA
BVHW091027300822
645842BV00001B/132